Integrating Language and Content

Edited by Jon Nordmeyer and Susan Barduhn

Maria Dantas-Whitney, Sarah Rilling, and Lilia Savova, Series Editors

TESOL Classroom Practice Series

 Teachers of English to Speakers of Other Languages, Inc.

Typeset in ITC Galliard and Vag Rounded
by Capitol Communication Systems, Inc., Crofton, Maryland USA
Printed by United Graphics, Inc., Mattoon, Illinois USA
Indexed by Butler Indexing Services, Overland Park, Kansas USA

Teachers of English to Speakers of Other Languages, Inc.
1925 Ballenger Avenue, Suite 550
Alexandria, Virginia 22314 USA
Tel 703-836-0774 • Fax 703-836-6447 • E-mail tesol@tesol.org •
http://www.tesol.org/

Publishing Manager: Carol Edwards
Copy Editor: Sarah J. Duffy
Additional Reader: Terrey Hatcher
Cover Design: Capitol Communication Systems, Inc.

ISBN 9781931185660
Library of Congress Control No. 2010923480

Table of Contents

How Do Teachers Integrate Language and Content?

How Do Teachers Evaluate Language and Content Learning?

Contents

How Do Teachers Collaborate to Integrate Language and Content?

Dedication

From Jon:

   This book is gratefully dedicated to my students, who humble me with their multi-lingualism, and to Cynthia, Gus, and Atticus, who inspire me every day.

From Susan:

   I dedicate this book to each of the authors of this volume, who worked so creatively and caringly to share their stories about their joy in teaching.

Series Editors' Preface

The TESOL Classroom Practice Series showcases state-of-the-art curricula, materials, tasks, and activities reflecting emerging trends in language education and in the roles of teachers, learners, and the English language itself. The series seeks to build localized theories of language learning and teaching based on students' and teachers' unique experiences in and out of the classroom.

This series captures the dynamics of 21st-century ESOL classrooms. It reflects major shifts in authority from teacher-centered practices to collaborative learner- and learning-centered environments. The series acknowledges the growing numbers of English speakers globally, celebrates locally relevant curricula and materials, and emphasizes the importance of multilingual and multicultural competencies—a primary goal in teaching English as an international language. Furthermore, the series takes into account contemporary technological developments that provide new opportunities for information exchange and social and transactional communications.

Each volume in the series focuses on a particular communicative skill, learning environment, or instructional goal. Chapters within each volume represent practices in English for general, academic, vocational, and specific purposes. Readers will find examples of carefully researched and tested practices designed for different student populations (from young learners to adults, from beginning to advanced) in diverse settings (from pre-K–12 to college and postgraduate, from local to global, from formal to informal). A variety of methodological choices are also represented, including individual and collaborative tasks and curricular as well as extracurricular projects. Most important, these volumes invite readers into the conversation that considers and so constructs ESOL classroom practices as complex entities. We are indebted to the authors, their colleagues, and their students for being a part of this conversation.

Integrating Language and Content is about how the definition of *English language classroom* is changing. When students have the opportunity to learn content and language at the same time, disciplinary boundaries overlap. Teachers are rethinking how they design courses, plan lessons, assess students, and collaborate with colleagues to support student learning and facilitate their own professional growth. In these chapters, contributors describe practical examples of integrating language and content in a variety of classrooms. Although these insights are neither new nor revolutionary, they emerge as consistent themes for classroom practice. The authors' honest reflections and their students' experiences help to show how integrating language and content learning can be an effective and meaningful way of engaging with English as a new language.

Maria Dantas-Whitney, Western Oregon University
Sarah Rilling, Kent State University
Lilia Savova, Indiana University of Pennsylvania

CHAPTER 1

At the Intersection of Language and Content

Jon Nordmeyer

Riding a bicycle in Shanghai is an education. Weaving among cyclists, fruit vendors and pedestrians, I am learning the nuances of turn taking, overtaking, and advantage taking. Intersections provide the most interesting challenges. Often, as I ride up to a crossroads, vehicles pour into my path from two opposite streets; however, after momentary and subtle negotiations, flow resumes and I find myself on the other side of the intersection, continuing my ride homeward. In the same way, when language teaching intersects with content learning, it can feel difficult to navigate or it can appear as if the two processes are moving in opposite directions. In diverse and integrated classrooms of the 21st century, teachers need tools for supporting all students' learning. Through collaboration and reflective practice, English language teachers can understand linguistic traffic patterns and work with colleagues to help students thrive within integrated learning environments.

CHANGING CONTEXTS, CHANGING INSTRUCTION

In classrooms around the world today, students are learning *through* English, that is, students are learning English as a new language while learning other subjects in English. Although the integration of language and content is not necessarily a new development in the field of English language teaching, what is striking is the extent and diversity of programs that have developed within the past 10 years (Freeman, 2005; Short & Fitzsimmons, 2007). Examining common questions and challenges reveals useful lessons and practical insights from teachers in the field.

In both English as a second language (ESL) and English as a foreign language (EFL) contexts, curriculum reform and demographic trends are introducing English language learners (ELLs) into classes where nonlanguage subject matter is taught through the medium of English. Educational policy in many

1

English-speaking countries has shifted "from assimilation to multiculturalism to mainstreaming" (Davison, 2001, p. 30). In countries where English is not a native language, teaching subject matter through English is a chance to develop content knowledge and English fluency at the same time. In many cases, teachers of English and other subjects are being asked to teach classes that may be new or unfamiliar and for which they may not have experience or training.

The chapters in *Integrating Language and Content* describe how the definition of *English language classroom* is changing and illustrate how students are acquiring English in a variety of different classrooms around the world. Contributors from North America describe how integrating language and content serves emerging bilingual students who need to learn grade-level academic material or valuable job skills, but cannot wait 5 or more years to develop the requisite English skills (Cummins, 1981a; W. P. Thomas & Collier, 2002).

In the larger global context, contributors to this volume share how young learners in Italy, the Netherlands, and Yemen are acquiring English as an additional language through the study of religion or science. The teacher authors who are university instructors in Turkey, Taiwan, and Russia describe students' opportunities to learn English for specific purposes—along with advertising, fashion design, or philosophy—in newly integrated classrooms. Instructors in both the United States and South Africa reflect on curricula that empower adult learners by integrating essential English skills with health literacy, conflict resolution, and social justice. These integrated English language teaching environments present rich opportunities to reconsider the role of language and the role of language teachers within larger professional contexts.

DEFINING TERMS

A primary challenge in discussing the integration of language and content is one of definition. Within this volume, as in the larger field of English language teaching, educators use a variety of terms to describe similar practices. In each chapter, the authors have defined program types with respect to the local context. Terminology is not standardized, even within a single national context, but three foundational terms are used to describe the wide variety of curriculum designs and instructional approaches used to integrate language and content.

Content-based instruction (CBI). Brinton, Snow, and Wesche (1989) define content-based instruction generally as "the integration of particular content with language teaching aims" and more specifically as "the concurrent teaching of academic subject matter with language teaching aims" (p. 2). The term *CBI* is used more frequently in North America and includes many different models and program types such as English for specific purposes and English for academic purposes (EAP). One challenge inherent in this label is that it implies primacy of teaching language rather than content.

Language as a medium of learning. As a way to synthesize the dual perspectives of language and content learning, Mohan (1986) proposes viewing English as neither a means nor an end but as a medium of learning:

> Since it takes a considerable amount of time to learn a second language for academic purposes, to learn to use it adequately as a medium of learning content and culture means that ESL students must learn language and subject matter *at the same time.* (Mohan, 2001, p. 107)

Viewing a language as a medium of learning helps to illustrate the interdependent and cyclical nature of English skills and subject matter knowledge.

Content and language integrated learning (CLIL). This is an umbrella term most commonly used in Europe. In most cases, it refers to students learning in a new language, one that is not spoken in the home or community. Marsh (2002) defines CLIL as "any dual-focused educational context in which an additional language, thus not usually the first language of the learners involved, is used as a medium in the teaching and learning of non-language content" (p. 15). The CLIL classroom creates a meaningful context for authentic academic communication. The dimensions of CLIL have been outlined as the four Cs (Coyle, 2002):

- *curriculum:* content or subject demands
- *communication:* language as a medium for both learning and communicating
- *cognition:* developing thinking and learning skills
- *culture:* defining pluricultural opportunities

Marsh, Cenoz, and Hornberger (2007) further explain that, in CLIL,

> learning outcomes tend to focus on achieving higher levels of awareness and skill in using language in real-life situations, alongside the learning of subject matter. This approach can be viewed as being neither language learning, nor subject learning, but rather an amalgam of both. (p. 233)

CBI, language as a medium of learning, and CLIL are different ways of describing the relationship between language and content, as illustrated in Figure 1. The top arrow represents content as a vehicle for language learning. An engaging theme or relevant academic subject area can provide a meaningful context in which students can master language objectives. In this case, content serves the language. The bottom arrow, on the other hand, represents how language can be adjusted or scaffolded to help students attain content objectives. In this case, language serves the content. Although depicted separately, the two arrows in Figure 1 represent interdependent processes that occur to a greater or lesser degree in all classrooms. All students can benefit from these processes. As Mohan, Leung, and Davison (2001) observe, "there is more recognition of areas

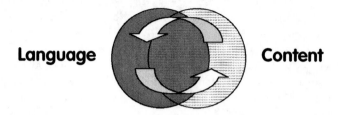

Language **Content**

Figure 1. The Cyclical Relationship Between Language and Content

of common ground: that, differences notwithstanding, both ESL learners and native speakers are learning language for academic purposes, and both groups are using language to learn" (p. 218).

RATIONALE FOR LANGUAGE AND CONTENT INTEGRATION

It is useful to consider established rationales for integration as well as problems inherent in framing a language/content dichotomy. In describing classroom practice, it is beyond the scope of this volume to provide an in-depth review of theoretical or research foundations for the integration of language and content, but several resources are available to readers interested in more extensive discussion of this topic (Brinton et al., 1989; Met, 1999; Mohan, Leung, & Davison, 2001).

Since the 1980s, the integration of English and other subject matter has been a consistent practice in schools. Teachers and researchers have recognized that teaching language and content together is an effective way of developing English language proficiency (Brinton et al., 1989; Genesee, 1994; Grabe & Stoller, 1997). Indeed, there are a number of reasons for using a content-based language curriculum focus on promoting the acquisition of English:

- It builds on the interests and linguistic needs of learners.

- It increases motivation by using content relevant to learners.

- It incorporates the eventual uses that learners will make of the target language.

- It teaches meaningful language embedded within relevant discourse contexts.

Another reason why teachers integrate language and content is to help students achieve academically and participate in a discourse community (Mohan, 2001; Stoller, 2002). From elementary school CLIL classes to university lectures, students can develop valuable thinking skills and build background knowledge in the context of learning English. Content-based language instruction motivates students through the interaction of English with content they need or want to learn; learners become connected to the learning communities in which they are studying. Additionally, through the use of Web 2.0 tools, ELLs can extend classroom dialogue through social media or personal learning networks. English can serve as a basic tool for academic literacy, cultural access, and economic opportunity, connecting students with people and ideas within a particular industry or academic context.

However, Davison and Williams (2001) caution that common rationales for content and language integration are "essentially intuitive, and there is a very limited research base to support these claims, despite their widespread face validity with ESL teachers" (pp. 53–54). The challenges of definition discussed earlier compound this problem because the integration of language and content is based on a convergence of practice rather than a unifying theory of language. Davison and Williams advocate for more comprehensive research "to both capture the diversity of practice and explore and articulate a principled basis for different approaches to language and content integration which take account of different teaching contexts, and accommodate different theories of language and language learning" (p. 69).

Even while putting language and content together, it is helpful to pull the two apart and consider whether language or content aims are driving the curriculum in any particular teaching context. This question of focus is the central issue that educators must face. Met (1999) and Davison (2001) have each described a continuum based on whether instruction is being driven by an emphasis on language or content (see Figure 2).

Where a particular program falls along this continuum has important implications:

> The relative priorities given to content, language or both, influence a number of decisions that program and course designers will make: who will teach and what teachers will need to know; whether students and teachers will be held accountable for the

	Content driven	←———————————————————→			**Language driven**
Met (1999)	Total and partial immersion	Subject courses taught in the second language	Subject courses plus language instruction	Language classes based on themes	Language classes with frequent use of content
Davison (2001)	Content teaching	Language-conscious content teaching	Simultaneous, integrated language and content teaching	Contextualized language teaching	Language teaching

Figure 2. The Language/Content Teaching Continuum

learning of content or language; how student progress will be assessed, by whom, and for what purposes. (Met, 1999, p. 21)

Met further contrasts the two ends of the language/content curriculum, as seen in Figure 3.

Content-Driven Curricula

On the content-driven end of the continuum, language acquisition is considered incidental. Language objectives, if they are used at all, are included only to support content learning. M. A. Snow, Met, and Genesee (1989) have defined content-obligatory versus content-compatible language objectives, distinguishing between the language skills or structures necessary to learn specific content (content obligatory) and the language that would naturally accompany a topic (content compatible). When content drives instruction, teachers need to scaffold content instruction in order to make key concepts more accessible for ELLs. One well-known resource for content-driven classes is the Sheltered Instruction Observation Protocol (SIOP). Short and Echevarria (1999) developed SIOP as a research tool for describing effective practice for teachers of ELLs. By rating teachers using the protocol, Short and Echevarria found that teachers who scored higher on the SIOP scale had a positive effect on students' narrative and expository writing skills.

Of course, in content-driven courses, language is still essential. The cyclical nature of language and content learning means that for content-driven curricula, comprehension of English texts and oral English allows greater access to subject matter. Improved speaking and writing skills allow students to perform better on content assessments. In reading or writing to learn, students use the language to acquire content, and subject area teachers are in a unique position to help them develop language skills in context. Mohan (1986) proposes that "the expert on writing to learn chemistry should be the chemistry teacher" (p. 12).

Content Driven	Language Driven
• Content is taught in the second language (L2). • Content learning is priority. • Language learning is secondary. • Content objectives are determined by course goals or curriculum. • Teachers must select language objectives. • Students are evaluated on content mastery.	• Content is used to learn the L2. • Language learning is priority. • Content learning is incidental. • Language objectives are determined by L2 course goals or curriculum. • Students are evaluated on content to be integrated as well as language skills and proficiency.

Figure 3. Content-Driven Versus Language-Driven Curricula

Note: Adapted from Met, 1999, p. 7.

Although many content teachers embed literacy skills and use language-across-the-curriculum approaches, collaboration with language specialists can provide additional support in differentiating for a range of English proficiency levels to create opportunities for language development.

Language-Driven Curricula

For language-driven curricula, on the other hand, "content learning may be considered a gratuitous but welcome by-product, but neither students nor their teachers are held accountable for ensuring that students learn it" (Met, 1999, p. 6). The curriculum may be organized around themes or topics, chosen specifically to maximize language development. For some teachers, an integrated approach means letting go of a grammar-driven syllabus. In a content-based language curriculum, Brinton et al. (1989) propose that English language teachers need to

> let the content dictate the selection and sequence of language items to be taught rather than vice-versa . . . [and] view their teaching in a new way, from the perspective of *truly* contextualizing their lessons by using content as a point of departure. (p. 2)

Changes in curriculum and assessment also support the integration of language and content. Recent revisions of English language proficiency standards have been linked to content standards, helping teachers understand and assess the academic English skills that ELLs need in order to learn math, science, social studies, and language arts. English proficiency standards from TESOL (2006) and the World-Class Instructional Design and Assessment (WIDA) Consortium (2007) are integrated with the content areas and anchored in academic content standards. These standards describe content-based language skills at different English proficiency levels and provide valuable support for teachers in both designing lessons and understanding student progress.

Integration and Collaboration

Most integrated classrooms fall somewhere along the middle of the language/content continuum. The reality is messy, complicated, and at times contradictory, presenting an exciting but challenging paradigm shift. Teachers are rethinking how they design courses, plan lessons, and assess students. When students have the opportunity to learn both content and language at the same time, disciplinary boundaries overlap. Viewing language teaching as an integrated process rather than a discrete discipline introduces new ways of engaging with colleagues. Collaboration across subject areas not only supports student learning but also facilitates professional growth.

When schools build intentional collaboration among language specialists and content specialists, they foster targeted professional development that is embedded in the daily work of teachers and aligned with existing administrative structures. To integrate language and content, learning communities can use tools such as the Critical Friends Groups protocols to support collaborative inquiry and embedded professional learning (Dunne, Nave, & Lewis, 2000). As teachers, researchers, and policy makers redefine the role of the language teacher, professional development should reflect these new realities.

In *English Next*, Graddol (2006) observes that integrating language and content alters "the working relationship within schools, and requires a cultural change of a kind which is often difficult to bring about within educational institutions" (p. 86). This challenge presents an opportunity: Greater cooperation within schools can enrich both student and teacher learning by bringing specialists together to share techniques and approaches across disciplines.

IN THIS VOLUME

All of the contributors represented in this volume have encountered situations requiring them to examine the interdependence of language and content learning and consider how their practice has changed in response. They describe the context of their work and explain personal, institutional, and theoretical rationales for implementing an integrated approach. Across continents and classrooms, they share several important observations about dual-focused learning environments:

- Students' needs should remain at the center of each curriculum.

- Assessment should inform instruction.

- Professional collaboration between disciplines supports student learning and teacher growth.

Although these insights are neither new nor revolutionary, they emerge as consistent themes for classroom practice. The authors' honest reflections and their students' experiences help to show how integrating language and content learning can be an effective and meaningful way of engaging with English as a new language.

Why Do Teachers Design Courses to Integrate Language and Content?

Reflecting on the genesis of a particular course, each author in this section shares the rationale for using content to support the acquisition of English and describes the skills and knowledge—beyond language—that helped students in their classes achieve success. The teachers trace their own thought processes and how they communicated their rationale to colleagues, students, and parents. In each case, students' needs served as a central organizing principle in course design.

In Chapter 2, "Content for Change: Integrating Radical and Socially Relevant Content Into a Business English Curriculum," Sedia Dennis describes the passionate advocacy that she brings to her experiences working with students in Winterberg, South Africa:

Students walk into the English language classroom with subject matter. It seems counterproductive to me if we, as their teachers, look past the material they bring—material so relevant to their lives and central to who they are as cultural beings—in search of material that may not be as connected to them or as urgent. (p. 29)

In Chapter 3, "Danger Learning: Experiencing ESL Through Conflict Resolution Techniques," Christopher Stillwell describes how an intensive ESL course in New York City, was designed to challenge advanced English language learners and provide "techniques useful in the negotiation of meaning in their daily lives to confirm understanding and repair communication breakdowns" (p. 38). Stillwell goes on to state that,

in the use of conflict resolution and mediation techniques as the subject of language study, the ESL seminar focused primarily on practices that would not only provide the most interesting content, but that would also prove transferable to the teaching and learning of language. (p. 32)

In Chapter 4, "A Pound of Prevention: Health Literacy for Beginning-Level Adult English Language Learners," Susan Dalmas and Judy Trupin outline a new health literacy course designed for adult students in New York. They agree on the following purposes for the curriculum: "to help students acquire the language necessary to navigate the health care system, to provide them with content-specific knowledge about the U.S. health care system, and to teach preventive health knowledge" (p. 45).

In Chapter 5, "Does Content and Language Integrated Learning Work With Young Learners?", Elena Pratissoli describes an interdisciplinary unit developed at her primary school in Italy. During initial planning meetings with her team, "it became clear . . . that there was a risk of the project expanding too much and losing focus" (p. 59). After choosing specific content for the project, Pratissoli and her team agreed that "the tasks may be cognitively demanding as long as they are concrete; they may be emotionally complex as long as they are experiential" (p. 72).

How Do Teachers Integrate Language and Content?

The second section of this volume considers some of the specific techniques and materials teachers use to help students navigate the intersection of language and content. Contributors provide examples of how some general terms such as *CLIL, sheltered instruction,* and *EAP* are applied to specific contexts. Although every chapter in this volume shares practical examples of how teachers have worked with a particular group of students, this section provides an additional window into teachers' approaches and their reflections.

In Chapter 6, "Two Birds, One Stone: Using Academic Informant Projects as English for Academic Purposes Content," Shawna Shapiro outlines a university course in Seattle, Washington, in the United States, that is built around the exploration of discipline-specific reading and writing:

> Whether they are explaining their academic majors, analyzing a document from an organization they have joined, or reflecting on their own writing process, students have an authentic reason to communicate as academic informants. In addition, this sort of work incorporates types of writing that students will likely use in other courses: exposition, analysis/evaluation, response, and reflection. (p. 84)

In Chapter 7, "A Short Course on the Miniskirt: Providing a Language Toolkit for University Instructors in Turkey," Steve Darn analyzes a CLIL project and explains its dual focus, defining CLIL in the following way:

> Content and language are learned simultaneously and in balanced proportions. A CLIL lesson is not a language lesson, nor is it a subject lesson transmitted in a foreign language. The second language is the means by which the content objectives are reached. (p. 93)

In Chapter 8, "Opening the Door: Making Mathematics Accessible to English Language Learners," Anita Bright describes a variety of strategies she used to teach math to middle school ELLs in Virginia, in the United States, including using students' home languages. She comments on how her collaboration with the math teacher resulted in growth for students and teachers alike:

> [It] take[s] thought, time, and perhaps even courage, but the dividends are well worth the investment because students are provided with multiple avenues to gain access to the curriculum. (p. 115)

In Chapter 9, "Links in a Food Chain: Guiding Inquiry in Science for English Language Learners," David Crowther, Lori Fulton, Joaquín Vilá, and Eric Hoose describe a unit on the food chain taught to fourth-grade students in Nevada, in the United States. The authors propose that inquiry-based science instruction can support ELLs through

- the use of real materials to build context,
- equality of common experiences among students,
- access to one's primary language to explore ideas,
- access to peer assistance through cooperative learning,
- comfort that not knowing the answer is accepted,
- the creation of a positive attitude toward learning.

Crowther and colleagues also explore the role that standards can play in shaping assessment and instruction.

In Chapter 10, "Building Bridges Between Language and Content in

Religious Education," Rosie Tanner and Lorna Dunn describe how they used language and content objectives to guide instruction in a religious education class for adolescents in the Netherlands. The authors observe that "learners used their academic English authentically to refine their understanding of lesson content, interacting in authentic ways to produce a real product . . . and through the various tasks gradually refined their understanding of the topic in a foreign language" (p. 141). They conclude with suggestions for getting started with a CLIL class when students are just beginning to develop English proficiency.

How Do Teachers Evaluate Language and Content Learning?

This section explores the tensions related to assessment and how teachers can address the critical decision about what will drive instruction. Contributors discuss how objectives and standards can inform teachers' work and provide useful guidelines for student learning.

In Chapter 11, "Big Ideas in Little Pieces: Science Activities for Multilevel Classes," Ann Fathman and Patricia Nelson discuss integrating the teaching of English and science to help adolescent English langauge learners in California, in the United States, think like scientists:

> Remembering any specific detail is not as important as for students to grasp the themes and to think back and say, "That was fun. I understand. I really like science." . . . Through scientific inquiry, students use English in various functions to express themselves while making observations, posing questions, planning investigations, gathering data, and communicating results. Students learn not only academic vocabulary related to the theme, but also sentence patterns for scientific discourse. (p. 158–159)

In Chapter 12, "Exploration: One Journey of Integrating Content and Language Objectives," Kate Mastruserio Reynolds reflects on a middle school mapping unit in Wisconsin, in the United States, which helped her see the richness of an integrated approach:

> By the end of the unit, learners mastered the language and content objectives, but the learning went far beyond what was written as objectives on paper. Learners were inspired and motivated by the material and began to engage cognitively with the future material as active classroom participants and generators of knowledge. (p. 173)

In Chapter 13, "Blending Digital Media and Web 2.0 in an English Advertising Class," Aiden Yeh explains how university students in Taiwan used Web 2.0 tools to develop their English skills in the context of advertising:

> The job list that the students submitted as part of the assessment also shows how tasks were divided and shared. But most important, this project enabled students to gain deeper awareness of their culture and society, and it provided them with the exposure to understand social issues that have direct impact on their lives. (p. 186)

In Chapter 14, "Developing Language Skills While Studying Cultural Identity," Pavel Sysoyev and Stephanie Funderburg-Foreman, describing an American Cultural Studies course in Russia, discuss how integrating language and content was

> an effective way to motivate and practice a second language while focusing on important issues that promote critical thinking and evaluation of one's self in the world today. . . . [S]tudents in this course gained a deeper understanding of their culture and how it impacts society, all while using a foreign language. (p. 206)

How Do Teachers Collaborate to Integrate Language and Content?

In this final section, contributors discuss strategies for collaboration as well as what competencies teachers need in order to most effectively work in integrated environments. Many teachers who learn new strategies to support ELLs remark, "This could help *all* my students." However, the authors of these chapters show how attention to the linguistic layer of instruction is more than just good teaching. Effective classrooms should be accessible to students who are still learning English and, at the same time, provide opportunities to extend language acquisition. Teachers must work together to develop the skills necessary for this complex, multilayered learning environment.

In Chapter 15, "What Counts as Good Math Instruction for English Language Learners," Kimberly Hunt and Linda Walsleben discuss the fine balance of shared professional growth that resulted from two teachers working together at a middle school in Vermont, in the United States: "Collaboration is not always easy. Both people in the collaboration must think carefully about the words they choose when giving advice to each other while at the same time being ready to learn about their own teaching" (p. 216).

In Chapter 16, "Sustained Content-Based Academic English Teaching Through Paired English and Philosophy Courses," Jerry Spring analyzes the effects of two parallel courses in a university in Turkey: a political and social philosophy course taught by a philosophy teacher and an EAP course taught by an English teacher. "By bringing together two rather different academic tribes (Becher, 1989), the project has valuable effects on both sets of instructors that feed back into enhanced teaching and learning," Spring says (p. 226). In describing successful collaboration, he says that "for all instructors, it is a chance to experiment with a wide range of solutions (and hear about other experiments) to the learning problems posed by the courses" (p. 226).

In Chapter 17, "Motivating Students to Develop Their English Literacy Skills Through Science," Eilidh Hamilton describes how she helped implement a new CLIL program with EFL and science teachers at secondary schools in Yemen. She outlines a number of specific competencies that language teachers need to develop when working in integrated environments, including "the necessary knowledge and ability to relate the language focus and choice of topic to what learners are covering in the broader school curriculum—making content work relevant and useful" (p. 237). Hamilton adds that teachers need to be able to "communicate across subjects and willing to coplan and codeliver where logistically possible" (p. 237). She concludes that "the collaborative planning work between departments laid an excellent foundation for the lessons, and the students' motivation to use English in class significantly increased when engaging with a relevant topic" (p. 236–237).

As a collection of classroom practice, *Integrating Language and Content* illustrates the trend toward greater integration and collaboration by bringing together educators from a variety of contexts and locations, telling their stories and sharing their excitement. Each chapter describes practical examples of how teachers approach language and content with a specific group of ELLs. Although the students and schools vary greatly, the authors have faced common challenges and reached many similar conclusions. As practitioners, these teachers share their work at the sometimes chaotic intersection of language and content by honestly reflecting on teaching, learning, and professional growth.

———————————————

Jon Nordmeyer is K–12 coordinator of ESOL at Shanghai American School, in China. He has a BA in classical archaeology from Dartmouth College and an MA in TESOL from the SIT Graduate Institute. He has taught ESOL and trained teachers in North America, South America, Europe, Asia, and Africa. He has also taught seminars for the Harvard Graduate School of Education, Tibet University, SIT Graduate Institute, and the Massachusetts Department of Education.

Susan Barduhn is a professor at the SIT Graduate Institute (School for International Training), in Brattleboro, Vermont, in the United States, and chair of the institute's Summer MA in Teaching program. In her global career in ELT, she has been a teacher, trainer, supervisor, manager, assessor, and consultant. She is past president of IATEFL; former director of The Language Center, Nairobi; and former deputy director of International House, London.

Why Do Teachers Design Courses to Integrate Language and Content?

CHAPTER 2

Content for Change: Integrating Radical and Socially Relevant Content Into a Business English Curriculum

Sedia Dennis

> Good teachers are effective because they understand their learners as well as they
> understand their content, and they are able to bridge the divide between what stu-
> dents already know and care about and what they need to learn. (Darling-Hammond,
> 2002, p. 89)

Because English has been used historically to colonize and dominate, I believe
that all teachers of language, particularly English language teachers, need to be
aware of the inherent connection between language and culture and to incorporate culture into the English classroom. I believe it is even more important for
us—as teachers of the socially and politically dominant language and the language
of power politics in the world—to recognize and realize in our teaching that, as
progressive educator and writer Lisa Delpit (1995) says, "power plays a critical
role in our society and in our educational system. The worldviews of those with
privileged positions are taken as the only reality, while the worldviews of those less
powerful are dismissed as inconsequential" (p. xv). Teachers and students bring
their entire selves into the language classroom; we therefore need to understand
who we are and what we bring, and who our students are and what they bring,
before we can holistically teach the language in a way that not only effectively and
sensitively promotes cultural awareness and intercultural communication, but also
does not perpetuate or reinforce ideas of imperialism or false notions of inherent
English superiority.

In this chapter, I explain my integration of socially and politically relevant
content into the Business English course curriculum I taught in rural Winterberg,

South Africa, for the Youth Empowerment Program (YEP), a part of the Winter-berg School Trust (WST).

I designed every 2-hour lesson so that students were learning the required curriculum but also learning and talking about their own community and the larger world. I wanted the course to be meaningful to them. I wanted them to feel that what they were learning was useful. And most important, I wanted them to dream, and dream freely, because I felt they had to visualize themselves doing whatever it was they dreamed of doing first and then take steps to make their dreams a reality.[1]

Throughout the course, I used articles that dealt with issues of race, hope, resistance, questioning, love, and overcoming adversity. I hoped not only to teach students how to read classified advertisements and bus timetables and write and take telephone messages (some of the requirements of the Business English course), but also to inspire them to question their social conditions. I decided to integrate content into the Business English curriculum that would, as required, introduce students to the required business practice skills that would enable them to better their futures economically, but I also wanted to integrate content that was relevant to their lives and reflected their realities. Essentially, this meant content that would encourage them to question the racially motivated hierarchical power structures and disproportionate distribution of economic wealth in their community. I wanted to engage students in a curriculum in which they could see themselves. Because I wanted them to be codesigners of that curriculum, I listened to them and learned from them daily so that I would know what to add to the already set Business English curriculum. I hoped that doing this would help them find their voices, give them confidence, allow them to dream, and encourage them to work on the English language with dedication enough to pass their exams and use it as a tool to help direct their lives.

Although I was only with these students for 5 months, we managed to cover all of the required topics for the year in the English textbook. In addition, students improved their grammar, writing, reading comprehension, speaking skills, and confidence. I strongly believe that their motivation to learn English was directly linked to their connection to the curriculum content.

In this chapter, I argue for conscious teaching and include ideas for implementing readings connected to issues of social justice and expanding on them to also teach reading, writing, listening, and speaking. As part of the required Business English curriculum, students needed to improve their reading comprehension, learn to take core notes and expand them, learn to summarize and write

[1] In an instructor meeting, I excitedly talked about a student sharing with me that she hoped to become a pilot. The other three YEP instructors laughed and rolled their eyes. One said that the students "need to have realistic dreams" and that the YEP would not enable them to become pilots and doctors. The other two agreed. I felt deeply saddened by their attitudes because I know that a teacher's belief, or lack thereof, in her students (and their dreams) is infectious, and the students can feel it. I became even more determined to provide a space for my students to dream.

summaries, and improve their speaking skills. To illustrate the methods I used to achieve these goals while infusing the curriculum with content relevant to the students and their lives, I focus on a particular lesson I taught based on Eboo Patel's (2007) essay "We Are Each Other's Business."

My hope is that this chapter will provide an example of how teachers can create an engaged, supportive, and encouraging learning environment that tangibly invites the whole learner into the classroom by integrating socially and culturally relevant content into any English curriculum.

CONTEXT

The legacy of apartheid permeates the social fabric of the Winterberg community, and race continues to dictate the social structure and most social interactions such as who owns what, lives where, receives what kind of education, and is "house friends" with whom.[2] All of the students in my class were Black and therefore belonged to one of the historically underprivileged and underclass ethnic groups, Xhosa, in a racially mixed community where they and their parents worked as farm laborers and domestic workers, and where literally all of the farms and businesses were owned by White members of the community.

The YEP was developed as part of the WST in partnership with Ikhala Public College, in Queenstown, South Africa. The aim was to help empower students with business skills who previously, due to socioeconomic constraints, had little opportunity of extending their studies beyond the ninth-grade general education level. The Business English class I taught met 4 hours a week and served 27 students whose ages ranged from 16 to 25.

In addition to Business English, the YEP offered Mathematics, Computer Practice, and Secretarial Catering courses. Once students completed their course of study at WST, they could take a national exam based on the courses and that, if passed, allowed them to receive National Business Studies Certificates, which would enable them to be more competitive in the larger South African workforce.

CURRICULUM, TASKS, MATERIALS

The First Step: Learning About Students and Their Lives

Conscious that I was preparing to teach in a postapartheid context, I wanted to begin by learning about the students, what mattered to them, and their hopes for themselves in the future. Darling-Hammond (2002) discusses how critical it is that teachers understand students' lives as well as their learning. She poses the following questions for thought and consideration:

---

[2] *House friends* is a term that some people in the Winterberg community use to refer to friends they would invite into their homes.

- How do students' home, family, and cultural contexts influence their experience of school (e.g., connections to the curriculum, connections to teachers, relationships with peers, feelings of belonging)?

- How might students' home and cultural contexts as well as their school experiences influence their sense of themselves as learners?

- What do we (teachers) know about students' home and family contexts? Their communities? Their prior experiences?

- How can we come to understand the needs of the communities in which we teach?

- How well can we explicitly affirm students' identities and develop their capacities in the ways they select materials, organize their work, and develop relationships among students and between teachers and students?

- How can we find out more? (p. 91)

I asked students numerous questions and listened to their answers. I facilitated many discussions, and again, I listened when they spoke. I created opportunities for them to write, and I let what they wrote guide me to decide where to lead the class.

What I learned about these students was that they were beautiful and intelligent, but many of them believed the opposite about themselves because they had internalized racism. Not only had most of them accepted their realities (i.e., that literally all the domestic and farm workers in the community were Black and the farm owners White), but they also believed those realities to be inevitable and permanent. They did not believe, for example, that as a result of the YEP they would earn money by means other than scrubbing floors or herding goats. Many of them did not even believe in their own abilities to learn and speak Standard English and, especially in the beginning of our course, often laughed at each other's pronunciation. But I learned that they had dreams. One young woman dreamt of becoming a pilot; she begged me not to tell her classmates. Another young woman, who happened to have the strongest English skills in the class, wanted to be a writer. I wanted them to envision themselves in those positions. But I knew that it would be particularly difficult for them to do so considering that the materials in their assigned texts hardly reflected their lives.

As cliché as one would imagine when thinking about lack of inclusion, all of the pictures in the textbook were of people of European descent except the one picture of a Xhosa man who was first a drug dealer and later managed to turn his life around. My students seemed accustomed to such portrayals of Xhosas. As a class, we flipped through each page of the textbook and simply looked at and discussed the pictures of people that it contained, noticing who was represented and who was underrepresented, misrepresented, or not included at all—specifically, people of color, people who looked just like them. Looking through that textbook with the students made me question how they were expected to ever dream big and envision themselves as business owners rather than simply as laborers. It made no sense to me to teach Business English to students who could not envision themselves owning a business.

The YEP graduates who were most economically successful went on to work as wait staff in some of the expensive cafés and restaurants in nearby cities. For them to be in such positions not only was a great step up in social status, but it also helped their families financially. However, I wondered what it would do for students in my class to see, read about, and discuss people who looked like them and came from backgrounds similar to theirs but who were successful writers, doctors, teachers, and so on. I knew I had work to do, so I substituted as many reading materials as I could, purposely choosing those that I hoped would encourage students to dream. I chose readings that were engaging, moving, controversial, provocative, concise, sufficiently challenging, and somehow related to their lives and social realities. I wove these throughout the course and linked them to the work in their Business English textbook. Students wrote about and discussed topics ranging from the importance of reading in their lives to the dangers of drugs and alcohol in their community. They learned about and read the work of people such as Thich Nhat Hanh, a Vietnamese Buddhist monk and radical teacher; Dr. Benjamin Carson, an African American neurosurgeon; and Nkosinathi Biko, a South African writer and son of renowned freedom fighter Steve Biko.

We Are Each Other's Business: A Lesson

The steps involved in this lesson can be spread out over several days or adapted to fit into a single lesson, depending on the length of the lesson. I prefer to keep lessons narrow and deep, meaning that I base them on as few materials as possible and try to get all I can out of the materials I use. For example, I would introduce students to a short text and design various activities and exercises around that text throughout the course of several days or even a week. I believe that doing this allows students to own the text and engage with it in various ways, essentially increasing its impact. Because I chose content that they cared about and could relate to, the students cared more about investing in the coursework. They engaged more deeply in the content because they felt more connected to it and consequently became more enthusiastic about expanding their vocabulary, working on grammar, and developing their reading, writing, listening, and speaking skills. I integrated activities that enabled students to improve all of these skills while engaged in written and oral reflections on issues that directly impacted their lives, a first step in becoming active participants in helping to design their futures.

Reading

I often chose essays from the National Public Radio series *This I Believe*, an international project based on a popular 1950s radio program that publishes essays by diverse people in which they discuss their deepest values and the beliefs that drive their lives. One such article I used was Eboo Patel's (2007) "We Are Each Other's Business." In his essay, Patel discusses people's collective responsibility to stand up for each other, particularly when another's culture, religious beliefs, or ethnic identity is being chastised. Given that my students and I were in a postapartheid context, I thought Patel's essay would be an excellent catalyst for thought and discussion about the blatant racism and social inequalities that define the structure of the Winterberg community. I knew that the students were not used to questioning such things and that they had only previously alluded to the racism in their community through jokes and knowing glances.

To help students develop reading strategies such as previewing texts, making predictions, speed reading, and summarizing, I handed out copies of the essay and asked that students first simply look at the entire essay, notice the title and topic sentences of each paragraph, and make guesses about the content. I then gave them ample time (10–15 minutes) to read the entire essay while I watched closely to make sure that the slower readers were given a chance to finish this task. I encouraged all of the students to read the essay all the way through without stopping to underline or look up words they did not know during their initial reading. I had already introduced them to basic speed-reading strategies (something I do at the beginning of every new term with all English language learners to help them strengthen their reading comprehension and develop reading fluency), so I encouraged them to practice these skills as they read.

To assess their speed-reading skills, I often had students do direct speed-reading activities in which I would give them a set amount of time to complete a reading. I would then ask them to share what they understood from the reading by going around the room and having each student discuss anything in the reading, from a new vocabulary word to an entire passage, or give a summary of the article. When I was sure that all of the students had read the piece, I introduced the next step: rereading.

I asked students to read the text a second time and underline vocabulary words that were new to them while trying to guess the meanings of the words from the context of the sentence containing them. I encouraged students to write question marks next to confusing passages, make comments in the margins, and put asterisks next to passages they liked or disliked and those with which they agreed or disagreed. I found that encouraging students to write on the actual essays freed them to further engage and connect with the texts. The level to which they internalized the content was evident in the ways they made connections between the class readings and assignments and themselves, and between the readings and assignments and the larger world.

Freewriting

After reading, rereading, and marking the text, I asked students to take out some paper to do a guided freewrite for which I provided the topic. Freewriting is a prewriting strategy I had taught early in the term and encouraged students to use. It helped them focus on putting their thoughts down on paper by writing as much as they possibly could without worrying about grammar, spelling, or punctuation.

I gave students approximately 15 minutes to write, without stopping, about anything that came to their minds as they read and thought about Patel's (2007) essay. I asked them to think about their friends and family, their communities, their lives, what the essay meant to them, how it made them feel, and whether they liked or disliked it and to explain their answer. To encourage students to write for fluency and for the sheer purpose of putting their thoughts down on paper, I allowed them to continue writing even if their thoughts wandered off topic. I told them to let the words flow through them onto the paper, but to at least try to make an effort to write about the topic. It helped students focus sometimes if I gave them a few minutes of unguided freewriting time before class to simply write about whatever was on their minds. In an effort to ward off any amount of writer's block, I instructed them to write "I cannot think of anything to write" repeatedly until they did think of something to write.

I included freewriting in many of my lesson plans because it gave students opportunities to write meaningfully without their internal editors interrupting the flow of their thoughts to paper by constantly focusing on their lack of English skills. I also included freewriting because it allowed students to develop writing fluency in English, and included in the course objectives of the Business English curriculum was for students to be able to write formal paragraphs, summaries, and business letters. I knew that freewriting would be a good way to help them first articulate their ideas before learning to organize their writing into these forms. In 5 months, students went from writing short and choppy sentences to writing more fluid sentences and longer, more expressive compositions. I witnessed how repeatedly writing about topics they cared about, such as our responsibility to each other as human beings, made them want to articulate their thoughts and ideas on paper and led them to write more fluently in English.

Comprehension Questions

I often guided students in using reading activities to enhance their comprehension. One basic method I used was to give them approximately 5–10 comprehension questions based on the reading. Because freewriting and answering comprehension questions help develop different skills, this method can be used in addition to freewriting but perhaps as homework or during the following class session in order to avoid too much all at once. Helping students better understand the content led to their being better able to think critically about it. Their understanding of the readings led many students, for example, to begin talking more openly about racial dichotomies in the nearby town of Tarkastad and the abject poverty in the all-Black Zola Township.[3] As I had hoped, the students' understanding of what they read led them to question set social conditions in their community and even dream of better lives for themselves.

Group Discussions

Throughout the term, our class engaged in countless discussions, often fueled by the readings and students' writings. Just as I had expected it would, our class discussion about Patel's (2007) essay raised many questions and comments about race, class, religion, privilege, and racial dichotomies. One student talked about a specific farm in the community on which an all-White home school was started in response to the previously all-White preschool in the nearby town of Tarkastad becoming integrated. Another student shared a childhood memory about how all of the Black farm workers, her parents included, were called out of the kitchens and their servants' quarters to sing and dance for the farmers and their families. After the performance, the farmers would throw candy onto their lawns, at which time the farm workers' children would run out and try to collect as many pieces of candy as they could. "Our parents encouraged us," she said. "They did not know better." A young man who considered himself colored spoke about the history of the farmland on which he had worked his entire life, saying that his family had owned that land at one time.

We all learned and felt and questioned and discussed. The beauty of the discussion was that the questions were raised at all among a group of Black students growing up in a rural postapartheid setting, students who had never before taken or been given the opportunity to voice their thoughts and opinions regarding issues that directly affect their livelihoods and socioeconomic status. I could see them thinking and hear them challenging each other's and their own notions of what was the norm and why. Brazilian educator Paulo Freire (1970) has said that all teachers teach from specific worldviews (i.e., one's outlook that is shaped by complex and sundry forces like educational background, religion, ethnicity, the media, popular culture, etc.) whether or not they explicitly recognize it. In my classroom, I chose to recognize this. I thought it was crucial for these students to know that I saw them, heard them, and strove to understand them and their world. I wanted both my teaching and the course content to reflect this. In *Teaching to Transgress*, bell hooks (1994) argues that

> [radical teaching] compels educators to recognize the narrow boundaries that have
> shaped the way knowledge is shared in the classroom. It forces us all to recognize
> our complicity in accepting and perpetuating biases of any kind. Students are eager

---

[3] In South Africa, a township is an underdeveloped urban location usually situated on the periphery of a more developed town or city. During the apartheid era, only blacks, "coloreds" (individuals of mixed race), and working-class Indians inhabited townships. Little has changed since.

to break through barriers to knowing. They are willing to surrender to the wonder of re-learning and learning ways of knowing that go against the grain. When we, as educators, allow our pedagogy to be radically changed by our recognition of a multicultural world, we can give students the education they desire and deserve. We can teach in ways that transform consciousness, creating a climate of free expression that is the essence of a truly liberatory liberal arts education. (p. 44)

If language is inherently linked to culture and politics (and the English language in particular has historically been used to oppress and continues to flourish as the dominant language of power politics in the world), then we as English language teachers should closely examine our teaching of English and teach it in ways that are engaged, participatory, culturally inclusive, and charged with enough power to effect change. Infusing the Business English course content with content that was socially and politically relevant for students was my way of doing this.

Choosing to facilitate charged discussions took a great deal of courage for me because I knew enough about the students' backgrounds and their history to know that we would more than likely touch on intense and deeply personal topics. But as a teacher who believes strongly in allowing students' entire beings into the classroom, I felt I needed to be prepared to facilitate such discussions. I also felt it was important for students not only to read and reflect, but to share their thoughts and hear themselves doing so because I wanted them to have a comfortable space in which to talk about issues that directly impacted their lives, issues to which they told me they had never before given voice.

It was incredible to witness them become braver and more articulate (without focusing on grammatical mistakes because they were so focused on their thoughts) as the term progressed. I saw students who had previously been quiet in class begin making connections to what others had said and providing examples from their own lives and connecting those examples to content we discussed. As the students developed confidence using English and their fluency improved, their grammatical accuracy improved as well. Because I encouraged them to both self- and peer-correct, and because we often explicitly practiced doing both in class, they were less reliant on me alone to provide feedback and they grew increasingly confident in giving and receiving it. I believe that learning such skills made them more aware of grammatical forms and meaning and subsequently helped them incorporate their awareness into their use of the language. They began to notice and point out to me and to each other that they were better able and less afraid to speak English.

Throughout the term, our group discussions took various forms. Sometimes I asked students to share their thoughts with the person seated next to them. I would give each partner approximately two minutes to share, and then I would open it up to the larger group and allow different pairs to voluntarily share what they felt were the most important insights that had come up for them. In having students first discuss their thoughts with their partners, I hoped to provide them with the comfort and practice of clarifying and articulating their thoughts in their second language to one listener first before sharing their thoughts with the larger group.

After a reading or freewriting session, I would often divide the class into groups of four. Each group assigned one member to be the group's scribe and another to be its reporter. The students would then go around in their groups and share their thoughts about the reading as the scribe listened carefully and took notes on each member's main points and later shared them with the group to check for accuracy. When all groups were finished with this discussion period, each group's reporter would stand and share some of the group's thoughts and ideas with the rest of the class. Doing this activity allowed students to practice speaking fluently by focusing on the content rather than being encumbered by their mistakes. It also allowed them to improve their listening skills because they had to first listen to each other and then listen to the scribe for accuracy. Listening for accuracy allowed them to discuss grammar, share knowledge, and essentially own the language, which in turn freed them to use it.

Way of Council

Another discussion technique we practiced throughout the term was Way of Council, which is a practice of listening and speaking from the heart that can be found in many of the world's indigenous cultures. Along with speed-reading and freewriting, I taught students the key principles of this technique early in the term: speak from the heart, listen from the heart, be spontaneous, and be lean of expression.

As a whole group, we went around the circle so that each person had an opportunity to speak. Not all students chose to speak, and I always allowed space for that. All students, however, listened intently. Because the nature of council usually creates an environment of trust and deep sharing, it can sometimes lead to the sharing of personal stories. For example, one student talked about her father's alcoholism and how it affected her family, and another student talked about how hard her mother worked in the "main house," the one on the property that belongs to the farmer's family, and how she helped her mother clean when she got home.

As facilitator of the council, I would listen for and summarize common themes while also taking notes on grammar mistakes. I usually listened for content during Way of Council and never used this time to point out students' mistakes unless that particular session was focusing on grammatical accuracy. At the end of the council, if appropriate, or during another lesson, I would use my notes to address common errors and mistakes the students had made.

I also gently guided the direction of the councils and tried to decide how many times the talking piece, an object that is passed around the circle and that gives permission to the person holding it to speak, needed to circle the room (often two times was enough, the purpose of the second time being to allow students to make connections to each other's stories and share any further thoughts). This is just one way that I used Way of Council in my class as a tool to help students connect to the content in the class and to each other while developing their confidence speaking in English. There are countless other ways to facilitate council (for many enjoyable, light, and serious ideas, see Zimmerman & Coyle, 1996).

It was common during the term for students to approach me and ask if we could hold a Way of Council session that day, which always illustrated to me the power of Way of Council as a tool for teaching language. Teaching social justice content using this technique helped students gain confidence and learn to clearly and concisely articulate their thoughts and ideas by providing a safe and supportive place to raise issues of concern to them.

A Follow-Up Fluency-Building Speaking Activity

I often picture myself wringing the water out of a washcloth when I plan lessons because I like to try to get all that I can out of the materials that I use. I believe that doing so helps students better retain information because it gives them opportunities to interact with the materials in different ways.

One activity I introduced to help students build speaking fluency was one that began with the whole class divided into two circles facing each other, one inside the other. To make the circles, one group of students encircled the room and stood at makeshift stations, leaving enough space in between individuals so that they would not interrupt each other's discussions. The other group would pair up with people from the first group and face them.

Before beginning the activity, I would ask students to think about, for example, a time in their lives when they stood up for a friend or when someone stood up for or helped them, purposely choosing a topic connected to Patel's (2007) essay. I would then ask the inside circle of students to be the speakers and the outside circle to be the listeners. Next I would give the speakers exactly 3 minutes to speak. While they spoke, I watched the clock, eavesdropped, and made sure all speakers continued to talk throughout their 3 minutes (just as they are encouraged to write without stopping for an entire freewriting session). The listeners were supposed to simply listen and save all of their questions and comments for when the speaker stopped. After the 3 minutes had elapsed, the listeners were given approximately 1–2 minutes to ask questions or make comments. I usually did not time this section, but rather assessed the energy of the discussions and let students share and discuss depending on the amount of remaining class time.

After the listeners' questions and comments, I would call out, "Rotate," and the inner circle, the speakers, would rotate to the next listener and tell the exact same story again but within only 2 minutes this time. The same process as the first round would ensue. Next came the third rotation, and the speakers only had 1 minute to speak. They would tell the exact same story, and the listeners would again be given 1–2 minutes to ask questions. After the speakers had told their stories three times and the listeners had listened to three stories, I would have the inner circle move to the outer circle, making the former speakers the listeners. We would repeat the entire process with the new speakers telling their stories. After completing this activity, when students had all returned to their seats, I would ask them to reflect on the process by answering the following questions:

- What did you notice during the first, second, and third rounds as a speaker and listener?

- What did you learn about speaking (fluency, grammar)?

- What did you learn about listening?

- How can you use what you learned in this activity in the future?

REFLECTIONS

I understand that delving below basic cultural presentations to discussing deeper, burning issues involving culture can be terrifying, for I, too, am often afraid when I do so. I worry about everything from the topics that will arise to my ability to effectively facilitate the discussions when they do. But I try to push through the fear, taking small steps if necessary, because I recognize that the reason for doing the work is much larger and more urgent than my fear and in many ways even trivializes it.

At the beginning of every new term, I feel nervous upon entering my new classroom because I do not yet know the students and they do not yet know me. But I also feel nervous because I feel such an overwhelming responsibility to meaningfully use our time together, guide them, and hopefully contribute to making their lives better at the end of the term. My desire to facilitate learning and teach for social justice and my knowledge that this work is more important than my nervousness help me move forward.

Many teachers argue that students do not want to discuss emotionally laden or controversial topics (that greatly impact their lives) in class. If students are resistant to discussing, for example, the social conditions that prevent them from making enough money to pay their rent, it could be because they think such a discussion could only lead to their feeling humiliated or embarrassed or, at best, feeling temporary relief from discussing such matters in class. I believe we as English language teachers can facilitate such discussions in ways that do not magnify one student's problems, but create spaces for questioning social concerns that affect us all through conversations safe enough (that is, respectful, not evasive) to encourage students to share their opinions and experiences. We need to have the courage to create such a class atmosphere. Whenever I facilitate discussions around sensitive topics, I notice that students are often completely engaged and eager to share. Conversations usually erupt, and the most challenging aspect for me is facilitating the discussion effectively enough for all students to have a chance to speak their own truths and share their thoughts and ideas about the topic.

Indeed, I have witnessed time and time again that, if given opportunities and space, students become enveloped in cultural and political discussions and materials. I can almost hear their collective sigh of relief for opportunities to respectfully and empathetically discuss issues crucially relevant to all of our lives. As another radical educator, Elsa Auerbach (1992), says, "people learn best when learning starts with what they already know, builds on their strengths, engages them in the learning process, and enables them to accomplish something they want to accomplish" (p. 39). I agree. Students walk into the English language classroom with subject matter. It seems counterproductive to me if we, as their teachers, look past the material they bring—material so relevant to their lives and central to who they are as cultural beings—in search of material that may not be as connected to them or as urgent.

bell hooks (1994) expresses concern that one of the biggest misconceptions about teaching for inclusion is that it simply substitutes "one dictatorship of knowing with another" (p. 32). The work should move far beyond merely substituting binary oppositions. And Peggy McIntosh (1989) warns that "disapproving of the [dominant] systems won't be enough to change them" (pp. 10–12). How can we combine our disapproval of the status quo with a curriculum that is multidimensional, multifaceted, and so inherently dynamic that it reflects our thirst for justice in the world? In South Africa, I strove to do this through infusing a Business English curriculum with progressive content. I tried to create a multidimensional curriculum that also reflected who my students were. Using such a curriculum to help them prepare to pass their Business English exams, which they all did, helped them develop not only fluency and accuracy in English, but also confidence in using it. All of this was evident in our class discussions and in students' own analyses of their command of the language at the beginning of the term compared to their abilities at the end of the term.

Incorporating social justice content into English courses does not have to be difficult. It is a matter of acknowledging the students, seeking to understand their realities, and then finding and using materials and resources that reflect who they are and that will help them achieve their goals. As advocates of progressive education, it is crucial for us to ensure that the content we teach is connected to a belief in a more just society. In doing so, our teaching will be reflective of our core values.

———————————

Sedia Dennis holds an MA in teaching from the SIT Graduate Institute and has taught a variety of English classes, from literacy to academic English. She has taught adults and youth in the United States and other countries and currently teaches developmental reading and writing in Washington, in the United States.

CHAPTER 3

Danger Learning: Experiencing ESL Through Conflict Resolution Techniques

Christopher Stillwell

There is a natural fit between the studies of English as a second language (ESL) and conflict resolution, for both involve a pursuit of enhanced skills with which to use and understand language effectively. Although the word *conflict* may conjure feelings of danger of physical or emotional harm and risk of damage to relationships, an ESL course in conflict resolution can promote an alternative view of conflict as a potential opportunity for enhanced communication and understanding. Insofar as conflict forms an inevitable part of daily life, such material can also have great power to stimulate interest and engage higher order thinking as learners use language not for its own sake but rather to communicate, negotiate, and mediate.

This chapter outlines content that can be used to relate conflict resolution principles to language learning. It proposes techniques for addressing simulated conflicts in the classroom and focusing on the appropriateness of specific language structures for particular contexts, all of which can lead to great strides in learners' vocabulary, fluency, listening comprehension, and pragmatic awareness. Sample tasks are provided that apply content knowledge to the analysis of disagreements found in the news, literature, and movies, and methods for helping students learn to conduct mediations for themselves are explored. Attention is paid to ways in which processes typically used by third-party mediators to help disputants resolve their differences might be used at the level of effective teaching practices. How a teacher begins the class, asks questions, and deals with the responses can all serve as models of good mediation practices, such that the medium of instruction serves equally well as the message.

CONTEXT

The material discussed in this chapter was developed in the United States for a 5-week ESL seminar for adult learners that I taught at an intensive English program in New York City. Having completed all the levels of study that the program had to offer, the learners were continuing to develop their language abilities in elective courses that used movies and television programs as the content for integrated language skill development, with their progress assessed through vocabulary-related homework assignments and in-class simulations. As we went forward, the need to find new and interesting ways of broadening their exposure to and practice with language structures became more pronounced.

Taking inspiration from Kressel's (2000) statement that conflict resolution skills are "of such demonstrable value that training in mediation can well be justified as part of the learning experience of the well-educated person" (p. 544), for "conflict in the workplace, school, home, and community is ubiquitous and would often respond well to mediation" (p. 541), I decided that a conflict resolution focus would be valuable both on its own merits and also as a fresh means of language study. In the absence of an ESL-friendly text on mediation and conflict resolution, the class would continue in its prior mold of using movies as the primary foundation for the lessons, but in this case the scenes would not only serve as sources of vocabulary, grammar, listening, and speaking practice, but also provide the structure for numerous discussions and simulations dealing with the nature of conflict and mediation. The content of the course would also be strongly influenced and guided by principles promoted by the International Center for Cooperation and Conflict Resolution (ICCCR) in a number of graduate level practica at Columbia University, which I had attended.

In the use of conflict resolution and mediation techniques as the subject of language study, the ESL seminar focused primarily on practices that would not only provide the most interesting content, but that would also prove transferable to the teaching and learning of language. Such common mediation practices as building rapport, using neutral language, listening actively, asking probing questions to tease out additional information, and debriefing to promote reflection and enhance learning were likely to yield similarly positive benefits in the language classroom. These techniques would lay the foundation for a safe environment in which affective barriers to class participation could be broken down, and they would provide additional strategies for the negotiation of meaning.

CURRICULUM, TASKS, MATERIALS

The first step for mediation, as for a language class about mediation, is to begin well. This can require building rapport, learning about the parties and the issues in need of mediation, and giving an introduction to the process to come (Kressel,

2000). Similar procedures that take place in the typical language classroom include the use of icebreakers to help the students get to know one another, assessment of needs, and analysis of the syllabus in order to outline the expectations and requirements of the class as well as how progress will be assessed. Setting appropriate expectations is important, and for a language class this involves explaining how grades will be assessed using unique materials such as these. A graduate-level practicum on conflict resolution typically requires a fair amount of participation in role-plays in class as well as completion of journals, papers, or both, to demonstrate reflection and growth. Such tasks can be equally appropriate in the language classroom, perhaps with specific language requirements overlaid to meet particular language goals.

The Teacher's Role

Throughout the conflict resolution literature, there are calls for the mediator (or teacher of mediation content) to "walk the talk, and in so doing . . . model the skills involved in constructive management of conflict" (Deutsch, 2000, p. 38). This is the principle of congruence, and it can be illustrated by the story in which a woman asked Gandhi to tell her child not to eat sugar (LeBaron, 2002). According to the story, Gandhi told her to bring the child back in 2 weeks for a talk because he had to follow the advice for himself first before he could pass it on to another. Such congruence played a crucial role in making Gandhi's lessons convincing and credible, and similar practice on the part of the teacher or mediator can prove equally effective. Therefore, it is essential for a teacher of conflict resolution content to incorporate its key principles in the routine operation of the class from the start, such that students learn from not only the subject matter, but also their experience of its execution.

Associations With Conflict

In a sense, second language learners may have an advantage over native speakers when it comes to the acquisition of conflict resolution skills, for so much of the work involves the development of effective habits in terms of language use. These habits can be incorporated as a part of the learners' nascent language practice, with new language structures analyzed in terms of the impact they might have in conflict situations. Still, learners surely have many preconceived notions about how to deal with conflict, and it is essential for the teacher to bring this to light at the outset. As Deutsch (2000) states, "before students can acquire explicit competence in conflict resolution, they have to become aware of their preexisting orientations to conflict as well as their typical behaviors" (p. 37).

In the intensive ESL class, a scene with an argument from a movie or story such as *Rain Man* (Johnson & Levinson, 1988), or even more family-friendly fare such as *Finding Nemo* (Walters & Stanton, 2003), can provide a useful context for discussion of the definition of *conflict,* as well as the connotations associated with the word. Students may be put into small groups to work out how the chosen situation qualifies as a conflict, all the while determining their own criteria for identifying what a conflict is. Each group may then be given a piece of chalk and a section of the chalkboard on which to post their list of the characteristics of conflict. Students can then take a "gallery walk," visiting the other lists and considering the various ideas that arose from everyone's group work. To increase the amount of language practice that takes place, each group could be split in half, with half of the members able to visit other groups while the other half stays behind and elaborates on their list for the visiting students. After a fixed period of time, the group members swap roles, with the first half now standing by their lists and talking to visitors. Whole-class discussion can then draw out the similarities and distinctions, reaching a consensus on a class definition of conflict. Further discussion may involve the challenge to think of a (conventional) story or movie that does not involve conflict, which should be a difficult task because drama typically requires conflict to define the main action of the plot. A logical following step is to consider the frequency of conflict in daily life: How many conflicts do we typically face in a single week? In a day?

A more direct way to find out students' orientations toward conflict that is used in conflict resolution practica and workshops, particularly those offered at the ICCCR in New York, is to ask them to list other words that they associate with it. In an ESL context, this task may include asking learners to share the connotations that the equivalent word typically has in their native language. Once a sufficiently large list of associated words has been generated, learners can take a step back to identify how many of the words could be considered negative; it will typically be a high percentage. (For further explicit attention to language, it may be useful to take an additional moment to identify common prefixes used in negative words, if indeed such a pattern exists.) In the end, the instructor should summarize the discussion and share that one aim of a course in conflict resolution is to reframe this negative perspective, such that learners see how conflict can have a positive side: It can lead to opportunities for deeper understanding, beneficial changes, strengthening of relationships, and growth.

Preparation and Body Language

If the course content is to be supplemented with the viewing of a conflict-ridden movie, a fair amount of additional preparation is required to make sure the experience is relevant and valuable. If the material is used effectively and interest can be nurtured, the teacher will have a memorable context within which to discuss the nature of conflict and to put principles into action with movie-inspired role-plays. However, if sufficient thought is not given to how to ease frustration and scaffold learners' successful introduction to the material, they may quickly lose patience.

The opening scenes of a movie are often a particular challenge for nonnative speakers, and it may seem natural for a teacher's plan to involve using the captions to provide textual support for the viewing. However, there are two potential drawbacks to such an approach. First, the use of subtitles can backfire, proving that the vocabulary is too difficult (depending on the level of the class) and reinforcing the feelings of frustration. Second, the use of subtitles does not have any parallel in the mediation process, so the film-viewing portion of the class may be experienced as something unrelated to the acquisition of mediation skills. Encouraging students to view the scene while practicing the listening strategy of paying attention to body language is an alternative approach that avoids those two drawbacks. It provides useful experience as learners consider the wealth of information that can be inferred just by paying attention to a person's posture, gestures, and the like. This strategy can broaden language learners' understanding of a scene, just as awareness of body language can attune mediators to the emotions and comfort levels of parties attempting to resolve a conflict. (For additional suggestions regarding the effective use of video in the classroom, see Stillwell, 2009.)

The Impact of Language: Identification of Conflict Vocabulary and Triggers

Parties committed to the resolution of conflicts need to be keenly aware of the impact (both intentional and unintentional) that various language choices can have. Exploration of this side of language can be of obvious benefit for English language learners as well, for it engenders a fuller understanding of many structures that have already been taught. Use of video can prove particularly helpful in this area because conflicts found in movies can provide powerful and memorable examples for analysis.

A simple approach involves providing students with a list of key vocabulary to listen for as they view a selected conflict in the film or having students make a list for themselves as they watch. The ensuing discussion of the words should focus on the words' degrees of neutrality and the likelihood that they will yield positive responses. In particular, the class should identify a number of words and expressions that can instantly provoke a negative response in the interlocutor, words that may be referred to as *triggers*. Although some triggers may be fairly obvious, such as the use of offensive or accusatory language, others will be far more subtle. For example, in recurring arguments between partners, one may characterize the other's (forgetful) behavior as a refusal to do what should be done. If the offending partner feels that it is not a case of conscious choice but rather of human error, the frequent use of the word *refuse* can become a trigger, causing feelings of irritation to build up and sending the overall conversation on a negative spiral.

As potential triggers are identified in the list of vocabulary, students can be asked to generate a companion list of more neutral alternatives that could be used in their place. For instance, direct language and accusations can be paired with softer and less direct versions, and direct attacks might be replaced with *I* statements (e.g., "When you say I am refusing to do something, I feel that you think my forgetfulness is intentional"). In addition, further target language structures can be explicitly taught and added to the list according to the various ways they can be used and misused. For instance, grammar structures and other language forms can be viewed as triggers and alternatives to triggers (see Table 1).

Paired role-plays of situations inspired by the movie can be used to help students experience firsthand the difference such choices can make. For instance, students may be asked to role-play an argument between Nemo and his father, Marlin, from *Finding Nemo*, in which Nemo's desire for freedom conflicts with Marlin's need to keep his son safe from danger. For the first attempt, students can be given 1 minute to improvise a conversation, using vocabulary from a list of emotionally charged words and triggers from the film, such as "You think you can, but you can't" and "I hate you." For the second attempt, students revisit the same scenario but shun the triggers in favor of more neutral alternatives used in a sensitive fashion. Having students put a mark next to each word they use while engaged in the role-play can keep them on task and scaffold the reflective discussion that occurs next, in which participants consider the impact that the vocabulary choices had on their emotions and inclination to cooperate. Class discussion, or homework journals, might then logically turn to reflection on the triggers that tend to come up in the students' own recurring arguments, with consideration of alternative formulations. Assessment of students' progress with use of these language structures could take the form of additional role-plays using the same word lists in new situations. For a variation on this activity that is not based on movie content, see Figure 1.

Further discoveries can be made in role-plays and simulations if a third party is employed to observe the conversation and lead the reflective discussion that follows, helping the participants focus on their experience of the activity and how the various uses of language made them feel. As the class progresses and students gain further experience with mediation techniques, these third parties can become

Table 1. Language Features, Triggers, and Alternatives

Features	Possible Triggers	Alternatives
Parallel structure	List of complaints	List of positives
Conditional	If you hadn't (been so stupid) . . .	If I were in your shoes . . .
Modals	Should/ought to/had better/must	May/might/could/can
Gerunds and infinitives	Threaten/warn	Appreciate/enjoy
Pronunciation	Deliberately enunciated and spaced due to irritation	Casual, calm, and connected speech
Direct or indirect language	Imperative, subjunctive for advice	Perhaps/maybe/you might consider . . .

Sister Trouble

Linda borrowed her sister Susan's jacket on Friday night, but she never asked Susan for permission. Linda returned the jacket later that night. Susan is angry.

Try to use these vocabulary words:

Hold on	Take it easy	Have to	C'mon
Whoa	Insult	What (are you), (stupid)?	Put up with
Make a scene	Be supposed to	The point	Upset
Change the subject	Take something personally	You (you, you)	Why?
	Who do you think you are?	Give (someone) an excuse	

Also, use three yes/no questions:

_____ ?

_____ ?

_____ ?

Sisters' Second Chance (Try It Again!)

Which words should you avoid this time? (Which words were triggers?)

Which words could you use in their place?

Try to use some probing questions, like:

_____ ?

_____ ?

_____ ?

If it's appropriate, you can also try to use an I statement.

When _____, I feel like _____.

Also, avoid ~~Why?, yes/no questions, sentences that begin with "you."~~

Extra information:

For Linda's Eyes Only

It's not uncommon for the sisters to borrow things without asking. In fact, Susan has been using Linda's bag for a few weeks.

Linda went to a diner on Friday night. She didn't notice any problems.

Linda has just gotten a big bonus at work.

For Susan's Eyes Only

Susan found ketchup stains on the jacket. Linda never said anything about it.

Susan wanted to wear the jacket on Friday night, but when she looked in the closet, she found it was gone.

This is Susan's favorite jacket.

Figure 1. Triggers and Alternatives Role-Play

more deeply involved in the role-plays. They can act as mediators, guiding the conversations and helping the disputants hear one another through use of active listening techniques.

Active Listening

After a mediator has made an opening statement in which appropriate expectations are discussed and ground rules are agreed upon, the disputants can each be given the floor to share their experience of the conflict. As the parties make their statements, the mediator engages in active listening, which is here defined as the use of paraphrases and probing questions to verify meaning and draw out additional information. These techniques are hardly exclusive to mediators; they can be used by unaided disputants to promote clearer communication in one-on-one discussions, and in the classroom they can be used to enhance the quality of students' contributions and participation. Language students will also find these techniques useful in the negotiation of meaning in their daily lives to confirm understanding and repair communication breakdowns.

Paraphrasing

Skill at paraphrasing can be essential to a mediator in a number of ways. First and foremost, it should be used to check assumptions and clarify meanings so that statements made by participants can be understood as they were intended. This repetition benefits the original speakers by helping them hear themselves as they sound to others, promoting reflection and making greater self-awareness possible. It is also useful for the mediator to revisit salient points to make sure that they are not missed. In addition, paraphrasing at times entails modifications to the language to make it easier for the opposing party to truly hear or to promote the discovery of new possibilities.

The teacher of such content should model the effective use of paraphrasing as a part of the routine management of classroom discussion. In this fashion, students can become familiar with the ways paraphrasing can be used to test assumptions, promote understanding among classmates, and allow speakers to reflect on their statements. It can also be an important means of enhancing student participation by making contributions of varying volume and intelligibility equally discernible to the rest of the class. Of course, paraphrasing can also be used as a technique for correcting student errors, but its effectiveness for this purpose may be limited if the teacher does not follow up to explicitly confirm that the correction has been noticed.

Students should be made aware of the benefits that paraphrasing practice can have as a part of the development of their language abilities. It can create opportunities for them to use the many redundant language forms that they have learned across the spectrum of grammar and vocabulary, and it can play an important role as a communication strategy, as speakers aim to find alternative formulations of their messages in order to match either their own or their interlocutor's linguistic limitations. It may be useful to introduce the classroom analysis of paraphrasing with a reminder to ESL students of the various ways that they will likely have already made use of it in their prior studies. For instance, their grammar lessons may have included work with indirect speech, and the students will undoubtedly have been asked to summarize content on numerous occasions. New opportunities to develop this skill (and develop fluency) can come from mediation role-plays based on such situations as the one in Figure 1 or movie conflicts like the earlier example related to *Finding Nemo*, in which the mediator parrots or modifies the disputants' statements. Paraphrasing work can also become a regular part of the video viewing activities, as students are given time to discuss and summarize what they've seen, confirming comprehension with their partners. Formal assessment of content knowledge and paraphrasing ability can be conducted simultaneously through similar summarizing tasks.

Probing Questions

The second skill involved in active listening is asking probing questions. During a mediation, the mediator uses probing questions to guide the discussion and get additional information on the table. Probing questions can be particularly effective when used to draw out details about what the experience of the conflict has been like for each individual, thereby helping all participants get a better idea of how it would feel to wear the other's shoes. Common questions for this purpose can be along the lines of "How did that feel?" and "What were you expecting to happen at that time?"

The effective use of probing questions requires skill and dexterity. The first rule for their use in mediation is to favor open questions over closed ones, which means that questions that offer limited choices (e.g., yes/no questions, *which* questions) should generally be avoided in favor of broader *who/what/how* questions. Not only do the former place limits on the amount of information that is given in response, making it difficult for accurate portrayals to come to light, they pose an additional risk when used in a chain: They can betray an agenda to the questioner's line of thinking. Something similar happens when teachers ask questions like "It's easy, isn't it?" and "Do you understand?" There can be little doubt that an affirmative answer is the desired response, and even students who have questions may remain silent out of a fear of being a nuisance. This situation can cause great frustration when misunderstandings lead to problems down the line. Teachers may have better luck following the mediator's approach by using more open queries such as "What do you think about that?" or "How does that seem?" or possibly even asking students to paraphrase the instructions with a partner.

Skilled use of probing questions also requires a delicate touch when it comes to *why* questions because these put the receiver in the position of having to defend an action or statement. Depending on the context, they can amount to an attack, particularly when used to directly question a person's choices or behaviors. Mediators try to avoid such circumstances as they seek to create a safe, comfortable atmosphere of sensitivity and understanding, so they favor alternative formulations like "That's interesting. Can you say more about that?" These questions invite the same sort of responses that a "Why?" might get, but with a mild tone that helps maintain a nonconfrontational atmosphere. In the language classroom, teachers may be surprised to find that using "Tell me more about that" in place of "Why?" can have similar results, particularly in classroom management situations (e.g., "Why didn't you do your homework?" vs. "You didn't do your homework. What can you tell me about that?").

For language students, practice with probing questions can yield great benefits. In terms of grammar, the subject-verb inversions can be a notorious source of confusion because they are required for questions but not for noun clauses (e.g., "What time *is it*?" vs. "I want to know what time *it is*" vs. "*Could you* tell me what time *it is*?"). Any additional practice with these forms in a fresh light will be a welcome source of review. Furthermore, because so much of learning involves putting forth the right questions, classroom practice with these forms will be time well spent, providing students with tools to continue learning on their own.

Mediation activities with probing questions, and also with paraphrasing, can entail having students share stories about conflicts they have experienced, with the listeners using active listening techniques to get a complete understanding of the situation before they have to join new partners and retell what they've learned. As a final step, these new partners recount the story to the original teller to check for accuracy. In the ICCCR conflict resolution practicum, another approach involves simulating calls to a phone helpline: The callers have prompts that indicate problems for which they are seeking advice, and the operators confirm understanding by paraphrasing what they hear and ask further questions to reach a deeper level of understanding. Further development and even assessment of these skills can be undertaken in practice mediations done in a fishbowl, whereby the whole class can benefit from sharing the same experience and having a group debriefing.

Debriefing

Mediators may find it useful to close with a group reflection, or debriefing, and in the classroom it can be equally useful to set aside time for participants to talk candidly about their experience of the processes that they attempted. Such activity is useful for reflection on the content and goals of the activities, which learners may not be explicitly aware of. According to Schmidt (2001), the "orthodox position in psychology is that there is no learning without attention" (p. 16), so these moments of reflection can provide a crucial opportunity for awareness to be raised regarding the lessons explored in a class session.

Kressel (2000) suggests that debriefing of simulated mediations begin with a "ventilation" stage in which the mediator initiates the reflective process by spontaneously sharing impressions of the experience. In the next stage, other participants of the role-play give supportive feedback, sharing specific and concrete comments on things that went well. The mediator then has an opportunity to share sources of surprise or frustration, and the other participants use active listening techniques to draw out deeper responses. As a final stage, participants may revisit the role-play and try again, attempting to make use of any lessons learned.

Debriefing can make another useful addition to the daily class routine. The teacher may invite students to take turns sharing one thing that they will remember from the day's class, something that they will take away with them. This stage can also serve as a useful point for the teacher to further model active listening, drawing out details with probing questions and paraphrases in such a way as to maximally benefit the rest of the class.

REFLECTIONS

A single chapter does not provide sufficient space to flesh out an entire course in conflict resolution as language learning content, but it may provide a sense of the significant overlap between the fields of language education and mediator development, as well as a useful idea or two for using this content to meet learners' needs for engaging language practice. Active listening skills can help students focus on messages and negotiate meaning, and the practice of using neutral language and avoiding triggers can provide a unique form of speaking, vocabulary, and grammar practice that gives students a fuller appreciation of the way language choices can affect outcomes. In addition, journals and reflective papers can provide regular practice with writing, and use of video can bring other voices into the classroom for authentic listening tasks.

There are also a number of ways to incorporate a reading focus into a course of this nature. First, written material such as short stories and newspaper articles can ground the class with a narrative arc and interesting contexts just as well as video can. In addition, there is a wealth of literature regarding the development of conflict resolution skills, and a sampling of chapters and articles can greatly enhance learners' experience. Of particular interest would be pieces dealing with key mediation concepts, such as the importance of distinguishing between positions (which are beliefs about what is simply right) and needs (which are often what a conflict is really about). An exploration of Maslow's (1954) hierarchy of needs can provide for interesting discussion and a strong foundation for additional active listening activities, as listeners attempt to use probing questions to discern the underlying needs that drive a conflict. These topics and other critical lessons are explored in Deutsch, Coleman, and Marcus's (2006) *The Handbook of Conflict Resolution: Theory and Practice*, though this text may require considerable support for all but the most advanced ESL learners. *Basic Skills for the New Mediator* (Goodman, 2004) is another option that provides an introduction to the field and includes some attention to legal issues. Many of the principles discussed in this chapter have referred to transformative mediation, so Bush and Folger's (2005) *The Promise of Mediation: The Transformative Approach to Conflict* is another potential alternative.

Above all, care must be taken not to overwhelm students with more details and theory than they can handle. Kressel (2000) notes that "foundational skills should be emphasized in mediation training programs where training time is limited," for they "are often sufficient to produce a collaborative orientation in the low-to-moderate-intensity conflict" (p. 542) that is most common. Although many of the principles may seem fairly simple, it would probably be best for a teacher to choose only one or two to work on during a set of classes and to carry those concepts forward into each new segment as part of the growing collection of tools. If this material is handled well, students should develop greater facility with various ways of using language for expression, enhancing their ability to appreciate more than surface-level interpretations of messages. In addition, students may be inspired to explore these concepts further on their own, becoming not only better language users themselves but facilitators of enhanced communication and understanding for others as well.

ACKNOWLEDGMENTS

I would like to express my deep appreciation to Beth Fisher-Yoshida, Leo Danny Mallonga, John Krister Lowe, and Columbia University's International Center for Cooperation and Conflict Resolution for making this chapter possible through inspired and inspiring instruction.

Christopher Stillwell has taught English language learners in Spain, the United States, and Japan for 15 years as well as TESOL graduate students at Teachers College, Columbia University. His interests include collaborative professional development and application of conflict resolution techniques to enhance language learning.

CHAPTER 4

A Pound of Prevention: Health Literacy for Beginning-Level Adult English Language Learners

Susan Dalmas and Judy Trupin

Teach health literacy to beginning-level English language learners (ELLs)? At first, this might appear to be a contradiction in terms. Even to consider teaching health basics to beginning-level speakers of English might seem impossible. Anyone who has taught adult ELLs knows that assistance with navigating the health care system is critical to students. Learners frequently rely on teachers for help—they bring their doctor's instructions to the teacher for explanation or ask for help making an appointment. Certainly, any good English to speakers of other languages (ESOL) class or textbook teaches *arm, stomach, knee,* and *I have a headache.*

But how could a full curriculum be introduced that incorporates terms and concepts such as *medical history* and *patients' rights and responsibilities*? How would a teacher communicate more abstract or technical concepts such as prevention and responsibilities? Or various names of diseases? In this chapter, we explain why the Queens Library Adult Learner Program (ALP) in New York City, in the United States, chose to undertake this task, and we describe our curriculum and results to date.

CONTEXT

Queens Library's ALP first became involved with health literacy in 2003, when five staff members participated in the Health Literacy Study Circle at the Literacy Assistance Center. Materials from this project were then incorporated into the ALP's ESOL classes. It quickly became apparent that although materials for health literacy were becoming available, most were written for either Adult Basic Education students—who are fluent in English but need to improve their reading and writing—or intermediate- or advanced-level ELLs. Therefore, in the spring of 2005, the ALP applied for and received funding from the Jacob and Valeria Langeloth Foundation to write and pilot a health literacy curriculum for beginners. This 2-year pilot would include writing an original 28-unit curriculum, testing it with 20 classes at Queens Library, and ultimately making it available on the web at no charge (see *Health Literacy Resources for Adult Education,* n.d.) to other adult education programs.

There are several reasons why we decided to create a separate health literacy curriculum. First, although the existing ESOL curriculum includes units on health, there is not enough time within a 12-week semester of 60 hours of instruction to devote more than one or two sessions to health topics, because the class must cover other themes to meet the survival needs of beginners. Additionally, if offered as a separate class, the in-depth health literacy curriculum could then be selected by those who need it the most, such as individuals with limited access to health care or those who are already struggling to manage the health care system for themselves or a family member.

What Is Health Literacy?

One widely circulated definition of health literacy is "the capacity of an individual to obtain, interpret, and understand basic health information and services and the competence to use such information and services in ways that are health-enhancing" (Joint Committee on National Health Education Standards, 1995, p. 5). It may be surprising to note that 36% of adults in the United States—fluent English speakers included—have only basic or below-basic health literacy (National Center for Education Statistics, 2003). And 12% of the U.S. adult population is estimated to have skills at the lowest level on the Health Activities Literacy Scale, an instrument designed to assess an individual's ability to perform various types of health-related activities, including understanding preventive health practices, following a doctor's instructions, reading medicine labels, and navigating the health care system. Individuals at this lowest level would not be able to do such things as determine how often to take medicine (Rudd, Kirsch, & Yamamoto, 2004). Other research indicates that nearly half the U.S. population cannot accurately follow medical instructions (Vastag, 2004). Nonnative speakers of English have also been found to be more likely to have lower levels of health literacy (Kutner, Greenberg, Jin, & Paulsen, 2006).

In our own survey of 35 students enrolled in a beginning ESOL class at Queens Library in 2004, 73% scored "inadequate" in their functional health literacy level. Another 18% scored "marginal," reinforcing the need to improve health literacy among our own student population.

Student Body

The students enrolled in our classes reflect the diversity of Queens County, New York, which has more than one million foreign-born residents—46.1% of the population. The most common languages spoken by the ALP's health literacy learners are Spanish, Chinese, Bengali, and Haitian Creole (New York City Department of Planning, 2004).

As is typical of the ALP, health literacy classes serve a mix of individuals, some with many years of formal education and others with limited prior formal schooling. Some learners are stay-at-home parents of young children, and others work as laborers or retail clerks. Some had been doctors, nurses, or pharmacists in their countries of origin.

Our target population for the health literacy classes is beginning-level students who know at least a few words of English and have some native-language literacy. We felt that those with absolutely zero English literacy would benefit more from a traditional beginning-level course and that the use of text would be too challenging for them.

CURRICULUM, TASKS, MATERIALS

The focus of the curriculum is threefold: (1) to help students acquire the language necessary to navigate the health care system, (2) to provide them with content-specific knowledge about the U.S. health care system, and (3) to teach preventive health knowledge.

Each unit consists of two to six sessions, beginning with background information for teachers. The background information—as well as content-specific professional development—was added after the first round of classes, when it became apparent that the teachers felt a little insecure about their own knowledge of health and were running to the Internet to refresh their knowledge. A summary of the health-related information pertinent to each unit was then added. For example, the unit on nutrition outlines the different kinds of fats along with a brief explanation of why trans fats are harmful to the body. The unit on taking temperature gives an overview on when it is generally considered advisable to see a doctor when one has a fever.

Following the background information for teachers, each lesson provides a detailed lesson plan and all the needed worksheets. There are also suggestions for web sites to visit and other textbook resources to support the unit. An accompanying audio CD was produced to provide listening activities for many of the units.

The curriculum begins with the basics: learning the parts of the body, describing symptoms, and making doctor appointments, much like the health care theme in most textbooks for beginners. Each unit includes all four skills and blends teacher-led activities with group and pair work. We made our own audio recordings and produced our own "Body Parts Bingo" game and student worksheets for the activities.

Starting at about the seventh session, the curriculum broaches topics that are different from the standard ELL beginner health units. We have attempted to impart a level of health-specific information generally not covered in "ordinary" ESOL classes. Some topics, such as options for obtaining health insurance, are rarely touched upon in any ESOL class, whereas others may be covered, but either not for beginners or not in the level of detail we have provided.

One topic that is often reserved for higher level students is filling out and reporting one's health history. The high level of vocabulary involved is too complex for beginners. However, it may be one or more years before ALP students are functioning at a high enough level to attend an intermediate class; in the interim, they are likely to encounter such terminology when visiting the doctor. We have therefore included a unit on filling out a health history with pictures and realia used for more concrete terms such as *blood pressure, X- ray,* and *injection.* However, some terms, such as *cancer* and *heart attack*—which might be familiar in the individual's native language—would be unduly challenging to teach through English and are therefore taught with translations.

In the classroom, students work with classmates who speak the same language to fill out a medical vocabulary worksheet, translating a list of words often seen on a health history into their native language. Students are not necessarily expected to retain all terminology on the worksheet; rather, they could bring this personal glossary to assist them with visits to their health care providers, which several students have reported that they have in fact done. And in a rather unexpected outcome, one student said that he took his worksheet to his next doctor's visit and asked the nurse—who spoke his native language—to assist him with translating the English words.

We also hoped that some terminology introduced that is generally not considered "beginner" vocabulary will be retained because the words are repeated through the course. For example, teachers do not usually teach the word *cholesterol* to beginners. But this term is introduced in the medical vocabulary session and later reappears in at least four other units—on health screenings, healthy eating habits, health goals (e.g., "exercise may help maintain healthy cholesterol levels"), and talking to the doctor. When the word reappears, the teacher is able to suggest that students refer to their medical vocabulary section, where they can quickly see its meaning. By the end of the course, most students seem comfortable using this word in English. They are able to both pronounce and recognize it in oral and written English.

In order to convey some of the more challenging vocabulary of the curriculum, we also rely more on native languages than would a traditional ESOL class. For example, it seems more expedient to ask learners to look in their dictionaries for the word *cancer* than to try to explain it using beginning-level English.

Another goal of the curriculum is to go into more detail on some health-related topics. For example, many contemporary ELL textbooks in the United States introduce the U.S. Department of Agriculture's (2009) Food Pyramid but cover only the basics, such as which foods are in each category (see Figure 1). Our curriculum goes into detail by, for example, providing information on the need for fiber and on healthy and unhealthy fats.

We also want to make U.S. content relevant to students' cultural backgrounds. One of the many pitfalls of teaching based on the Food Pyramid is that the recommended foods do not necessarily correspond to the traditional diets of many ALP students. For example, the Food Pyramid has milk as a main category, and although it does mention calcium-fortified foods such as orange juice or soy milk, there is little emphasis on alternative calcium sources. Because the traditional diet of many ALP students does not include milk products, we provide additional information on nondairy sources of calcium.

Sometimes, challenging abstract terminology such as *patients' rights* needs to be explained in English. Asking learners to look up a word like *rights* would be impossible, given the many meanings of the word in English. So to teach this concept, we introduce other examples of rights that students might be familiar with, such as the right of a citizen to vote.

Figure 1. U.S. Department of Agriculture Food Pyramid

Health care rights is another example of a term that may be a culturally new concept to some students. Once the English vocabulary is understood, the ideas of health care rights, such as the right to a translator or to treatment in an emergency, may be explained.

The curriculum makes use of both realia and pictures. Some of the hands-on activities are the most enjoyable to students. For example, in Unit 5, students use single-use thermometers to learn about normal body temperature in Fahrenheit. Although some of the students are familiar with the Celsius scale for normal temperature, few of them know the Fahrenheit scale. Following a demonstration of how to take one's temperature, students take their own temperatures and subsequently practice saying and responding to the question "What's your temperature?" by interviewing several classmates.

For a number of units, we developed our own wordless or minimal-language picture-based stories, similar to Ligon and Tannenbaum's (1990) *Picture Stories* or Singleton's (n.d.) *Picture Stories for Adult ESL Health Literacy.* Each story is related to the theme and is also used to reinforce previously introduced vocabulary. For example, in a story about talking to the doctor, the first series of pictures shows the nurse checking the patient's blood pressure and heart rate and taking his temperature, because this had been taught in the prior two lessons.

Each of the picture stories ends with a box with a question mark. This technique is used as a means of eliciting different responses from students about what should or might happen next. A typical sequence with a picture-based story is as follows:

1. As a class, the teacher elicits text for each of the pictures, writing key words on the board.

2. In small groups, students write one or two sentences for each of the pictures and discuss ideas for the question box. The teacher walks around to assist the groups.

3. Students share their results as a class.

4. The teacher asks various students to write the text on the board, and the class makes corrections as needed.

5. Students work in small groups to role-play the situation.

6. Volunteers share their role-play with the whole class.

In the initial phase of developing the curriculum, we collaborated with Elmhurst Hospital, in Queens, New York. Hospital staff provided us with photos, hospital maps, and brochures, and gave us input from the hospital departments as to which topics they considered critical for their patients to know. Queens Health Network (QHN; a health and hospital corporation comprising two major facilities in Queens, 15 community-based medical centers, and six school-based health centers) was also a resource for us; QHN staff worked with Queens Library staff to develop a brochure on health programs for the uninsured in New York City.

Typically, a four-skills English course attempts to cover grammatical or functional skills in every lesson. We made a conscious decision not to do this because the health literacy class was not designed to replace a four-skills course; rather, it was designed as a supplement. We introduce grammatical functions only when needed to convey a particular unit theme. For example, the word *should* for advice is introduced in several units, such as the one on treatment of colds and flu (e.g., "You should call the doctor") and emergency care (e.g., "You should/shouldn't call 911—the emergency number in the United States").

Short true/false quizzes are given after each unit. These units assess both language acquisition (e.g., an arrow pointing left, accompanied by the statement "This means go straight") and health knowledge (e.g., "Your cat is in a tree. Call 911").

REFLECTIONS

Following each health literacy unit, the students complete an evaluation of the unit, writing in either their native language or English. From these evaluations, as well as from teacher comments and the results of a focus group after each quarter, we have learned about some of the individual successes of ALP learners.

Many students have reported that they now felt more comfortable making appointments and talking to their health care provider. A number of students found out about available methods to pay for health care and signed up for programs. Others mentioned that they now knew they had the right to a translator and understood the importance of giving their name and address correctly. Others commented on what they had learned about practicing preventive health. One student wrote, "I always buy white rice and white bread. After this class, I buy wheat bread and brown rice." One teacher reported that her student had never gone to a doctor because he thought doctors were only for women. After a unit on health screenings, he went to the doctor—and discovered he had high blood pressure.

To assess the success of the program statistically, we relied on the results of true/false quizzes as well as the Short Test of Functional Health Literacy in Adults (S-TOFHLA; Nurss, Parker, Williams, & Baker, 2003), which was given as a pre- and posttest. We chose the S-TOFHLA because it is one of the few standardized assessments for health literacy available for ELLs. Another widely used assessment, the Rapid Estimate of Adult Literacy in Medicine, scores the ability to read 66 health and medical words aloud (Columbia University School of Nursing, n.d.). We rejected this instrument because of its emphasis on pronunciation rather than comprehension.

A health researcher who served as a consultant on the pilot curriculum evaluated the data from these tests. As of this writing, data are available from the first two rounds of classes; the two later data cycles are not yet available. On most of the true/false quizzes, the majority of students scored above 80 percent. When we found that students did not score well on a particular item, we reexamined the assessment question and the teaching of the concept. In some cases, the question had been misleading. In a few cases, such as determining when to go to the emergency room, we realized that students were having trouble distinguishing when it was medically necessary to go and therefore added materials to the curriculum to reinforce the concept.

To date, the results of our S-TOFHLA posttests have not shown a statistically significant improvement in health literacy. However, we feel there are a couple of reasons why this is the case. First, the level of the test is so high that for beginning-level learners, even if they score a higher number of correct answers on their posttest, that gain may not be sufficient for them to reach the next level—namely, to move from "inadequate" to "marginal" literacy. Second, although the test has been validated for use with ELLs, several researchers have pointed out that it does not assess the full range of skills needed in health literacy, including listening and speaking skills, or cultural differences (Columbia University School of Nursing, Center for Evidence-Based Practice in the Underserved, n.d.; Nielsen-Bohlman, Allison, Panzer, & Kindig, 2004). Our curriculum covers these aspects of health literacy, but they are not measured by the standardized test.

One unexpected outcome has been how the program affected the ALP teachers. Most of them reported increasing their own knowledge of health. One said, "I love teaching this class because I always learn something new." For many of the teachers, the experience gave them more insight into the students they teach. One surprise was that, although most of the class participants knew about health care options for their children, they were not aware that there were programs available in New York City to assist all adults—even those without immigration documents.

One of the biggest challenges of running the health literacy classes has been maintaining attendance. This is often a problem in adult education programs due to the nature of these students' lives—they get jobs that interfere with schooling or have childcare issues or health problems. Furthermore, some students were not aware that it was a special class and, despite our calling the class English for Your Health, they thought they were signing up for a regular beginning-level ESOL class. After the first round, we distributed flyers detailing the course content in simple English. Nonetheless, some continued to enroll only because they were closed out of the regular beginner ESOL classes, only to leave when they discovered it was not what they were expecting.

After reflecting on our experience with the first year of health literacy classes, we would like to make a number of improvements. First, we would like to offer this course as an elective to individuals enrolled in beginner ESOL classes. In this way, learners who now enroll in twice-a-week beginning-level classes would have the option of adding a health class once or twice a week.

Second, we now feel that certain topics may be too challenging for a beginning-level class. The issues of rights and responsibilities probably should be part of an intermediate-level class. However, we do feel that some of the more advanced content may still be important to provide to beginners, so we may consider providing short explanations of these topics in learners' native languages.

In terms of assessment, we have not been satisfied with the S-TOFHLA as a pre- and posttest instrument. The level of the S-TOFHLA is so high that many learners were frustrated by taking it. More than once at the pretest session, a student wanted to withdraw from the class because the test was so difficult that the individual assumed the class would be too difficult as well. Furthermore, some of the questions seemed not to be related to health literacy, but rather to grammar. For example, one multiple-choice question asks test takers to complete the blank in a sentence with either *are, has, had,* or *was.* A learner could certainly understand the health concept and still mark the wrong answer. Additionally, the S-TOFHLA page design seems difficult to read, and items tested do not look like real materials. For example, one item asks questions about an appointment card, but the text does not look like a card. Another issue is that the test assesses only reading and numeracy skills and does not assess listening comprehension, which is an important component of health literacy for ELLs.

For future classes, we plan to devise our own pre- and posttest, which will reflect our curriculum more accurately. The questions will not only correspond more closely with what we teach, but also include some simple questions so that we are able to see progress for someone that begins the class with almost no health literacy. We will test learners' ability to work with health-related materials that closely resemble those they will encounter in the real world. Our test will also include a listening component. This test, currently in draft form, will assess learners' ability to understand health-related language as well as health content.

Our experience has led us to believe that a health literacy class for beginning-level ELLs can be an effective part of the ESOL curriculum. As mentioned earlier, a health literacy class is ideally an elective course, running concurrently with a beginning-level ESOL class. In setting up such a curriculum, it is important to keep several things in mind (see Appendix for additional useful resources):

- Learners should be fully informed as to what the focus of the course will be.

- Where possible, this information should be provided in both English and a learner's native language.

- Potential participants' English skills should be assessed to screen out individuals with extremely minimal writing skills as well as those with zero English literacy.

- Teachers need to be trained specifically in how to discuss potentially sensitive health information and should be provided with appropriate health information resources.

Teaching health literacy to beginners is a challenge, but it is one worth undertaking. Learners cannot afford to wait until they are fluent speakers of English to learn how to navigate the health care system. Their health care needs are immediate, and methods of addressing them should be a component of any adult education curriculum for beginning-level ELLs.

ACKNOWLEDGMENTS

Special thanks to all of the Queens Library Adult Learner Program staff who lent their voices and images for our audio recordings and visuals; the Langeloth Foundation for funding the development of the health literacy curriculum and the field testing of the health literacy classes; pilot teachers Geremias De La Cruz, Stephanie Chellapen, MaryAnn Gottlieb, Sandra McElvey, Beatrice Osterer, and Jennifer Wieland; production designer David Ford; illustrator Maryam Shabaaz; and for helping to develop background information for teachers, Kate Goheen, Health Literacy Fellow 2007, and Leslie Short, Health Literacy Intern 2006, New York City Mayor's Office of Adult Education.

Susan Dalmas has an MA in TESOL and has taught all levels of ESOL; developed curricula, materials, and assessments; provided teacher training; managed programs; and supervised ESOL teachers and support staff. She is currently the manager of the Adult Literacy Program for the Queens Library, in New York City, in the United States. She initiated and implemented the health literacy curriculum described in this chapter.

Judy Trupin has an MS in TESOL and has taught all levels of ESOL, developed curricula, and supervised preservice teachers. Currently, she is the assistant manager of the Queens Library Adult Learner Program, in New York City, in the United States, where she has developed the English for Your Health course and a curriculum for teaching computer skills to adult learners.

APPENDIX: RESOURCES FOR TEACHERS

Ganong, E., & Ingram, D. (2003). *Grab bag of health activities.* Toronto, Ontario, Canada: Canadian Resources for ESL.

Gianola, A. (2007). *Health stories.* Syracuse, NY: New Readers Press.

Harvard School of Public Health. (n.d.). *Health literacy studies.* Retrieved from http://www.hsph.harvard.edu/healthliteracy/overview.html

Health module introduction and project ideas. (n.d.). Retrieved from http://www.aelweb.vcu.edu/publications/ELCivics/health/index.htm

Literacyworks. (2008). *California health literacy initiative.* Retrieved from http://www.cahealthliteracy.org/

National Center for the Study of Adult Learning and Literacy. (n.d.). *Skills for health care access and navigation.* Retrieved from http://www.ncsall.net/?id=891

City of New York. (2009a). *NYC health literacy campaign.* Retrieved from http://home2.nyc.gov/html/adulted/html/health/campaign.shtml

City of New York. (2009b). *Take care New York: A policy for a healthier New York City.* Retrieved from http://www.nyc.gov/html/doh/html/tcny/index.shtml

Trupin, J. (2008). *Health literacy resources for adult education.* Retrieved from http://qlhealthlit.blogspot.com/

CHAPTER 5

Does Content and Language Integrated Learning Work With Young Learners?

Elena Pratissoli

The improvement of understanding is for two ends: first, our own increase of knowledge; secondly, to enable us to deliver that knowledge to others. (Locke, 1703, p. 1)

When English was introduced as a foreign language in the Italian primary school system in the late 1980s, there were many pilot projects scattered all over Italy. It was only in 1992 that English became a compulsory subject in the primary school curriculum. From the beginning, it was clear that parents welcomed this change, but they were also sceptical about how English would be taught to young children and the competence they would achieve. After many years, several doubts still survive, and in a way they are evidence of the expectations that parents have. These are only a few of the many questions parents usually ask when their children start learning English in primary school:

- Can young children pick up foreign languages easily? Does "the sooner, the better" really work in terms of teaching modern languages to young children?

- Are young children able to imitate new sounds effortlessly?

- Will they pick up only words, or will they be able to understand and speak English?

- Will my child become bilingual?

- Will the children study enough grammar and syntax to be linguistically competent when they reach secondary school?

- What comes first when you teach English to young children? What linguistic benefits might I expect culturally, cognitively, socially, and educationally?

Being involved in both teaching children and training language teachers, I keep looking for new ideas and readings about methodology that could work better to meet children's needs. When I first heard of content and language integrated learning (CLIL), I understood it as using a modern foreign language as the language of instruction for nonlanguage subjects, and I couldn't help thinking that integrating content and language would help increase children's motivation and make their learning more stimulating. My main questions, as a teacher, were as follows:

- Would CLIL work with young children?

- Would it be all right to try it out in our school system?

- How would colleagues see it? Would they cooperate?

- Would parents think it was a waste of time?

Starting a CLIL-based project was indeed a new way of teaching and learning, and many aspects had to be considered, including how to assess the results to be achieved. Taking for granted that we all, as teachers, agreed on the importance of enhancing language competence in young learners of English, we asked ourselves if better results might be achieved via a CLIL approach and project work. What if the CLIL project helped us learn a new set of teaching skills but did not result in increased student learning? And was one goal more important than the other: increased language learning or content learning?

Being responsible for the whole project and for delivery of the lessons in English, I had to make sure that parents were informed of the rationale for learning English through an interdisciplinary project. I invited them all to a school meeting to illustrate it in detail so that they would be aware of the following:

- the aims of the project

- the team of teachers working on the project

- how the timetable would be adjusted

- the activities that children would be doing in class

- the skills they would be practising, the language they would be learning, and how it would integrate within the national curriculum syllabus

- the importance of raising cultural awareness through motivating activities

- how the children's progress would be evaluated and how parents would be informed of their children's progress

- the end product to be achieved, underlining that more emphasis was going to be given to the process of developing the project than to its final output

I also explained that the language outcomes were going to be especially related to thinking skills and learning strategies that could help enhance language competence about information gathering and questioning; organisation skills about categorising and comparing; and analysing skills about identifying main ideas, key elements, relationships, and patterns.

The parents were a bit puzzled about this new way of teaching and learning, which was so different from their own learning experiences. They were also concerned that it might be an experiment that would waste their children's time or learning opportunities. It became important to make parents understand that the children were going to use the language in a more motivating context, one that would offer a need to speak in English while they were learning other topics. So it was crucial to emphasize that exposing the children to more English would enhance their language competence.

CONTEXT

In the Italian context, the main integrated strands of a primary school modern language curriculum are communicative competence, language, and cultural awareness. The children should learn the language within authentic, appropriate contexts, and the teacher should act as facilitator in the language learning experience. The children should also explore a variety of cultural aspects and become aware of the lives and interests of children their age in other countries (*Nuove Indicazioni per il Curricolo,* 2007).

In recent years, interest in understanding and developing CLIL has been growing in Italy, although it has not been widely piloted in schools (Eurydice, 2006). Teachers with a more innovative outlook regard this type of educational approach as a means of reinforcing the study of foreign languages and enhancing the quality of teaching and learning. In broader terms, CLIL is currently considered in tandem with the concept of bilingual education. More specifically, it is seen as an approach associated with the communicative use of a foreign language.

The project work I describe in this chapter was carried out at the Scuola Primaria "Italo Calvino" in Reggio Emilia, Italy, and lasted the whole school year. A total of 22 children ages 7–8 were involved. They were beginners in English, in their second year of primary school. As the specialist English teacher, I was personally responsible for the project and its results, and I worked as a member of the team with the classroom teachers. I was quite lucky to find myself working with a team of teachers who believed in teaching English to young learners and were willing to work on a yearlong project that would involve integration of language teaching into the learning of other subjects.

CURRICULUM, TASKS, MATERIALS

When the teacher team started looking for links in curriculum areas that might help enhance language competence, we soon realized that there were many links and that we had to plan our cross-curricular project carefully in order to focus on sets of self-contained units that could be built up sequentially into a final project outcome.

Curriculum contents must be "appropriate to the grade level of the students" (Curtain & Pesola, 1994. p. 35). Genesee (1994) suggests that content "need not be academic; it can include any topic, theme, or non-language issue of interest or importance to the learners" (p. 3). Met (1991) proposes that "'content' in content-based programs represents material that is cognitively engaging and demanding for the learner." CLIL can also have an impact on conceptualization, that is, how students think; the results from working in another language may lead to different thinking horizons and allow better association of various concepts. Thus, the broad aims of our CLIL project were as follows:

- to help children develop communicative abilities in English

- to favour the introduction of multimedia technologies

- to enhance the teaching and learning of English as a foreign language

- to integrate the teaching of English with other subjects

- to develop cross-curricular approaches

- to raise cultural awareness

- to introduce the teaching of curricular subjects through English

- to encourage children to develop creativity and learning through problem solving and learning by doing

- to use the computer as a tool to produce materials

We therefore agreed about the importance of organising the lessons in such a way that would incorporate individual work, pair work, group work, class work, information and communication technology (ICT) activities, and the integration of students with special needs. We selected the aspects we would cover from the following curricular subjects:

- *Math:* Eulero-Venn diagrams; calculus of probability; mathematical ideas such as number, geometry, patterns, and movement; basic programming rules of LOGO; problem solving activities; mind mapping

- *Science:* animals and their habitat; classifying animals (tame/wild), where they live (farm/forest/water), what they eat (carnivorous/herbivorous)

- *Environmental Studies:* rubbish collection differentiation, recycling rubbish and household waste, visiting the local incinerator

- *Italian:* narrative text and its main elements: theme, plot, conflict, resolution, character, setting; sequence identification; mind mapping

- *Geography:* identifying where Italy is and where the United Kingdom is, figuring out how to get to the United Kingdom

- *Music:* discriminating sounds, associating music with narrative contexts and characters

- *Arts and Crafts:* creation of the materials needed to build the multimedia story, backgrounds, characters

- *Physical Education:* body segments, development of laterality, space orienteering, problem-solving activities, creating patterns to make the LOGO "turtle" move

- *ICT:* use of multimedia computers (Windows platform), use of Micro-Worlds JR (a version of LOGO) tools to create the project's final output

- *English:* communicative functions such as greetings, introductions, describing physical appearance, colours, numbers, likes, dislikes; main topics such as animals and pets and related British cultural aspects; IT vocabulary to create the final output in English

We first agreed on using a project-centred approach. This would allow the children to relate what they know to a concrete problem that they would work through in the target language and to take greater responsibility for their own learning. In addition, this approach offered the incentive to become personally involved and to cooperate with peers, and it might enhance students' motivation and help them develop their intellectual, motor/physical, and social skills.

We decided that I would work alone with the class for 3 hours per week to meet the amount of English instruction required by the national curriculum. I would give children the language background as well as introduce, practise, and revise vocabulary and structures related to age, colours, names, animals, onomatopoeic sounds, likes, and dislikes. The students would cover the other subjects with their classroom teachers, and I would follow a monthly rotation to be able to cooperate with the teachers in order to integrate some English into their lessons.

The team then planned the interdisciplinary units so that I would know exactly what the classroom teachers would be teaching in terms of content and specific language used. This was a demanding but essential step in order to know the concepts and specific language the children had already learned in Italian and to be able to present, recycle, reinforce, revise, transfer, or develop this into an English context.

At this planning stage, it became clear to all of us that there was a risk of the project expanding too much and losing focus. We therefore decided to have a final product that would give parents evidence of some of the steps of the project work. The children would create an interactive multimedia story in which the several inputs from the CLIL lessons would converge so that activities could blend together. This final product would also give the children a focus for their work.

The work carried out in English specifically focussed on animals and pets, and it was aimed at developing language competence while incorporating aspects of other curriculum areas and disciplines. Figures 1 and 2 show the related project webs, and in the remainder of this section I describe some of the CLIL activities we created.

Speaking and Listening: Developing Oral Fluency and Phonemic Discrimination

The students learned that animals, like people, make different "noises" depending on the country they come from. They discovered what onomatopoeic sounds are and learned some through a song (see Figure 3). We played guessing games to

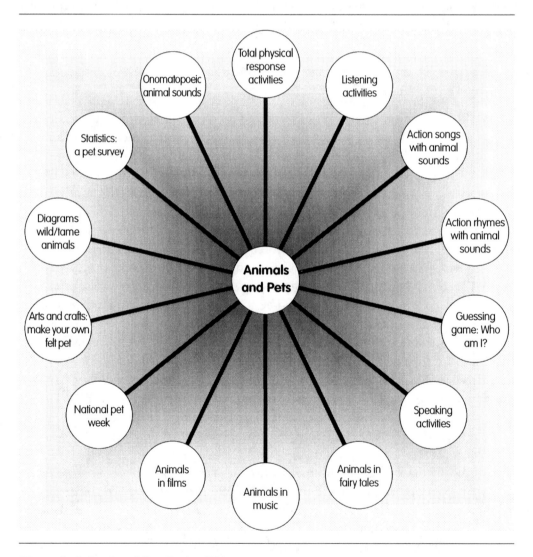

Figure 1. Animal and Pets Project Web

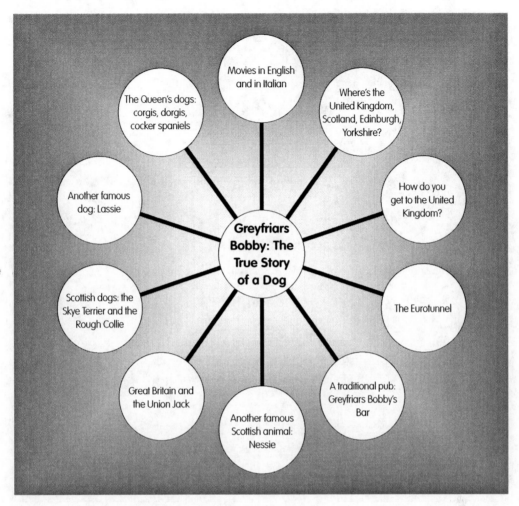

Figure 2. Project Web Focusing on Related Cultural Links

help children improve their speaking skills: by miming, making sounds, saying the animal's colour or number of legs. They also had to guess the name of the animal.

Vocabulary Development

Some of the children's artwork was used to make flashcards, cards to play Pelmanism (Concentration), Bingo cards, board games, worksheets, and wall displays. Figure 4 shows an example of a matching activity created by the children to learn basic vocabulary and improve their reading skills.

Speaking Accuracy

The students completed a survey based on an activity in their English course book, *I-Spy English* (Ashworth, Clark, & Lawday, 1996; see Figure 5) by going around the room and interviewing their classmates. The structures they had to

Figure 3. Students Singing the Onomatopoeic Sounds Song

practise were *"Have you got a pet?" "Yes, I've got [a dog, two cats, a white rabbit]"* or *"No, I have no pets."*

The children next built a graphic to illustrate the answers they had received, and they worked out statistics about the most common pet, the least common pet, how many of their classmates had pets, and how many did not.

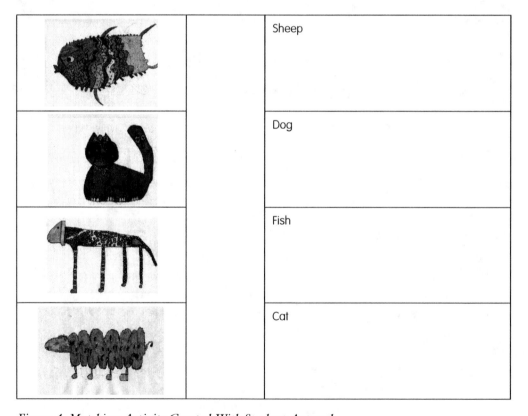

Figure 4. Matching Activity Created With Student Artwork

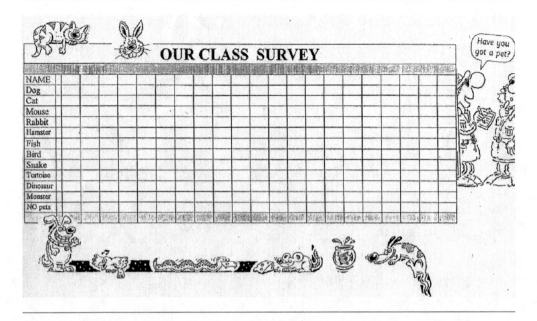

Figure 5. Class Survey About Pets

Speaking Fluency

As an arts and craft activity, children made finger puppets by following oral instructions in English. Figure 6 shows the puppets that were then used to create communicative activities in context.

Figure 6. Finger Puppets Made by Students

Using their finger puppets, the children created conversations assembling the communicative structures they had learned. They loved practising so much that they soon became fluent and even tried to add funny bits to their conversations. The following is an example of a conversation that I recorded:

Chicken:	Hi!
Lion:	Hello!
Chicken:	What's your name?
Lion:	My name is Simba. What's your name?
Chicken:	My name is Chick. What colour are you?
Lion:	I'm brown. What colour are you?
Chicken:	I'm white. Do you have scales?
Lion:	No, I have brown fur and an orange mane. I'm a mammal. Do you have fur?
Chicken:	No I have feathers. I'm a bird.
Lion:	What's your favourite food?
Chicken:	Corn! What's your favourite food?
Lion:	Chicken!

Academic Vocabulary: Task Language and Following Directions

As a follow-up to science lessons about garbage, reusing, and recycling, the children were asked to bring to school objects made of different materials. During the CLIL lesson, the children labelled them and classified them into four categories: wood, plastic, metal, glass (see Figure 7). Each child filled in a related grid in his or her own notebook.

An arts and crafts activity followed this classification exercise. Students had to read a worksheet, selecting what they needed to make their own mobile and then following the steps to assemble it (see Figure 8).

After creating their mobiles, students had to assess themselves and provide feedback on the activity. Figure 9 shows a sample feedback form filled in by one of the children.

Figure 7. Classifying Materials Brought From Home

1. Draw what you need		
Wood Sticks	String or Ribbons	A pair of scissors
Draw objects made of ⇒	Wood	Plastic
	Metal	Glass

2. Follow Instructions
1. Select the stick.
2. Select the strings.
3. Select the materials.
4. Make knots.
5. Hang your mobile.

Figure 8. How to Make a Mobile

Academic Reading

As a follow up to geography lessons, the students learned where Italy and the United Kingdom are, and we formulated a hypothesis about how we could travel from one country to the other. We used maps written in English, and students had to answer specific questions to improve reading skills:

> Look at the map:
> 1. Where is Italy?
> 2. Put a cross where Reggio Emilia is.
> 3. Where is the United Kingdom?
> 4. Put a cross where Edinburgh is.
> 5. Go to www.mappy.com.
>   a. Think of all the possible means of transport you could use to go from Reggio Emilia to Edinburgh.
>   b. Calculate your route from Reggio Emilia to Edinburgh.

DIFFICULT ☹ • hang objects • make knots • thread beads with small holes • make the objects balance
EASY ☺ • choose the objects to hang • borrow objects from my friends • help my friend to make knots
I liked: • all the objects and their different colours and shapes and materials • try and try and try to learn how to make knots
I didn't like: • ask for help to make knots
I felt… • sad because I lost the only real pearl I had
I need to improve: • making knots • learn how to balance objects

Figure 9. Sample Feedback Form

Academic Writing

The children discovered that there is a tunnel between France and the United Kingdom, so they looked for information about it on the Internet, formulated questions, and found answers to them. This activity was a particularly interesting part of the project, but it generated quite a bit of interlanguage; English was used but in an approximate way at times because children incorporated aspects of Italian, their native language. This most probably happened because information was gathered either in Italian or in English. The main difficulty I found was in making the children formulate easy, simplified sentences with the English they knew. I had to be careful that there was as little interference as possible from Italian to English. Figure 10 shows some examples of the materials students produced to reinforce their speaking and writing skills.

Cultural Aspects of the Foreign Language

Through looking at pictures, watching films, answering the teacher's questions that were intended to encourage reflection and comparisons, and engaging in problem-solving activities, the children had opportunities to observe and notice cultural aspects that they could compare with their own experiences in order to discover differences and similarities. Some of their comments about the main cultural aspects were recorded and reported by teachers through observation sessions and note

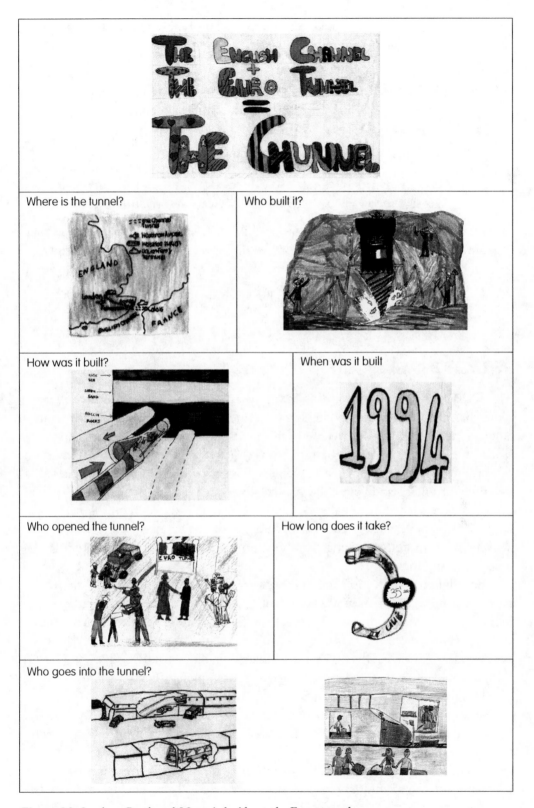

Figure 10. Student-Produced Materials About the Eurotunnel

taking during the various activities (Appendix A shows the grid used to keep a record of teachers' observations):

- The children thought it was quite obvious that British animals spoke a different language from Italian animals! They also pointed out that noises are different in English, and they looked for examples in children's magazines and cartoons:

  — "An Italian dog says 'bau-bau.' An English dog says 'woof-woof.'"

  — "Like in my video game! Also cats speak English in my video game. Cats say 'meow-meow' in English. My cat says 'miao-miao.'"

- Looking at pictures on web sites or children's magazines, they noticed that in Britain children tend to have more pets than in Italy and, surprisingly, most dogs live inside the house and not outside:

  — "My dog lives in the garden. He has a small house in the garden."

  — "My cat Nina can't sleep in my bed."

REFLECTIONS

This CLIL project was a rewarding teaching experience, even if it did require more than the usual amount of lesson planning and preparation. As the foreign language teacher, I was able to spend more time with the children, and this helped me get to know them better. It was easier to respond to their needs and offer them adequate support and feedback. This strong involvement also eased discipline problems and kept children actively involved in all the lessons. Because activities were carried out in a less traditional way, all the children took part and felt less academically tested and assessed. Even the special needs children were actively involved in the activities, and group work helped them feel more integrated and supported.

The children's motivation and interest were always quite high. Using the Internet to search for information was stimulating, and they expressed their enthusiasm in the artwork they produced. There was the potential to get carried away by the children's enthusiasm and broaden the project too much if we were to develop all their ideas. So we had to make sure to plan and adhere to detailed lesson plans that we could all share. (Appendix B shows an example of a completed lesson plan template.)

Assessment was an important issue because we realised early on that we would test the children in three areas: their English skills, the extent to which they learnt in Italian, and the extent to which they learnt that content in English, too. So we had to plan sets of testing materials that were strictly related to the topics covered but that took into account several skills and that could all converge toward a global evaluation of each child's progress. The fundamental need was to devise a broad continuum of assessment modes in order to create a spectrum that reflected the full range of each child's progress, achievement, and development. Such a continuum included teacher observation; teacher-designed tasks and tests; work samples, portfolios, and projects; curriculum profiles; standardised tests; and diagnostic tests.

Collaboration was another key part of the interdisciplinary approach we used. The teachers involved in the project met once a month to do the following:

- exchange feedback on the several phases of the project

- define evaluation criteria to measure the effectiveness of the project

- monitor learning process

- keep a record of each child's progress and attainment

- revise strategies

- plan teaching units

- develop materials

- discuss assessment strategies

- elaborate forms of assessment and evaluation of individual outcomes

- define how to communicate assessment information to children and parents

According to feedback received from the team of teachers, parents, and the children themselves, this project enhanced the children's concentration and attention span during the activities, their cooperation was spontaneous, and the children approached the several disciplines with a different state of mind because the different subjects were all entwined and presented in practical and concrete ways. The children cooperated and encouraged their friends to communicate in English more, offering instantaneous feedback and participating willingly in turn taking. There was no need to set the scene for role-plays or drama activities; conversation was spontaneous and came from a real need.

Several doubts arose and triggered discussion or critical analysis in our team. We all agreed that learning by doing should be favoured by teachers for the development of language and subject learning. Developing language learner self-confidence was undoubtedly very important, and an early experience with integrated media offered a great opportunity for language learning and culture awareness raising. The cross-curricular activities offered the opportunity for a critical look at practices in classes and a chance to teach cooperative and collaborative learning techniques.

In the future, I will focus my attention on planning in advance how to record activities and outcomes in a more systematic and detailed way, where to physically keep the records, and how to organize them so that every step and relevant activity of the project can be substantiated. I'm glad I could work on this project because from my professional point of view, it was a demanding but enjoyable teaching experience.

Most of the teachers agreed on how a CLIL approach should be planned and developed on a more regular basis. The trust parents put in us was a fundamental influence because it meant that they were cooperating, too, and the children were supported and living in a constructive environment. We involved the parents at the beginning, during different stages of the project, and at the end. Figure 11 shows the final questionnaire that we distributed to parents, with sample responses from various parents.

Defining a target language for CLIL was complicated. One main problem was connected to the use of Italian and English and the mixing of the two languages. Alternating between the two is what in linguistics is referred to as code-switching,

---

What aspects/activities of the CLIL project did your child enjoy most? Why?
- He liked working in groups.
- He liked doing things, more than sitting down quietly.
- She realised she could actually use English to talk to her friends.
- He liked the way subjects were correlated.

What aspects/activities didn't your child like?
- At the very beginning he didn't know who was teaching what.

Two positive aspects of this CLIL project:
- It made my child more aware that English is a language he can use even outside language lessons.
- Learning topics more in-depth

Do you think your child's workload increased because of the project?
- It did in the sense that homework was given on a more regular basis.
- The work increased, but I don't think my daughter felt it as a "load."

Did the work help your child remember facts and skills better? Why?
- Well, he certainly told me what had been happening in school, and that meant a lot since [previously] any time I would ask him, "What did you do today?" his usual answer would be "Nothing."

Do you think the CLIL activities helped your child develop a wider language competence in English? Why?
- They certainly did! They spoke some English at last!
- My child was feeling so confident about her English that she felt the right to test mine!

Did you receive enough feedback about how the project was developing?
- Regular feedback was given during parents' nights.
- We had a few meetings [about] this project, and I finally understood what CLIL was.
- The materials produced during the lessons were brought home regularly.

Continued on p. 71

Did you feel involved in the project? Why?
- My son was so enthusiastic about it that he asked me if I could help him at several stages.
- We knew exactly what our children were doing while in school.

Were your expectations met? Why?
- Yes, absolutely. Glad I agreed about carrying out the project.
- Seeing my child going to school in a good mood was a real joy.

Other
- Video recording should be considered as another possible way of documenting the experience.
- Thank you for making this school year so special.

Figure 11. Final Questionnaire and Sample Responses

and this often occurs in bilingual contexts. Code-switching was therefore adopted to explain difficult concepts and to boost the children's confidence and allow them to express their opinions fully and freely. One of the key skills in relation to producing better learning appeared to be that of *translanguaging* (Baker, 2000). Input was received in one language and, via cognitive or other processes, output was produced in the other language, which triggered a learning stimulus. Because of these factors, I found myself organising lessons and activities in different ways:

- One of my colleagues would deliver a unit in Italian, and I would then deliver complementary lessons in English.

- I would deliver oral lessons in Italian, inserting key words in English.

- I would ask the children to do reading and writing activities in which key English words were used.

- The children would find information from materials in English, and I would help them with the language they would need to express themselves more fully in English.

Language competence can be increased at early stages and with young learners as long as the tasks given and the experiences offered are selected in accordance with the learners' stage of development. I have found that in CLIL lessons the tasks may be cognitively demanding as long as long as they are concrete; they may be emotionally complex as long as they are experiential.

Elena Pratissoli taught English as a foreign language for 20 years to children in several primary schools in Reggio Emilia, Italy, and she taught Italian in Scotland. She trained primary school teachers of English for 18 years. Currently, she teaches Italian as a foreign language to migrants at CTP Pertini, in Reggio Emilia.

APPENDIX A

Date	Group/class	Activity	Discipline	Teacher
Description of activity				

Child's name	Interaction			Comprehension			Production		
	Interest (specify if shown in L1 or L2)	Cooperation (specify if in L1 or L2)	Autonomy (specify if only in L1 or also in L2)	Global comprehension (in L1)	Global comprehension (in L2)	Understands sentences related to the topic in L2	Can answer questions only in L1	Can answer questions in L2	Can ask/answer questions in L2

☺ always	☺ sometimes	☹ never

Notes:

APPENDIX B: SAMPLE LESSON PLAN

Subject: Science

Topic: Animals

Class/group of children: 20 children

Teacher: English teacher

General aims: Classifying animals

Reference to the national curriculum:

- Finding criteria to classify animals
- Grouping animals (mammals, fish, amphibians, birds, insects, reptiles)

Prerequisites:

- Classification abilities
- Ability to fill in classifying grids
- English vocabulary related to animals, food, body parts, colours, numbers

Specific topics: Vertebrates and invertebrates

Linguistic aims:

- English vocabulary about animals: *vertebrate, invertebrate, mammal, fish, bird, insect, reptile, 2–4 legs, swim, run, jump, fly, climb, eggs, babies*

- *How many legs has it got? It has . . .*

- *Can it . . . ? Yes, it can. No, it can't.*

- *What does it like? It likes . . . +food.*

Interdisciplinary aims:

- Understanding instructions

- Classifying criteria

Skills:

- Listening

- Reading

- Writing

- Speaking

Number of lessons/hrs: three 1-hour lessons

Space: Classroom

Materials:

- Pictures of animals

- Worksheets

Forms of testing:

- Oral questions (oral comprehension + oral production)

- Multiple-choice activity (reading + writing skills)

Assessment: Grid

Records of activities to be kept for portfolio: Individual worksheets

Anticipated problems: Too much vocabulary

Unforeseen problems (to be filled in after the activities for future reference)

APPENDIX C: EUROPEAN CLIL WEB SITES

CLIL Compendium
   http://www.clilcompendium.com/

European Network for Content and Language Integrated Classrooms
   http://www.euroclic.net/

Translanguage in Europe: Content and Language Integrated Learning
   http://www.tieclil.org/

Science Across the World
   http://www.scienceacross.org/

Teaching English
   http://www.teachingenglish.org.uk/

Multilingualism: Many People Speaking Many Languages
   http://ec.europa.eu/commission_barroso/orban/index_en.htm

How Do Teachers Integrate Language and Content?

CHAPTER 6

Two Birds, One Stone: Using Academic Informant Projects as English for Academic Purposes Content

Shawna Shapiro

One of the greatest delights of teaching university-level English for academic purposes (EAP) is getting to work with students from a diverse range of academic majors. My most recent class included future businesspeople, doctors, architects, engineers, linguists, teachers, and research scientists. This sort of diversity is both exhilarating and a bit overwhelming, particularly as I have become increasingly aware of the many differences among these fields of study. How am I, as a generalist, supposed to support these students in the various language tasks they will encounter as they pursue their academic careers? (For more discussion of these concerns, see Braine, 1988; Spack, 1988.)

This question led me to develop what I call the Academic Informant Project, in which students use their own academic experiences as the content for our language course. In this chapter, I describe how I have implemented this project in my classes, highlight some of the students' most successful projects, and reflect on the benefits and challenges of this type of work.

CONTEXT

The question of how to meet students' specific needs within the generalist framework of academic English has been discussed frequently in TESOL literature. Educators and researchers know that language and content are codependent and highly integrated, but they often struggle to balance the depth of that content with the language objectives of the course (Hyland, 2002; Spack, 1988). In essence, the issue of content represents a conundrum for language teachers: As we incorporate more specialized content, we have less time to address the important language issues that emerge from that content. Yet if we try to avoid specialized content altogether, our classes may lack the academic authenticity and cognitive challenge that students most need in order to reach more advanced academic language proficiency (Pally, 1997). It often seems as if either content or language takes a back seat in our classrooms.

In recent decades, second language scholars have sought solutions to this quandary by designing curricular activities that ask students to bring their own wealth of academic experiences into the English language classroom. Johns (1990), for example, requires students to keep an academic *journalog* in which they reflect on their mainstream coursework, describing what they are learning and how they feel about their progress in the course. Hirvela (1997) assigns a *disciplinary portfolio* in which students compile and reflect on work they have completed in mainstream courses. Taking what she calls a critical approach to this sort of work, Benesch (1996, 2001) has developed class activities targeted more closely at areas of potential conflict in mainstream courses, such as communicating with professors and understanding assignment expectations. Hence, she sees her language course as a place for problem solving and advocacy in relation to content courses. Learning about these projects inspired me to develop a set of my own activities so that students in my classes can engage more deeply with their academic work, both inside and outside our language classroom.

CURRICULUM, TASKS, MATERIALS

Because most of the EAP courses I teach are focused largely on writing, the Academic Informant Project usually has a written component, although that writing is often accompanied by an oral presentation and other preparatory activities. The aim of the project can be to inform, analyze and critique, reflect, or a combination thereof.

Informative (Expository) Projects

In these projects, students use their own academic interests as the basis for continued research, with the aim of informing their classmates about a topic in their own area of study. Students first submit a proposal in which they discuss the relevance of the topic to themselves and their audience of classmates (see Appendix A for sample proposal questions). They then complete a short research paper and an oral presentation based on one or more narrowed research questions.

One of the most memorable examples of this project was completed by a Taiwanese student named Charles, who chose to define the field of "marine resources" for his classmates because he sensed that students from other disciplines often thought his work involved "just going fishing." Whether or not this perception was accurate, Charles was quite enthusiastic about the opportunity to address possible misconceptions about his discipline and to persuade his classmates that his field will, as he put it, "become a hottest technology in the future." In his final presentation, he explained how marine biology can contribute toward medical research, energy conservation, and global politics. In completing this project, Charles confronted particular linguistic challenges: To make his case, he needed to define key terms in his field in a way that was comprehensible to an audience of nonscience majors. In addition, he had to develop an organizational structure to present his information in a logical way. Charles experimented with various organizational structures that included subtopics such as methods, issues, and future directions.

Carrie, a Taiwanese business student in the same class, used her paper and presentation to explain the rationale behind the use of paid consultants for non-profit organizations. Her project explored a prevalent concern in the nonprofit world about the ethicality of using funds for this purpose. In both the spoken and written components of her project, Carrie used persuasive language and various forms of evidence to convince the audience that hiring a consultant can indeed be a worthwhile use of nonprofit funds, particularly when it results in more effective fundraising efforts. Because her undergraduate studies in business had given her a number of opportunities for public speaking, Carrie's presentation was an excellent model for other students who were less confident in organizing and conveying relevant information. It also offered a chance for her to bring together two intellectual worlds that many students might not have considered complementary: business administration and social activism.

Informative projects like these offer an ideal starting place for practicing language functions such as definition, explanation, cause/effect, and problem/solution. Because students often possess substantial knowledge about their topics, this project allows them to represent and expand on what they know, thus gaining confidence in both language use and content knowledge. At the same time, the project presents a real challenge for students: They must consider the relevance of their academic studies to a diverse, interdisciplinary group of classmates. Hence, they begin to develop a greater awareness of audience. I imagine that this sort of project might also be useful in preparing students to rationalize their choice of major to potential employers, graduate admissions committees, and—perhaps most difficult of all—their own families.

Analytical/Critical Projects

Although informative projects offer potential for some degree of persuasion and audience awareness, this second type of project reflects a more explicit attempt to move students toward an analytical mode. For many students, this transition from knowledge telling to knowledge transforming is particularly difficult, both culturally and cognitively (Bereiter & Scardamalia, 1987). Students can often discuss the *what* of texts, but struggle to address the *why* and *how*. This struggle is made easier, though, when students are guided from concrete observation toward more abstract analysis. One of the best ways for students to practice this analysis is by bringing their non-EAP textbooks (or other readings) into the EAP classroom. In language classes, they can learn the skill of textual analysis and begin to recognize how writing differs by discipline. Significant aspects of writing that might be considered in this analysis include the location (or absence) of theses and topic sentences, the types of supporting evidence most commonly used in a given discipline, and the ways that other publications are referenced. Students can also be guided to notice more nuanced linguistic features such as the use (or avoidance) of the first person, the passive voice, idiom, slang, and metaphor. Even the length or syntax of sentences can be a focal point of this sort of analysis.

Students can accomplish this type of activity individually or in disciplinary groups. Once an inventory of linguistic features has been completed, students can put their observations into practice with imitation activities in which they write in a style similar to the one they have analyzed. In this way, students can begin to see textual analysis as a valuable skill for learning inductively the conventions of a particular writing situation. They learn to truly notice the language of their disciplines.

Other possibilities for textual analysis exist as well. In a more advanced composition class comprising native as well as nonnative English speakers, I recently assigned the students a more complex rhetorical analysis in which they looked for hidden messages in an academic artifact (a document or web site from a campus course or program; see Appendix B). Students first took detailed notes on the artifact, noticing content, organization, and language features, as well as visual elements where appropriate. Next, they looked for common themes and unexpected elements in their observations. Finally, they developed a paper about the obvious and less-obvious messages that the artifact conveyed to its readers.

The papers resulting from this project reflected a variety of student interests. For example, Salyse, an African American student in a special section of composition for underprepared writers, chose to examine the syllabus from her Spanish class and discussed the instructor's commitment to creating a collaborative learning environment, as evidenced in the description of course objectives and activities. In her paper, Salyse discussed the importance of this environment in easing students' anxieties about language learning. Ultimately, she was able to make a claim about the effectiveness of this professor's more collectivist approach to language instruction by comparing her own experiences to the language in the syllabus.

Another student, a Somali immigrant named Anwar, examined the web site of our university's Young Democrats organization. Although he struggled at first to locate something out of the ordinary in the web site, he eventually zeroed in on the group's use of the word *sexy* as a descriptor for one of its environmental projects. His paper discussed the ramifications of this particular linguistic choice for an audience of college students.

In another class, an Ethiopian student named Eden analyzed the flyer for an Afro-Caribbean talent show in which she was a participant. She looked in particular at the photo the sponsors were using to market the event and discussed how it inaccurately represented African cultures as largely homogenous. In her paper, she discussed the pros and cons of this particular representation and critiqued other aspects of the flyer as well. In her portfolio reflection on this paper, Eden wrote the following:

> This paper challenged my writing ability massively because it was difficult to write a paper or develop my claim since I was part of this show: Afro-Caribbean Night and I knew too much of what the purpose of this show was. So, instead of focusing on the advertisement and write about it, the whole paper was focused on the purpose of the show and why it was important. . . . But through peer review and the instructor's feedback, I manage to differentiate my ideas.

As Eden's comment shows, this sort of project helps students build on their own interests to develop an academic analysis. It also increases their understanding of audience because they must consider the ways in which particular individuals or organizations represent themselves. Such an analysis could easily be expanded into a redesign project in which students create an alternative or extension for the artifact they have critiqued.

Another analytical assignment I have used in several courses asks students to visit one of our campus writing centers and write an evaluation of their experience (see Appendix C). Students are encouraged to offer specific examples to support their overall evaluation. A Korean student named Misun was particularly pleased with her writing center visit, commenting that her tutor had helped her clarify and organize her thoughts. She concluded her evaluation with the following positive evaluation:

> Overall, visiting the writing center helped me a lot in many ways. First, my tutor and I outlined my research paper and made solid claims; later, it aided me to grasp the big concept and picture of my research. Moreover, concrete outline were useful to find various example in an appropriate way. The only thing that I can suggest for the writing center is to hire . . . as many [tutors] as possible for every single students to obtain this wonderful opportunity.

This assignment gives students an impetus for visiting the writing center and evaluating it as an academic resource. If the evaluations are intended to be shared with writing center administrators, then students also have an authentic purpose and audience for their writing.[1] The administrators, in turn, receive valuable feedback that helps them evaluate their own work. The writing center evaluation can easily be adapted to other academic experiences as well, such as library visits, advisor appointments, and campus lectures. Although I tend to ask for a written product on this assignment, I have found that it can easily be presented as a

---

[1] I remove student names and/or ask their permission before sharing these pieces of writing with administrators.

short oral presentation, which often sparks lively discussion. In one case, several students attended a large campus lecture and shared with the rest of the class their challenges in understanding the speaker. This led to a class brainstorming session on how to increase listening comprehension using pre-, during-, and postlecture strategies. Sometimes students bring back syllabi or other artifacts from these experiences, which the class can then examine for disciplinary differences.

Reflective Projects

A final category of the Academic Informant Project involves writing that is more metacognitive in nature, that is, it deals with "cognitive self-knowledge," or "what individuals know about their own thinking" (Kasper, 1997, p. 1). Reflective writing has become one of my most valuable assessment tools in EAP because it offers a window into students' minds and gives me a sense of each student's learning processes. Furthermore, reflective assignments incorporate many of the elements of more formal writing (e.g., overall thesis, specific examples, transitional phrases) but in a slightly more personal way. Hence, they can bridge the gap between expressive or creative writing and more formal academic prose. In their reflections, students are asked to make claims about what they have learned and how, and to explain the relevance of such learning to their future study or professions.

When students turn in a larger assignment or project, I often ask them to write an in-class memo to me, discussing questions such as the following:

- How did the process of this assignment work out for you? Which parts were easiest? Most challenging?

- At this point, how do you feel about the work you are handing in?

- If you had more time, what else would you do for this assignment?

- Did this assignment raise any additional questions, concerns, or realizations for you?

The first time I asked students to write this memo, I thought they would groan in annoyance. They had just turned in a full research paper, and now I was asking them to write more? But I was surprised to see their engagement in the writing. Many of them seemed to find the exercise almost cathartic because it gave them a chance to "talk" to me (and to themselves) before I read their work and to step back from the intensity of the writing process to engage in self-reflection. This type of writing is focused on process more than product. I do not correct the work in any way, but only respond as an interested reader. Occasionally, the memos reveal intense anxieties and frustrations, such as when one student admitted, "I am scared to come to you with my questions. . . . I think it's because I also feel intimidated and I'm not comfortable at all with my writing." Prior to reading this, I was unaware that this student was struggling, especially because her bubbly personality masked much of this frustration. I was able to talk with her to ease some of her concerns and to clarify some points for her. Later in the course, the same student wrote the following: "I also wanted to thank you for your support that you have given me. . . . I feel a lot better about my work now!"

Additional reflection questions can be given throughout the quarter, including the following:

- What have you learned in this class thus far that you use (or might use) in your other classes?

- What differences have you noticed between this class and your other classes?

- What challenges are you facing in your other classes, and how do you think we might address them in this class?

Benesch (1996) has found that this sort of reflection often becomes the starting point for class projects aimed at improving communication with mainstream professors. In one particular case, she worked with several students to compose a letter that expressed general concerns and made specific suggestions for modifications that would support students.

At the end of the course, these reflections can be compiled and expanded into more structured essays or portfolio cover letters, because each offers a snapshot of the student at a particular point in the course. To help students incorporate their reflections into a more formal essay, the instructor can guide them through the following steps: First, students reread their own reflections, looking for themes and points of overlap. Then they develop one or more of those points as central claims for this new piece of writing, identifying examples in their previous work that support these claims. In drafting the reflective essay, students may benefit from scaffolding in the form of "sentence starters." Typical examples include the following:

- At the start of this course, I felt . . .

- Some of my most significant learning in this course has been . . .

- In future quarters, I plan to use these skills . . .

- Although this course has been . . . , it has also been . . .

In later drafts, students revise these reflective essays for organization, use of supporting evidence, word choice, and grammar. This revision is often completed in conjunction with analysis of a sample essay so that students learn inductively what is typical in reflective writing. In particular, the semiformal nature of the work offers an opportunity to discuss how language can be used to strike an appropriate balance between formality and familiarity, because reflective writing represents a midpoint between the two.

REFLECTIONS

What I enjoy most about using students' academic experiences as content is the relevance that it has for students. Whether they are explaining their academic majors, analyzing a document from an organization they have joined, or reflecting on their own writing process, students have an authentic reason to communicate as academic informants. In addition, this sort of work incorporates types of writing that students will likely use in other courses: exposition, analysis/evaluation, response, and reflection. I also have found that these projects can easily be extended into larger research projects with broader questions. For example, when it was time to choose a research topic, a Japanese student named Momoko realized that in many of our class activities she had focused on the topic of education. So for her larger project, she decided to do more research on alternative schools in the United States.

Perhaps the greatest benefit of Academic Informant Projects is the increase in confidence they can create for students. Each student has something different to share because the project is based on his or her own interests and experiences. Many of these projects actually ask that students teach the class by explaining terms, giving examples, and finding points of relevance for their peers. For many students, the opportunity to talk and write about what they already know contributes significantly to their sense of pride and accomplishment. Often, students are surprised by the interest shown by their peers. For example, Ming, a computer science student from Taiwan, gave such an effective presentation about the benefits of open source software that he was bombarded afterward with questions from his peers about how they might access such software for themselves. He was both surprised and proud as he realized that he had truly accomplished his persuasive aims for the presentation.

Assessment of Academic Informant Projects tends to be centered around evaluating students' vividness and clarity. Although I have used a variety of rubrics to assess the speaking and writing components of these projects, most tend to include the following categories: content, organization, style and word choice, and clarity and grammar. I often find it necessary to highlight clarity in the grading because many students are so immersed in their fields of study that they forget to consider the needs of a more generalized audience. To increase clarity, we spend time working on defining terms, giving relevant background information, and referencing sources.

The issue of citation tends to be a significant challenge in Academic Informant Projects because students often struggle to distinguish between their own ideas and those that need to be cited, particularly when the latter have become largely commonplace to them through their disciplinary studies. However, this challenge has its benefits because it provides the opportunity to have important conversations with students about plagiarism, audience expectations, and building authority as a writer.

Another struggle is topic selection. Although some students gravitate easily toward a topic within their realm of academic experience, others jump from one idea to another or are convinced that they have nothing to say. This is particularly true of freshmen, who are often in a highly exploratory phase of their academic careers and therefore struggle to select a particular discipline on which to focus their work. One solution that seems to help is to give students a small selection of on-campus educational experiences (e.g., lectures, colloquia) that they can attend jointly. This enables them to compare notes before preparing written or oral projects. Another possibility is to guide students collectively through the analytical process, using a common textbook, syllabus, film, or web site. This provides a concrete model and an opportunity for practice before students embark on their own projects.

The greatest struggle that students face in becoming academic informants, though, is that of going beyond the obvious. Many students are quite comfortable reporting what they see and do in academic situations but struggle to find greater meaning in their experience. I am still developing ways to guide students toward deeper analysis, but I have found that simple questions such as "So what?" and "Why is this significant?" can be useful starting points. Asking students to write in more authentic genres, such as letters to the editor, advice columns, or advertising pamphlets, may also help them engage with the relevance of their experience in deeper ways. Similarly, giving students ample opportunities to talk about their academic work and experiences increases the likelihood that they will see these larger implications.

As instructors in academic English classes, we sometimes forget the wealth of experiences that students have in the context of their other courses and other academic activities. Using Academic Informant Projects, we can tap into this wealth so that students feel a greater sense of connection between our classes and the campus at large. (See Appendix D for additional resources along these lines). This allows us to individualize the content of our courses while still encouraging advanced language acquisition for all students. Just as valuably, the content of these projects increases our own awareness of what is happening outside our EAP classrooms. Now that's what I call educational multitasking!

ACKNOWLEDGMENTS

I would like to thank Dr. Ann Johns, whose inspiration—both in publication and in person—contributed greatly to my interest in disciplinarity as a focal point for TESOL and EAP instruction.

Shawna Shapiro is a visiting assistant professor of writing at the Center for Teaching, Learning, and Research at Middlebury College, in Vermont, in the United States. She has taught English, ESL, social studies, and Spanish at middle school, high school, and university levels. She also facilitates a variety of courses and workshops for teacher and tutor training.

APPENDIX A: RESEARCH PROPOSAL QUESTIONS

1. What topic have you chosen? What are your research questions associated with that topic?

2. Why is this topic relevant to you?

3. How can you make this topic relevant to your audience of classmates?

4. What sources have you located so far? How did you find them?

5. How do you feel about the research process so far? What concerns or needs do you have?

APPENDIX B: RHETORICAL ANALYSIS OF AN EDUCATIONAL ARTIFACT

1. Choose a written artifact from a course, program, or campus organization. This could be a syllabus, pamphlet, advertisement, web site, or other document.

2. Using terms from our course reading as a lens or frame, identify and discuss one or two of the more implicit arguments evident in that artifact (this is your claim). Give specific examples to support this reading of the artifact (support). Also discuss the significance for students in that course or context to know this (stakes).

3. Bring a rough draft to class for peer review.

APPENDIX C: WRITING CENTER EVALUATION

Please schedule an appointment as soon as possible to work on brainstorming ideas, to work on an assignment, to work on a skill or strategy, and/or to develop a paper. Make sure to take a copy of your assignment sheet, any relevant class notes or handouts, and your writing when you meet with a tutor.

I. Getting Ready

Before you meet with the writing consultant, define a few things you would like to work on during your session. Do you want help breaking down a difficult reading assignment? Organizing your ideas? Brainstorming? Working on grammar or language clarity? Do you need tips on paragraph development? Critical thinking?

These are just a few starting points for defining your goals. Before your meeting, please list your session goals here:

II. Reflection

After your session, please write a one- to two-page description and evaluation based on your experience. Consider the following questions: What did you work on during your session (please be specific)? What tips, strategies, or other assistance did the tutor offer? How did your session help you with your assignment? Do you have new strategies you can now put to use or new things to think about when you read or write? What comments or critiques do you have about your experience with the Writing Center? What suggestions can you give so that the Writing Center continues to meet students' needs?

APPENDIX D: RECOMMENDED SOURCES

Herrington, A., & Moran, C. (Eds.). (2005). *Genre across the curriculum*. Logan: Utah State University Press.

Robertson, W. (Writer/Director). (2005). *Writing across borders* [DVD]. Available from http://cwl.oregonstate.edu/writing-across-borders

Zamel, V. (1995). Strangers in academia: The experiences of faculty and ESL students across the curriculum. *College Composition and Communication, 46,* 506–521.

Zamel, V., & Spack, R. (Eds.). (2004). *Crossing the curriculum: Multilingual learners in college classrooms*. Mahwah, NJ: Lawrence Erlbaum.

CHAPTER 7

A Short Course on the Miniskirt: Providing a Language Toolkit for University Instructors in Turkey

Steve Darn

A lecture on the miniskirt at a Turkish university? The Turks often suffer from outsiders' uninformed image of a Muslim country, characterized by mosques, headscarves, economic instability, and conservatism. In the west of Turkey at least, the reality is quite different. Westernization is accompanied by a growing educated middle class and a high level of technology integration. There are large numbers of female students in tertiary education, and jeans, bare midriffs, and short skirts are common sights on university campuses. Fashion consciousness is high, and Turkish fashion designers rank among the best in the world.

Consider, then, a group of fashion and design instructors who require training in overcoming language barriers to the comprehension of their subject matter, keen to add to their own knowledge and skills, and culturally aware enough to know that something happened to youth culture in England in the 1960s. What could be a more appropriate theme than the fashion revelation of the period: the miniskirt!

This chapter is an account of one part of a pilot project designed to build a bridge between subject teachers and language teachers working in the context of a private English-medium university. Designed by language teacher trainers, but targeting instructors on the faculty, the project focused on teacher development, though the methods and tasks involved could easily be transferred from the training room to the classroom.

The project, designed and implemented by the Teacher Development Unit in the School of Foreign Languages at Izmir University of Economics, focused on raising instructors' awareness of the need for ongoing language support while teaching subject-based content, and providing them with a toolkit of techniques for the classroom. The training program used methodology from communicative language teaching in an English as a foreign language context. The training itself relied heavily on loop input techniques, a specific type of experiential teacher training process that involves an alignment of the process and content of learning (Woodward, 2003), in this case involving the use of tasks that would be equally appropriate to the classroom, but with language and content aimed at the level of the target group. The overall approach was based on content and language integrated learning (CLIL), emphasizing a balance of language and content together with additional elements of cultural awareness and cognitive skills development, all of which are fundamental to CLIL practice. It was felt that CLIL would play a key role, having emerged as an umbrella term covering both learning a language through a content-based subject and learning a content-based subject through the medium of a foreign language. Whether one takes the language or the subject perspective, interdisciplinary cooperation, awareness raising, and training are prerequisites. The project aimed to give subject teachers the tools necessary to provide ongoing language support to students who were unable to gain maximum benefit from studying in the English medium.

CONTEXT

Located on the Aegean coast of Turkey, Izmir University of Economics is by no means unique. Students in the various faculties study in undergraduate and postgraduate programs delivered in the medium of English. In order to gain entry to these programs, students must either demonstrate a predetermined level of language competence by passing a proficiency-style entrance examination or, as is the case for some 1,300 students per year, embark on a 1-year intensive preparatory language program. A key difference between this and foundation programs elsewhere is that students here concentrate entirely on English rather than a combination of language and subject studies.

There are inevitable problems. For decades, the Turkish private education system has seen English as a pivotal subject in the curriculum. Successive attempts to teach English to a high level in the space of 1 year, first at the age of 11 and then later between middle and high school, have been for the most part unsuccessful, largely due to the inertia of an entrenched rote-learning system, poor teacher education facilities, and norm-referenced testing. Hence, the majority of students entering university are not yet capable of studying effectively in a foreign language. Nevertheless, a bilingual program is a major marketing point for private institutions, and preparatory schools within foreign language departments are expected to do the job that high schools were unable to do.

This scenario has produced a gap between expectation and reality. Despite a history of English-medium teaching, the prevailing education system, involving a national curriculum imposed by the Ministry of Education, does not bring the majority of students up to a level of language competence at which they are able to acquire language through their subject studies or to fully comprehend the content of their subject courses. Under these circumstances, critics of bilingual education would have some justification in pointing out that students might well be disadvantaged both in their language development and in their subject expertise. In the absence of a framework within which to address the problem, the following factors contribute to a chasm that is widening as a result of increased numbers of students opting for English-medium instruction and the proliferation of institutions attempting to meet the demand:

- It is almost impossible to bring students from elementary level to a point at which they can function academically in English in the space of a year, however intensive the program may be. Research suggests that it takes 5–7 years in a quality bilingual program to achieve this (Cummins, 1981b) and 7–10 years to achieve reading comprehension and language use levels comparable to that of native-speaking peers. An ongoing debate suggests that intensive learning may even be detrimental to content learning. These conclusions are drawn largely from empirical studies of immigrant groups in immersion programs in North America and the United Kingdom, and the time scale might well be reduced for academically able undergraduates working toward a common goal in a monolingual teaching context. Subsequent research reveals a variety of affecting factors and sees native-speaker language proficiency as a moving target (Collier, 1995a). However, it remains clear that long-term learning is involved, that content and language integration needs to begin at a relatively early age, and that in order to learn content through a foreign language, students in CLIL programs need to have a basic threshold level of proficiency that enables them to acquire new language rather than learn it formally.

- Language instructors are not aware of the subject-specific language that students will be expected to know, nor perhaps of the surrounding academic language or the tasks that students will be asked to perform using that language. Preparatory programs tend to consist of general English plus English for specific purposes (ESP), where ESP is defined as academic reading and writing without a specific subject focus.

- Faculty lecturers (subject teachers) are not aware of the task facing language teachers, nor of the adjustments they need to make in order to compensate for the low standards of language competence they are likely to face. Rather than confront the issue, these instructors commonly carry on regardless, teach in the mother tongue, and blame the language teachers.

- A lack of interdisciplinary cooperation and communication clearly persists. There is a prevailing perception that the School of Foreign Languages at the university is a department that services the faculties and is thus essentially nonacademic. There is reluctance on both sides to be proactive in the process of liaising. Consequently, the communication gap results in a lack of knowledge of the content of individual faculty courses on the one hand, and of the necessity for ongoing language support on the other. Attitudes and beliefs take time to change, but in the near term it is necessary to exchange the concept of blame for that of mutual responsibility. Given the reluctance of both sides to be proactive, there is a clear need for a catalyst to initiate a policy of closer cooperation.

CLIL is about teaching a subject through a foreign language while simultaneously increasing learners' language competence so that they may go on to learn more about the subject. It therefore has the potential to provide a platform for solutions to the four complicating factors I just delineated. Content and language are interrelated in such a way that language learning becomes immediately relevant to learner's needs, thus increasing motivation and providing a purpose for learning in both areas.

CLIL makes good sense for many economic, political, intercultural, and pedagogic reasons, but it is still in a relatively embryonic state, and as an umbrella term it lacks precise definition. It is perhaps best viewed as an assimilation of ideas and methods from a variety of existing language teaching and learning modes, including immersion, ESP, content-based instruction, and even *translanguaging*, whereby input and output in each language are alternated on a regular basis. From an ideological point of view, CLIL might be viewed as a more efficient means of education and a response to the linguistic and intercultural requirements of globalization. From the practitioner's point of view, it might be more profitable to see CLIL as a meeting point between language and content in the classroom, in which case a more coherent methodology and more purpose-designed materials are the teacher's immediate requirements. The project at Izmir University of Economics offers subject teachers some of the techniques required to deal with language issues and the option of adapting and fully exploiting existing materials for both language and content.

The language toolkit project is also an initial attempt to address the problem of the lack of appropriate teacher education, which currently inhibits the spread of CLIL. Given that language is a vehicle for learning content, it seems rational that subject teachers should be provided with this training. With younger age groups, because language and content are both relatively simple, teachers are on fairly safe ground, but at the university level language teachers are unlikely to have the specialist knowledge required to exploit content. So it falls to subject teachers to adopt a dual-focused approach and to language teachers to provide consultancy, ideally through team teaching.

Fundamental to CLIL is the premise that content and language are learned simultaneously and in balanced proportions. A CLIL lesson is not a language lesson, nor is it a subject lesson transmitted in a foreign language. The second language (L2) is the means by which the content objectives are reached. If content is the goal, then training in language support is essential for subject teachers.

CURRICULUM, TASKS, MATERIALS

The language toolkit for subject teachers has four main components:

1. *How to deal with vocabulary and lexis:* This involves raising awareness of the subject-specific and academic vocabulary that students need and of existing tools such as the Academic Word List (AWL). This corpus-based list of high-frequency academic vocabulary originally developed by Averil Coxhead (2006) at Victoria University of Wellington often provides a basis for generating language learning materials such as the highlighted and gap-fill texts produced using technology developed at the University of Nottingham. This component of the toolkit also draws attention to the *lexical approach,* a term coined by Michael Lewis (1993), which views language as chunks rather than discrete items and encourages the learning of real-life language rather than grammar. Learners are asked to notice set phrases, expressions, and collocations that they need to function efficiently.

2. *How to make lectures and presentations more interactive:* Here, English language teaching (ELT) methodology is used to demonstrate how different styles of lecture, using techniques such as skeleton notes (headings and/or key phrases to guide students' note taking), buzz groups (short breaks in a lecture for small groups to discuss content), and visual lecture frameworks (mind maps or diagrammatic summaries), can give students the opportunity to assimilate and comprehend a large body of information (Woodward, 1991).

3. *How to create an awareness of teacher and learner classroom language:* Training is given in techniques for creating a learning environment that is as close to immersion as is feasible, in ways of formulating concept questions to check meaning and understanding and of selecting and adjusting (or grading) language by the teacher to make comprehension easier for learners.

4. *How to deal with texts:* Reading remains the major learning and research skill in most subjects and is identified as the key skill in CLIL, primarily because texts are the dominant source of language and provide the opportunity for learners to acquire lexis. Listening is treated as a skill essential for understanding input such as lectures and discussions, and

the emphasis in terms of speaking is on communication and fluency rather than accuracy. Writing is viewed as a means of recycling previously noticed lexis and structures. Subject teachers learn about the ways in which language teachers deal with reading texts, the stages and tasks involved, the relationship between text and task, and applications to their own subject matter.

It is this fourth part of the toolkit that I describe in detail here. The pilot training sessions involved a group of instructors from the faculty of fashion and design (although in the long-term view, the instructors from other faculties would be involved), with adjustments made according to their needs and subject material. Most group members were Turkish speakers with an advanced level of English proficiency. Content was chosen with subject relevance, language level, and interest factors in mind. Training focused on dealing with texts and aimed to introduce instructors to ELT methodology that might be useful in providing language support. The participants had already learned about the different types of lexis in a text and been introduced to the AWL. In a previous session they had looked at the sublists most closely related to their subject and run a number of fashion- and design-related texts through the Nottingham University AWL Highlighter to identify the high-frequency vocabulary in the subject area.

The instructors were introduced to the following common ELT practices, transferrable to CLIL programs, exemplified through the tasks in each stage of the training session:

- using visuals as a lead-in to a topic through brainstorming and prediction of content

- using matching tasks to identify key concepts and lexis in a text

- drawing attention to subject-specific vocabulary

- categorizing lexis and structures according to topic, language function, or both

- introducing knowledge structures; identifying key content and using ideational frameworks and text mapping to provide a visual representation of the text (Such devices, also known as graphic organizers, are commonly used in the early stages of a writing task but less often in reading for content.)

- providing examples of ELT-style pre-, while-, and postreading tasks

- analyzing language, drawing attention to collocations and semifixed expressions, and producing highlighted and gap-fill texts using the AWL

- demonstrating how to record and store lexis in meaningful ways, such as maintaining a lexically organized or personalized notebook

- suggesting follow-up activities such as student-generated interactive texts

Tasks demonstrating the techniques were "looped," in that the instructors were asked to complete tasks that students might be asked to do, but at a content and language level appropriate to academics with a high level of linguistic and communicative competence. The classroom applications of the techniques, along with their strategies and rationales, were elicited and discussed following the series of tasks. Tasks were based on a text tracing the history of the miniskirt, which was determined to be appropriate to the pilot group, manageable in terms of subject and language content, interesting, and enjoyable.

Stage 1: Lead-In Through Visuals

The use of visuals is one way to stimulate interest in a topic and activate schemata by eliciting collective background knowledge and vocabulary (see Figure 1). Words and phrases that might arise included *60s, pop art, geometric, colours, mini,* and *pop groups.* Participants were told that they were going to read about some or all of these things.

Stage 2: Matching

Matching tasks were used to draw attention to key vocabulary, engage the readers with the text, and encourage a variety of strategies for determining meaning. Participants were given the text and a set of topic-related pictures (Appendix A) and then asked to scan the text to find words or phrases that matched the visuals. The specific purposes of this task were to provide further visual stimulus and reveal existing knowledge, but primarily to engage the readers with the text and provide an initial reason for reading. The task can be done individually and answers compared; preexisting knowledge, visual clues, elimination, and guesswork are all involved. This task also offered the opportunity for readers to identify specific interests that might form the basis of subsequent project work. There was also rich social and cultural content to be explored.

Figure 1. Lead-In Visuals

Stage 3: Text Mapping

Text mapping was used both to organize key knowledge from the text and to provide a basis for note taking. This activity assisted visual learners, developed understanding of text structure and organizational skills, and provided a reason to read the text again. Participants were asked to produce a visual representation of the text, which could take the form of a mind map, network, tree diagram, or other form of ideational framework (see Figure 2).

Stage 4: Looking at Lexis

Categorization is a meaningful way of listing important or new lexis and drawing attention to thematically or lexically related words. Participants focused on the first paragraph of the text and were asked to find examples of language under three headings (see Table 1).

Subject specialists would be able to identify subject-specific items, and academic vocabulary could be identified from the AWL. The same text that they had worked with in the previous tasks was given to them, but this time with various words highlighted in the text (see Appendix B). Alternative categories could be suggested, and there is likely to be some overlap. It would be equally valid, for example, to categorize lexis in terms of function, the emphasis then being on the language rather than specific content (see Table 2).

Attention could even be drawn to use of passive and nondefining relative clauses in this type of text. The main focus, however, is on collocation, set phrases, and fixed or semifixed expressions, concepts that may be unfamiliar to subject teachers but that represent the simple notion that language, whether it be everyday or academic, occurs in groups of related and sometimes inseparable vocabulary items. Participants were thus reminded of the difference between vocabulary items and lexical units. The remainder of the text was analysed similarly, with the task divided between pairs or groups and findings shared.

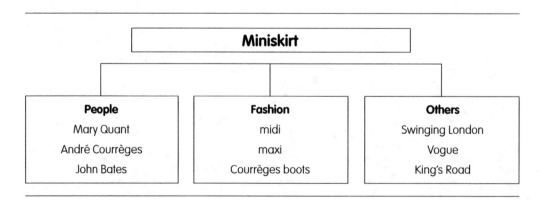

Figure 2. Simple Text Diagram

Table 1. Language Categories for the Lexis Task

Subject Specific	Academic Words	Other Language
miniskirt	credited	above the knee(s)
hemline	designer	credited to
knee level	cited	inspired by
fashion designer	inspired	cited as
	invented	disagreement as to

Participants were encouraged to record and store the lexis either as a thematic notebook page or in a personalized, visual style (see Appendix C), given a number of principles:

- Organized material is easier to learn.

- New words are more easily learned when they are incorporated into language that is already known.

- Word pairs can be used to learn a great number of words in a short time.

- Knowing a word entails much more than knowing its meaning.

- The words and phrases must be retrievable.

- Different students have different learning styles.

Stage 5: Text and Task

Tasks provide a reason to read a text and help to ensure detailed comprehension. Participants were reminded that their subject lectures and materials were also vehicles for language learning, and they were introduced to the classic pre-, while-, postreading model for dealing with a text. Participants reflected on the tasks they had completed so far in light of this model and identified task types and purposes from a chart (Table 3). The need to stimulate interest, provide reasons for reading, and give consolidation tasks was emphasized, as was the text–task relationship whereby the difficulty of the task is more important than the difficulty of the text.

Table 2. Functional Categories

Identifying/Naming	Referring	Describing Location	Describing Function
is credited to	often referred to	high above the knees	provide coverage of
called	often cited as	on _____ Road	incorporate into

Table 3. Reading Tasks and Purposes

Prereading	While-reading	Postreading
Purposes		
• Provide purpose • Stimulate interest • Activate prior knowledge • Add background knowledge	• Provide reason for reading • Develop reading strategies and skills • Improve control of second language	• Integrate with other skills • Check comprehension • Deepen analysis of text • Transfer skills to other texts
Tasks		
• Discuss author, text type • Brainstorm topic • Consider illustrations, titles, headings • List expectations • Skim for gist • Scan for facts	• Determine meaning from context, word structure • Do dictionary work • Find key lexis • Predict content • Confirm predictions • Read for specific information • Analyze reference words • Complete "read and do" tasks • Answer true/false questions • Take notes	• Do vocabulary/lexis exercises • Discuss • Debate • Role-play • Do parallel writing • Give presentations • Conduct research projects • Listen to a lecture

Stage 6: Follow-Up Activities

These activities were designed to consolidate and recycle both knowledge and language and thus concentrate on the productive skills of speaking and writing rather than extending knowledge through further reading. Participants were given a gap-fill exercise based on the highlighted text they had worked with in the earlier task (Appendix D). The difficulty of the task can be increased by omitting the selection of vocabulary to choose from. Discussion then focused on follow-up activities such as a project on a similar fashion item, a different fashion era, parallel writing, or a talk. Project work leading to a talk or written assignment was a popular option, and web-based texts provided the opportunity for students to follow links according to their interests. Such interactive texts may be prepared but are often readily available via *Wikipedia* (n.d.) and similar online reference sites.

REFLECTIONS

This project set out to meet the demands of a difficult teaching and learning context while adhering to basic principles of good practice in CLIL. Evaluation therefore involved not only feedback from the participants, but also a consideration of which CLIL aims and objectives had been met and to what extent. These objectives are wide ranging and well summarized by the CLIL Compendium (n.d.), which recognizes five dimensions: culture, environment, language, content, and learning (see Table 4). The importance placed on each individual aim will vary according to learners' ages and learning context (monolingual, bilingual, multilingual).

Apart from language and content aims, proponents of CLIL are committed to and address broader issues of long-term learning, life skills, holistic development, and globalization. There is no such thing as a "CLIL curriculum"; the syllabus is dictated by the subject matter. The materials and tasks used in the project at Izmir University of Economics would fit equally well in a general studies, social studies cultural program. However, CLIL lessons should reflect the dimensions in Table 4 and contain elements of the four Cs: content, communication, cognition, and culture. Guidelines for CLIL best practice are evolving, with implications for both syllabus design and lesson planning (Coyle, 1999).

The content in this project was clear and relevant to the target group, and participants found it interesting and motivating. Tasks were interactive, and there were opportunities for participants to engage with the text. What became apparent to participants was the extent to which a relatively short text can be exploited with respect to all of the four Cs and the amount of work required for full comprehension. In the text's opening definitive statement ("The miniskirt is a skirt whose hemline is high above the knees"), not only do readers need to note

Table 4. Content and Language Integrated Learning Dimensions and Objectives

Dimension	Objectives
Culture	• Introduce the wider cultural context • Build intercultural knowledge and understanding • Develop intercultural communication skills • Learn about other countries and societies
Content	• Provide opportunities to study content through different perspectives • Access subject-specific target language terminology • Prepare for future studies, working life
Language	• Improve overall target language competence • Develop oral communication skills • Deepen awareness of both mother tongue and target language • Develop plurilingual interests and attitudes
Learning	• Complement individual learning strategies • Diversify methods and forms of classroom practice • Increase learner motivation
Environment	• Prepare for internationalization • Access international certification • Enhance school profile

Source: CLIL Compendium, n.d.

the use of the singular subject, the correct relative pronoun, and collocations, but they also need to decode the meaning and message: miniskirts are short. Also apparent in this project was that any text can be exploited for language, providing that the tasks are relevant, manageable, and have a clear purpose.

Tasks such as text mapping not only provide a reason to read, but also develop cognitive organizational skills and an understanding of how a text is structured, offering subsequent opportunities for guided and parallel writing activities. With this project, the importance of self-study, project work, study skills, and thinking skills was emphasized in line with the underlying notions of long-term learning and life skills that are inherent in CLIL.

In CLIL, the subject matter determines the language to be learned. Thus, there is no graded or structural syllabus, a feature common to many conventional ELT course materials. The tasks here were not designed to focus on specific language structures, and language was not graded. Language relevant to content was noticed and recorded, as might be the case in an ELT lexical approach. There was a balance of language and skills development, with reading seen as the essential input skill, and a balance of content and language. The potential for output was seen in follow-up activities and project work.

Benefits to the university were made clear in terms of understanding and cooperation. In these circumstances, a number of positive developments are facilitated:

- Motivation for teaching increases.

- Each discipline becomes stronger on its own merit.

- Teachers expand their repertoire of teaching techniques and strategies.

- Mutual respect among teachers of various disciplines increases.

- Teachers, students, and the institution become more international in outlook.

Participants felt that there were opportunities for team teaching that would consolidate relations between language and subject teachers. Various permutations were discussed, including lessons coplanned and codelivered by language and subject teachers; a language consultant working with a group of subject teachers; and, ideally, a three-way partnership between a subject teacher, a language teacher, and a vocational trainer. The trainers fully appreciated the difficulties faced by subject teachers but, more important, that assumptions are made about commensurate levels of subject knowledge and language competence. Participants openly admitted that, despite being given the task of lecturing to foreign language learners, this project had been their first taste of being instructed in language teaching methodology and that they had previously given little thought to alternative means of imparting knowledge that might increase comprehension and therefore alleviate their own and their students' difficulties.

Positive responses to this project have so far come from three levels. At the level of individual lecturers, some have sought advice and consultancy about language issues and others have successfully implemented some of the techniques from the project. At the institutional level, there has been a call for interdisciplinary cooperation, closer communication between faculty and language instructors, and further instruction for faculty in alternative teaching techniques as well as teaching and learning in a foreign language. Perhaps most important, at the departmental level, language support courses for faculty have largely been redesigned using content-related materials, some of which have been purposely written to meet the needs of particular subjects. This process required initial consultation with individual faculties. It will be some time before improvements in teaching and learning outcomes can be measured, but, to a certain extent, the project has been successful in setting the wheels in motion.

ACKNOWLEDGMENTS

I would like to thank Keith Kelly, at Norwich Institute of Language Education, for permission to reproduce materials from the FACTWorld web site; Robert Ledbury, at Izmir University of Economics, School of Foreign Languages, Teacher Development Unit, for ideas on vocabulary teaching and for the vocabulary notebook page; and Sixties City (www.sixtiescity.com) for permission to use its photographs.

Steve Darn has lived and taught in Turkey for 25 years, in the high school, private language school, and university sectors. He currently works as a freelance trainer and consultant. He also trains teachers and trainers for the British Council and is a tutor and assessor for Cambridge ESOL Teaching Awards. He writes and reviews for a number of ELT publications.

APPENDIX A: TEXT AND PICTURES FOR MATCHING TASK

The miniskirt is a skirt whose hemline is high above the knees (generally 200–300 mm above knee level). Its existence is generally credited to the fashion designer Mary Quant, who was inspired by the Mini Cooper automobile, although André Courrèges is also often cited as its inventor, and there is disagreement as to who invented it first. Some credit the miniskirt to Helen Rose, who made some miniskirts for actress Anne Francis in the 1956 science fiction movie *Forbidden Planet*. Recently, Marit Allen, an editor for *Vogue* magazine, has credited the miniskirt to John Bates, whose costumes and accessories for Diana Rigg in *The Avengers* defined "mod style."

Mary Quant ran a popular clothes shop on London's Kings Road called Bazaar, from which she sold her own designs. In the late 1950s she began experimenting with shorter skirts, which resulted in the miniskirt in 1960, one of the defining fashions of the decade.

Owing to Quant's position in the heart of fashionable "Swinging London," the miniskirt was able to spread beyond a simple street fashion into a major international trend.

The miniskirt was further popularized by the French designer André Courrèges, who developed it separately and incorporated it into his mod look for spring/summer 1965. His miniskirts were less body hugging, worn with the white "Courrèges boots" that became a trademark. By introducing the miniskirt into the haute couture of the fashion industry, Courrèges gave it a greater degree of respectability than might otherwise have been expected of a street fashion.

In the United Kingdom, the increasing interest in the miniskirt in the 1960s necessitated a change in the way skirts were taxed. Previously, skirts were taxed by length, with the miniskirt qualifying as tax-exempt by effectively being a child's length.

The miniskirt was followed up in the mid-1960s by the even shorter micro skirt, which covers not much more than the intimate parts with the underpants. It has often been derogatorily referred to as a belt. Subsequently, the fashion industry largely returned to longer skirts such as the midi and the maxi. However, miniskirts remain popular. Miniskirts are also seen worn over trousers or jeans, or with strap-on trouser "leggings" that provide coverage of each leg from above the knee.

(Text adapted from http://en.wikipedia.org/wiki/Miniskirt)

Write a name, word or phrase from the text under each picture.

Note: Visuals from www.sixtiescity.com. Reprinted with permission.

APPENDIX B: HIGHLIGHTED TEXT

The miniskirt is a skirt whose hemline is high above the knees (generally 200–300 mm above knee level). Its existence is generally **credited** to the fashion **designer** Mary Quant, who was inspired by the Mini Cooper automobile, although André Courrèges is also often **cited** as its inventor, and there is disagreement as to who invented it first. Some credit the miniskirt to Helen Rose, who made some miniskirts for actress Anne Francis in the 1956 science fiction movie *Forbidden Planet.* Recently, Marit Allen, an **editor** for *Vogue* magazine, has credited the miniskirt to John Bates, whose costumes and accessories for Diana Rigg in *The Avengers* **defined** Mod **style**.

Mary Quant ran a popular clothes shop on London's Kings Road called Bazaar, from which she sold her own **designs.** In the late 1950s she began experimenting with shorter skirts, which resulted in the miniskirt in 1960, one of the **defining** fashions of the **decade.**

Owing to Quant's position in the heart of fashionable "Swinging London," the miniskirt was able to spread beyond a simple street fashion into a **major** international **trend.**

The miniskirt was further popularized by the French designer André Courrèges, who developed it separately and **incorporated** it into his mod look for spring/summer 1965. His miniskirts were less body hugging, worn with the white "Courrèges boots" that became a trademark. By introducing the miniskirt into the haute couture of the fashion industry, Courrèges gave it a greater degree of respectability than might otherwise have been expected of a street fashion.

In the United Kingdom, the increasing interest in the miniskirt in the 1960s necessitated a change in the way skirts were taxed. **Previously,** skirts were taxed by length, with the miniskirt qualifying as tax-exempt by effectively being a child's length.

The miniskirt was followed up in the mid-1960s by the even shorter micro skirt, which covers not much more than the intimate parts with the underpants. It has often been derogatorily referred to as a belt. **Subsequently,** the fashion industry largely returned to longer skirts such as the midi and the maxi. However, miniskirts remain popular. Miniskirts are also seen worn over trousers or jeans, or with strap-on trouser "leggings" that provide coverage of each leg from above the knee.

(Adapted from the Academic Word List Highlighter at Nottingham University. http://www.nottingham.ac.uk/~alzsh3/acvocab/awlhighlighter.htm)

APPENDIX C: PERSONALIZED VOCABULARY
NOTEBOOK PAGE

mini   midi   maxi

midi-skirt
midi-tansas

popularise (v)
necessitate (v)
incorporate (v)
innovate (v)
innovation (n)
creativity (n)

(include)

SKIRTS

COOL ACADEMIC STUFF

microskirt
= beltskirt ⊖
very revealing
intimate parts!
underpants
hemline

hipline

leggings

above the knees

KEY

PEOPLE

fashionable phrases

the London design scene
the fashion industry
fashion house
swinging London
street fashion
body hugging skirt
haute couture

"Mod style"

Mary Quant
André Courrèges
John Bates
Marit Allen/"Vogue"

APPENDIX D: GAP-FILL TEXT

The miniskirt is a skirt whose hemline is high above the knees (generally 200–300 mm above knee level). Its existence is generally _____ to the fashion _____ Mary Quant, who was inspired by the Mini Cooper automobile, although André Courrèges is also often _____ as its inventor, and there is disagreement as to who invented it first. Some credit the miniskirt to Helen Rose, who made some miniskirts for actress Anne Francis in the 1956 science fiction movie *Forbidden Planet*. Recently, Marit Allen, an _____ for *Vogue* magazine, has credited the miniskirt to John Bates, whose costumes and accessories for Diana Rigg in *The Avengers* _____ mod _____.

Mary Quant ran a popular clothes shop on London's Kings Road called Bazaar, from which she sold her own _____. In the late 1950s she began experimenting with shorter skirts, which resulted in the miniskirt in 1960, one of the _____ fashions of the _____.

Owing to Quant's position in the heart of fashionable "Swinging London," the miniskirt was able to spread beyond a simple street fashion into a _____ international _____.

The miniskirt was further popularized by the French designer André Courrèges, who developed it separately and _____ it into his mod look for spring/summer 1965. His miniskirts were less body hugging, worn with the white "Courrèges boots" that became a trademark. By introducing the miniskirt into the haute couture of the fashion industry, Courrèges gave it a greater degree of respectability than might otherwise have been expected of a street fashion.

In the United Kingdom, the increasing interest in the miniskirt in the 1960s necessitated a change in the way skirts were taxed. _____, skirts were taxed by length, with the miniskirt qualifying as tax-exempt by effectively being a child's length.

The miniskirt was followed up in the mid-1960s by the even shorter micro skirt, which covers not much more than the intimate parts with the underpants. It has often been derogatorily referred to as a belt. _____, the fashion industry largely returned to longer skirts such as the midi and the maxi. However, mini-skirts remain popular. Miniskirts are also seen worn over trousers or jeans, or with strap-on trouser "leggings" that provide coverage of each leg from above the knee.

defined	designer	major	defining	decade	editor	credited
style	previously	designs	subsequently	trend	cited	incorporated

(Adapted from the Academic Word List Gapmaker at Nottingham University. http://www.nottingham.ac.uk/~alzsh3/acvocab/awlgapmaker.htm)

APPENDIX E: ADDITIONAL RESOURCES

Clegg, J. (n.d.). *Providing language support in CLIL*. Retrieved from http://www
.factbg.hit.bg/issue6/f6-clegg.pdf

Coonan, C. M. (2003). Some issues in implementing CLIL. *European Language
Council Bulletin, 9*. Retrieved from http://userpage.fu-berlin.de/elc/bulletin/9/
en/coonan.html

Dalton-Puffer, C., & Nikula, T. (Eds.). (2006). Current research on CLIL [Special
issue]. *Vienna English Working Papers, 15*(3).

Darn, S. (2006). *Content and language integrated learning (CLIL): A European
overview*. ERIC Document Reproduction Service No. ED490775

Darn, S. (n.d.). *Exploiting an interactive text*. Retrieved from http://www.factworld
.info/turkey/jeans/exploiting_an_interactive_text.htm

Georgieva, M. (1999). *Processing and producing language through content: Ideas for
preparing tasks for content and language integrated learning*. Retrieved from http://
www.factworld.info/materials/papers/CLIL_tasks.htm

Gürüz, K. (2006). The development of private higher education in Turkey.
International Higher Education, 45, 11. Retrieved from http://www.bc.edu/bc_
org/avp/soe/cihe/newsletter/Number45/p11_Guruz.htm

Haynes, J. (2004). *Graphic organizers for content instruction*. Retrieved from http://
www.everythingesl.net/inservices/graphic_organizers.php

Haywood, S. (n.d.). *Academic vocabulary*. Retrieved from http://www.nottingham
.ac.uk/~alzsh3/acvocab/index.htm

Jacobs, J., & Mueller, W. (2001). *Design principles for interactive texts*. Retrieved
from http://www.math.duke.edu/education/ccp/resources/write/design/

Maljers, A., Marsh, D., & Wolff, D. (Eds.). (2007). *Windows on CLIL: Content and
language integrated learning in the European spotlight*. Graz, Austria: ECML.

Marsh, D., & Langé, G. (1999). *Implementing content and language integrated
learning*. Jyväskylä, Finland: University of Jyväskylä.

Marsh, D., & Langé, G. (2000). *Using languages to learn and learning to use
languages*. Jyväskylä, Finland: University of Jyväskylä.

Mehisto, P., Marsh, D., & Frigols, M. J. (2008). *Uncovering CLIL*. Oxford, England:
Macmillan.

Schmitt, D., & Schmitt, N. (2005). *Focus on vocabulary: Mastering the academic word
list*. White Plains, NY: Longman.

Stoller, F. L. (1997). Project work: A means to promote language content. *Forum, 35*(4), 2–9.

Wilkinson, R. (2005, March 18). Where is English taking universities? *Guardian Weekly.* Retrieved from http://www.guardian.co.uk

CHAPTER 8

Opening the Door: Making Mathematics Accessible to English Language Learners

Anita Bright

The mathematics teacher was talking about *half*, a word Magaly thought she recognized. "Who can use the word *half* in a sentence?" Magaly cautiously raised her hand. "Magaly, wonderful! Use *half* in a sentence."

Tentatively, Magaly spoke. "I half long hair."

The teacher smiled and said, "Ah, Magaly has found a very similar sounding word! *Have* sounds a lot like *half*, doesn't it? Good ear, Magaly. Bravo!"

"Mathematics is a universal language." This simple phrase is used in schools throughout the world. Adherents to this generalization are typically good-hearted, intelligent, experienced educators, but woefully unaware of their blind spot with regard to the challenges of language in mathematics, as illustrated in the previous example of the minimal pairs (*have* and *half*). This chapter explores some of the ways that one mathematics teacher highlighted the centrality of language in mathematics and illustrates specific ways to support students in gaining the academic register and lexicon necessary for success in mathematics in English.

CONTEXT

This lesson took place in a large, suburban public high school in Northern Virginia, just outside of Washington, D.C., in the United States, with a total enrollment of approximately 1,200 students in Grades 9–12. Around 240 of these students (approximately 20% of the student body) qualified for English to speakers of other languages (ESOL) services.

The 19 students that participated in this lesson were from nine countries (mostly in Latin America and East Africa) and spoke six different primary languages. Although they were all learning English, about half of them were already bi- or multilingual, with English being their second, third, or even fourth language. They ranged in age from 14 to 17, though most were in ninth grade. Most had been in the United States for approximately 6 months and were at the developing level of English language proficiency (TESOL, 2006).

All 19 students were working at the elementary level in mathematics and for this reason, in addition to their limited English proficiency, had been placed together in a sheltered mathematics course. Sheltered content courses (mathematics, science, social studies) differ from standard content courses in that they not only help students access grade-level content, but also simultaneously promote English language development (Echevarria, Vogt, & Short, 2004). This teaching of English through content is valuable for students because subjects are not taught in artificial isolation, but rather in more authentic, readily applicable ways, building in language that transcends the content. To facilitate students' learning of the mathematics content and the English language objectives, the lesson was taught by a teacher who was dually certified by the state of Virginia in both mathematics and ESOL.

The first part of the school year had been devoted to building background knowledge and establishing a safe, comfortable, and interactive classroom environment (Krashen, 1982). Each student was well known to the teacher and was a valued member of a cohesive, interdependent classroom of learners. These students needed to be able to take risks and have frequent and regular opportunities to practice not only honing their receptive skills in the language of mathematics, but also their productive skills (Cummins, 2001). To this end, the teacher included low-pressure activities so that students could speak, read, write, and hear the key vocabulary multiple times each day. By the time this lesson took place in the middle of the school year, the rhythm of the class was well established, as was a comfortable but serious tone.

Because these students were preparing to begin taking algebra, they required a complex series of mathematical skills, conceptual understandings, and academic language in English. Specifically, they were working toward TESOL's (2006) Standard 3: "English language learners communicate information, ideas, and concepts necessary for academic success in the area of mathematics" (p. 28).

For a week before this lesson, the class had been focusing on fractions. They had started out by using real-world items in the classroom and had practiced the requisite vocabulary, including *numerator* and *denominator,* and the difficult-to-hear pronunciation of fractional parts. This one week was a significant time investment, but the teacher recognized the importance of this content for success in algebra, which is considered a gatekeeper course in that successful completion of it is essential for success beyond high school (National Council of Teachers of Mathematics, 1998). Time spent on fractions would pay off in their future work in mathematics.

CURRICULUM, TASKS, MATERIALS

The physical environment was rich with visuals and tools that students needed to learn English, including bilingual and picture dictionaries and student-made glossaries of mathematics terms with heritage language definitions. In addition to many manipulatives (mathematical tools), the classroom also featured posters with labeled illustrations for each type of manipulative. Because the class was currently studying fractions, a full-color poster of the "fraction circle" kits was displayed in a central location. These nonlinguistic representations helped reinforce the key ideas and vocabulary that students were learning.

Another set of posters featured sentence starters. These important scripts were for students to use when discussing or writing about mathematics. The first poster, labeled "Asking for Clarification," had prompts such as *What do you mean?* The second poster, titled "Expressing Opinions," gave students the structures necessary for sharing their original ideas, and included stems such as *In my opinion . . .* and *It seems to me that . . . .* These stems, adapted from Kinsella (2006), supported students in implementing the academic register necessary for coursework in English, and because the teacher had made their use part of the daily classroom routine, students were confident in using the phrases and trying new ones. This emphasis on the use of oral academic English in mathematics aligns with TESOL (2006) Standard 3 in the domains of speaking and listening.

As the class began, the teacher reviewed the agenda and objectives written on the board. This daily orientation is an important element in sheltered instruction because it provides students with the expectations for the class period and additional opportunities to reinforce vocabulary in English. It takes just moments each day, but this ritualized activity can help make newcomers feel more at ease as the routines become familiar. This activity also addresses Level 1 of TESOL's (2006) Standard 1 in the reading domain: "preview visually supported text to glean basic information (e.g., menus, schedules, announcements)" (p. 88).

To begin the lesson, pairs of students retrieved a set of fraction circles. These plastic commercially available manipulatives fit together to form a series of 3-inch circles, each divided into color-coded halves, thirds, fourths, and so on. The teacher explained that the class was going to play a few rounds of Ms. Denominator Says. This variation of Simon Says is played with a recent mathematics vocabulary word in place of *Simon*. The target word (in this case, *denominator*) is attached to the leader of the game using a large sticky note, like a name tag.

Indicating the wall poster that showed illustrations and names of the fraction circle manipulatives, the teacher said, "Remember, use the poster if you need help." On the overhead, the teacher had written "Find _____" and "I found _____." She then said, "Ready? Ms. Denominator says find one-half."

The students consulted the pieces spread out on their desks and held up one-half pieces. Although some students were confident and reached quickly for the proper pieces, others hesitated and casually glanced at their neighbors before settling on a piece themselves. The teacher noted this, mentally assessing who understood the spoken forms of this fraction.

"Very good. Tell your partner, 'I found one-half.'"

Turning to their partners, students said in unison, "I found one-half."

"Wonderful. Ms. Denominator says, find one-eighth." Students looked at the various pieces in front of them and held up one-eighth pieces. "Excellent. Now tell your partner, 'I found one-eighth.'"

To change things a bit, the teacher then said, "Brilliant. Ms. Denominator says, find a green piece." This shift in focus, from naming fractional parts to naming a color, made some students pause, so the teacher repeated the phrase. Looking around, the students who had been confused now understood.

"Lovely. Show me a yellow piece," the teacher said. Several students smiled broadly and folded their hands, while others reached for yellow pieces. In mock surprise, the teacher addressed a student. "Lucia, you did not find a yellow piece! Why not?"

Laughing, Lucia said, "*Porque no dijiste*, 'Ms. Denominator says!'"

As the class groaned, the teacher seamlessly translated, "That's right. I didn't say 'Ms. Denominator says.' Bravo, Lucia! Now you're Ms. Denominator. You can come alone, or you can bring a friend. What is your choice?"

Lucia, eager but with limited English, chose to bring her partner, Norma, with her to the front of the room. Norma whispered directions into Lucia's ear, and Lucia directed the class. It was important for Lucia to feel successful in this activity, and because she wasn't quite ready to do it on her own, letting her lean on a peer, without shame or secrecy, was valuable. This kind of academic risk-taking behavior is important for students as they gradually move into classes with greater proportions of students who are not English language learners (ELLs).

Ms. Denominator Says took approximately 10 minutes. During this short time students had the opportunity to hear, speak, listen to, and read mathematical language and engage in an interactive, low-pressure mathematical activity, addressing TESOL (2006) Standard 3 (communication in mathematics) at Level 1–2 language proficiency level (starting to emerging). This standard corresponds to the National Council of Teachers of Mathematics (2000) number and operations standard for PreK–2: "All students should understand and represent commonly used fractions, such as ¼, ⅓, and ½" (p. 78). It also allowed students to briefly review an earlier term (*denominator*) in a playful, memorable way.

Indicating the agenda, the teacher said, "We've finished with our warm-up. Now it's time for equivalent fractions. Take a minute to talk with your partner about what equivalent fractions are. You may choose to speak in English or another language." By explicitly allowing students to speak in a language other than English, the teacher was drawing from extensive research that supports the use of heritage language in academic settings for ELLs (Collier, 1987; C. Snow, 1990; W. P. Thomas & Collier, 1999). Content knowledge and higher order thinking skills may transfer to the target language (in this case, English) once students acquire the appropriate vocabulary and structures of English (Cummins, 2001; C. Snow, 1990), so discussing conceptual issues in their heritage languages, if they choose to, is beneficial.

The teacher wrote on the overhead and then read aloud, "Choose any fraction. Write equivalent fractions. You have 1 minute." She further explained, "For example, you may choose one whole, two-thirds, eleven-seventeenths— any fraction you want." This corresponds to a National Council of Teachers of Mathematics (2000) number and operations standard for students in Grades 3–5: "Students should recognize and generate equivalent forms of commonly used fractions, decimals and percents" (p. 148).

By giving students the opportunity to select their own fractions to begin, the teacher employed student-directed differentiation, allowing multiple points of entry to the activity (Tomlinson, 1999). Not only did this permit the students to exert some level of control over their own learning and participation, it also allowed the teacher to informally evaluate students' levels of comfort and confidence in selecting and writing equivalent fractions in a timed, independent situation.

As students moved into small groups, the teacher both wrote and said the directions. "Explain to your group why you picked this fraction. For example, Lydia will explain why she chose one-half, and Melvin will explain why he chose one-fourth."

Next, the teacher guided students in talking about what strategies they used for this activity. "In other words, what exactly were you thinking when you wrote down each fraction? How did you know what to write next? Talk with your shoulder partner." The teacher circulated, listening quietly. Most students spoke in English, but a few same-language pairs chose to speak in a language other than English, which the teacher followed as best she could, listening for key vocabulary.

The teacher had built in multiple opportunities for both receptively understanding and actively producing English (Collier, 1995b; Walqui, 2000), and the inclusion of heritage language was a way to honor the multilingual skills and wisdom of each student, which contributed to students' overall feelings of receptivity toward the content (Moll, Amanti, Neff, & Gonzalez, 1992). In addition to the affective impact, the use of heritage languages was also a scaffold for learning the content by permitting students to link new ideas to prior learning and to verify and clarify their emerging understandings. This use of classroom discourse fits into TESOL (2006) Standard 3, in the domain of speaking, at Level 3: "Explain steps used in problem solving assisted by mental math or think-alouds" (p. 92). Although using English was clearly part of this lesson, heritage languages were welcome and valued as well.

After the partner discussions, the teacher guided students in writing their strategies, in alignment with TESOL (2006) Standard 3, in the domain of writing, at Level 2: "Describe simple equations, inequalities, or expressions from real-life situations with a partner" (p. 93). She provided the prompt, "The strategy I used to make my equivalent fractions was . . . ." As the students wrote, in English, for approximately 5 minutes, the teacher visited each student, checking to gauge his or her progress and helping when asked. As students finished, they read their writing to their partners, who were instructed to make any necessary suggestions for improvement.

Students spent the next 10 minutes working on this task, ending with a quick rewriting of their final drafts. The resulting texts would be displayed on the classroom wall, near the pencil sharpener, for easy viewing. With 5 minutes remaining in the period, the class began their cool-down. Students wrote in their journals in response to three prompts:

1. What did you do? Today I _____.

2. What did you learn? I learned _____.

3. What was interesting?

Because students responded daily to these same prompts, they had learned to elaborate on their thoughts. They used the agenda on the board as their guide to review what they had done and conferred quietly with their peers about their learning. In this way, they reinforced their learning for the day and reviewed the language they had practiced. This writing also helped the teacher gauge how well students had understood the content and plan for the following day. Additionally, the responses to the third item ("What was interesting?") helped provide important feedback to the teacher about what changes might make things more engaging or relevant for students. Although the responses were often humbling, the teacher appreciated this candid feedback.

Beyond this formative assessment, the teacher also administered a summative assessment of the relevant vocabulary and the mathematical content. As a way to empower students and have them share ownership, the teacher would have them work with partners to write quizzes that focused on the vocabulary and content. Given a set of parameters (including the specific vocabulary words to be used and a minimum quantity of items in the content portion), students would create a quiz (along with the answer key) and then decide whether it was easy, medium, or difficult.

After careful evaluation of each quiz by the teacher, students would choose which one best reflected their level of expertise and take it. Their results would be recorded as grades. This way, the teacher ensured that students had ample opportunity to become familiar with the vocabulary and content and were able to express what they had learned in an empowered, student-centered fashion.

REFLECTIONS

This lesson did not spontaneously erupt. It took great thought, planning, and rehearsal before the students and teacher were able to work in this focused, inter-dependent manner. Because preparing to teach a sheltered content lesson involves identifying and planning how to teach two objectives simultaneously (one content and one English objective), planning often takes longer than it might for a standard course. Within this complex planning process, the teacher must consider many factors, including the TESOL (2006) standards and knowledge of individual students and their strengths, and decide how to best use the available materials and resources.

Realistically, this type of hybrid English-mathematics lesson is a paradigm shift for many teachers of mathematics, and the example described in this chapter required long-term collaboration with the ESOL teacher. This collaboration included not only academic discussions about English language acquisition, but also heart-to-heart conversations about the often untapped or unknown strengths and challenges of each student, especially those students with limited or inter-rupted schooling. Although these types of interdepartmental relationships are often difficult to navigate (because priorities and values across departments are not universal), they are both valuable and necessary for supporting ELLs in their transition to grade-level mathematics.

Sheltered content lessons like this take thought, time, and perhaps even courage, but the dividends are well worth the investment because students are provided with multiple avenues to gain access to the curriculum in a manner that is both meaningful and respectful. Furthermore, the language focus is not limited to the content-obligatory vocabulary, but also includes communicative language that is intended to be used in various academic and social settings. This type of tightly integrated instruction not only supports students in learning content, but also equips them for success outside the classroom.

ACKNOWLEDGMENTS

Thank you to Tara Ross and Erik Behrens for reading drafts, and Shelley Wong and Jorge Osterling for inspiration.

Anita Bright has a PhD in multicultural/multilingual education and is a National Board Certified Teacher in early adolescence mathematics. Her work as a teacher educator focuses on meeting the needs of English language learners in second-ary mathematics. She is affiliated with Fairfax County Public Schools and George Mason University, in Virginia, in the United States. Her research explores the track-ing of students with historically marginalized identities in mathematics.

CHAPTER 9

Links in a Food Chain: Guiding Inquiry in Science for English Language Learners

David T. Crowther, Lori Fulton, Joaquín S. Vilá, and Eric Hoose

> Mr. Hoose calls his class of fourth graders to join him in a circle on the floor to begin the science lesson. He begins the lesson by telling students that they are going to talk about food chains today and asking them to take a minute to record their thoughts about what they think a food chain might be. A few minutes later, there is a buzz around the circle in both Spanish and English as students share their ideas with one another. One student has heard the term before but is not sure what it might mean; others admit they have never heard this before and propose that it must be some sort of chain made out of food or something to lock up food.

Can effective science instruction help with language acquisition as well as engage and interest students—all while enhancing conceptual understandings? Most teachers would immediately say yes, but how all of this is accomplished may not be entirely clear. The purpose of this chapter is to outline what an appropriate guided inquiry lesson may look like, the components that accompany it, and suitable standards-aligned learning outcomes for English language learners (ELLs).

The learning cycle is foundational to most current inquiry-based science programs. Developed in the mid 1960s, the learning cycle demonstrated that teaching science through inquiry was far more effective than more traditional direct instruction modes of teaching (Atkin & Karplus, 1962). Recently, to better serve the learning needs of ELLs, the learning cycle has been blended with the learning theories of Vygotsky and Krashen (Wallstrum & Crowther, 2009).

Inquiry as a form of teaching science has many faces. With open-ended inquiry, or full inquiry, students choose their own area of interest in science, write questions, lead their own investigations, collect data, and formulate conclusions based on the data. As ideal as this kind of learning may be, the only real time that students actually get the opportunity to choose their own subject and questions to research seems to be the annual science fair. For most science instruction, teachers are held accountable to standards and assessments that demonstrate proficiency of student learning. Which leads us to guided inquiry, in which the teacher chooses the standards-based subject to be learned and then provides an opportunity for students to ask questions and conduct investigations, perhaps using a kit-based program with real materials. The process is still inquiry, but with more teacher guidance.

In science there are two kinds of standards: content and process. Content standards can be thought of as the "nouns" that list the particular content facts that are to be explored in the lesson. Process standards may be viewed as the "verbs," or how the content will be learned. This portion of the standards ranges from particular tasks and skills to be developed or used in the investigation, along with how the investigation will be conducted (guided inquiry), to the nature of science or epistemology of the particular subject being explored.

The use of content and process standards in science instruction has become mainstream practice since the publication of the *National Science Education Standards* (National Research Council, 1996) and the subsequent development of state-level standards for instruction. When working with ELLs, the teacher must keep in mind that although science standards are written for a particular grade level or grade band, some adaptations may be needed in order for students to be successful with the lesson. These adaptations allow teachers to meet the specific language needs of students while addressing curricular goals. This differentiated instruction is supported by the *PreK–12 English Language Proficiency Standards* (TESOL, 2006), which were developed to integrate content and language learning standards in the domains of listening, speaking, reading, and writing.

The goal of this chapter is to explore a science lesson that follows a guided inquiry format and uses many strategies to promote language learning. First, a guided inquiry lesson used in a classroom with a majority of ELLs is shared. Then there is discussion of the key components and related research that validate this method while connecting relevant standards with integrated language and content area instruction.

CONTEXT

The Clark County School District, in Nevada, is the fifth largest district in the United States. With the influx of people has come a diverse population, as represented at Jay W. Jeffers Elementary School on the northeast side of Las Vegas. In the 2006–2007 school year, 812 students were enrolled in the school; approximately 5% were Caucasian, 5% were Black, and 89% were Hispanic. And more than 72% of students enrolled in the school were classified as limited English proficient (LEP).

Mr. Hoose, a fourth-grade teacher, and Ms. Fulton, the science mentor at the school, are preparing to coteach a lesson on food webs and food chains. Mr. Hoose has 28 students in his class—25 Hispanic and 3 Caucasian. All but 10 of these students were born in Mexico, 24 of them entered the school system as kindergartners, and 20 are classified as LEP and receive language services. Even after being in U.S. schools for up to 4 years, many students in Mr. Hoose's class still seem to lack the minimal academic language proficiency expected for their grade level.

CURRICULUM, TASKS, MATERIALS

Mr. Hoose begins the lesson by telling students that they are going to talk about food chains and asks them to take a minute to record their thoughts about what they think a food chain might be. Some students begin to jot down their ideas immediately, while others seem less responsive, wondering what these words might mean when used in this way. A few minutes later, Mr. Hoose invites students to discuss their thoughts about a food chain with a neighbor sitting next to them. Using both English and Spanish, students share their ideas with one another. After sharing, students go back to their science notebooks to jot down a few more thoughts, which they are then invited to share with the whole class. Most have written their thoughts using words, but some have drawn pictures, including an actual chain.

Having a sense of where the students are in their thinking, Mr. Hoose and Ms. Fulton are ready to move forward. They begin the lesson by engaging students in the song "There Once Was a Daisy" (2007), breaking them up into teams to sing the various parts (see the Appendix). After a quick read-through and modeling of the rhythm, the teachers practice the first line with the students and then have groups practice their parts. The whole class works together to sing the song, and it is evident from the expressions on their faces that students are putting ideas together and coming up with new thoughts about what a food chain might be. At the end of the song, students are asked to describe the links in the food chain they were just singing about in their small groups. They then share their ideas as a whole class and begin naming the various animals (fox, snake, bird, bugs, daisy) on a small whiteboard for visual reference. The students go on to explain that they now think a food chain is made up of different animals that eat one another.

Now that they have a better idea of what a food chain is, it is time to explore the concept a little further. Each student receives a 3 x 5 card containing a picture and label of part of a food chain. Out of the 28 students, 11 represent grass, 9 represent grasshoppers, 4 represent field mice, 2 represent snakes, 1 represents a hawk, and 1 represents a vulture. The instructors explain that students will use a ball of yarn to connect the links of the food chain (see Figure 1), starting with grass. The ball of yarn is handed to one of the students holding a grass card, and the class is asked who would eat the grass. There is a hesitant response of "grasshopper," and holding the loose end of the yarn, the grass girl tosses the ball to one of the grasshoppers. The lesson continues, with the instructors questioning students to see who would be the next link in the food chain, until finally the yarn arrives at the hawk.

Figure 1. Students Using Yarn to Link the Food Chain Together

At that point, Mr. Hoose and Ms. Fulton pause for a moment to ask students what they have just created. Students eagerly say, "A food chain." The instructors proceed to review the parts of the food chain and talk about the fact that the hawk is the top of our food chain and that there is nothing in our environment that would eat the hawk. With this information, students determine that they need to begin a new chain, so the yarn is tossed back to someone with a grass card and the process begins all over again.

Students begin to notice that the yarn looks like a web, and upon questioning, several students state that when many food chains are created they look like a spider web. The instructors explicitly reinforce the idea that when many food chains interact, a food web is created. While holding a section of the web, the instructors have students sway back and forth to feel the interdependency of the web. As individuals move, they can feel the tug on their section of the yarn.

It is now time to introduce the vulture, "the garbage man of the animal kingdom," who sweeps in and cleans up all of the dead animals. As the vulture picks up the string, students are excited and ask if they can do the activity again. As the yarn is rewound back into a ball, students take a minute to record in their science notebooks what they now understand about food chains. Again, most use words to describe a food chain while some draw a diagram or picture of the example that was just explored.

As they finish rewinding the ball of yarn, Mr. Hoose and Ms. Fulton provide some explanation to students about the elements of a food chain. First, they write "grass/plants" on the board and explain that scientists call these organisms *producers* because they can make or produce their own food using the sun's energy through photosynthesis. Next, they list "grasshopper/bugs" and explain that scientists call these organisms *consumers* because they must rely on something else for their food; they are also called *herbivores,* or plant eaters. The instructors also label the mouse a consumer, too, explaining that this type of consumer is different because it eats plants as well as meat, which means that it is an *omnivore.* Then comes the snake, which students state is also a consumer.

Next, Mr. Hoose and Ms. Fulton explain that *carnivores* eat meat only. They point out that this word looks similar to a word students might know in Spanish, *carne,* which means meat. This sort of acknowledgment of learners' native language not only validates their linguistic backgrounds, but also provides for increased motivation because learners are encouraged to formulate further hypotheses about the possible meanings of the new words encountered by drawing on the lexicons of both English and Spanish. Each time the instructors introduce a word, it is added to the diagram on the board and is constructed as part of a sentence strip to go on the science bulletin board word wall.

By this time, the yarn is back to its ball shape, so the instructors pass out the cards and have a student representing grass begin the process all over again. As students toss the ball to various parts of the food chain, they are asked to share whether they are tossing it to a producer or a consumer and, if it is a consumer, which type. Again, the students start responding to these questions quietly but end with strong voices. It appears as though they really understand the concept of a food chain.

To elaborate on the idea, the instructors ask students to work in groups to create posters showing a variety of food chains. Using *National Geographic* magazines, students look for pictures of items that would be part of a food chain. They use the pictures to construct a poster of food chains, which will ultimately make a web. The poster task becomes an alternative assessment that provides a nonverbal way for ELLs to share their grasp of food chains.

At first, it seems as though all of the students are looking for examples that match the diagram on the board or the example that was created earlier in the lesson; however, it does not take long before they start to branch out. This branching out seems to raise many questions—What exactly does a kangaroo eat? What would eat a butterfly? Is it a food chain if there are only two links? This task is proving to be a little more challenging than Mr. Hoose and Ms. Fulton anticipated.

The students have little experience with the types of animal pictures they find in the *National Geographic* magazines. For some of them, it seems as though they are organizing their chains based on the size of the animal, which usually seems to work, but then animals such as the rhinoceros pose a challenge. These issues are identified through constant monitoring and observing and then cleared up through small-group discussions that help the students understand the types of food these animals eat—reinforcing not only the idea of food chains, but also the terminology (e.g., carnivore, omnivore, herbivore, consumer, producer) as it relates to different organisms.

By the end of this activity, the groups have a variety of food chains on their posters (e.g., plant-insect-frog-bird-cat, grass-horse-wolf, gazelle-hyena). Some groups have even labeled the pictures on their posters as producers or consumers. To finish the lesson, the instructors have groups share their posters with the class. Everyone has an opportunity to ask questions, which pushes students to think about whether a tiger is considered a herbivore, an omnivore, or a carnivore or to explain which link in their chain is a herbivore and why. Mr. Hoose and Ms. Fulton are excited to see that students understand the main idea, regardless of their English language proficiency, as made evident by the varied assessments used.

In closing the lesson, Mr. Hoose and Ms. Fulton ask students to return to their science notebooks and reflect on what they now understand about food chains. Some students write their reflections (Figure 2), offering comments such as, "A food chain is animals eating outher animials [sic]," "The food chain is about an animal eating another animal," "A food chain is a pattern, like if there wasn't no mouse the snake will die and there will be a lot of grasshoppers," and

Figure 2. A Student Writing in Her Science Notebook

"If there's grass a grasshopper will eat it then a field mouse will eat the grasshopper then a snake will eat the field mouse then a hawk will eat the snake." Other students draw pictures of food chains (Figure 3), and some list the food chains they examined earlier in class (Figure 4).

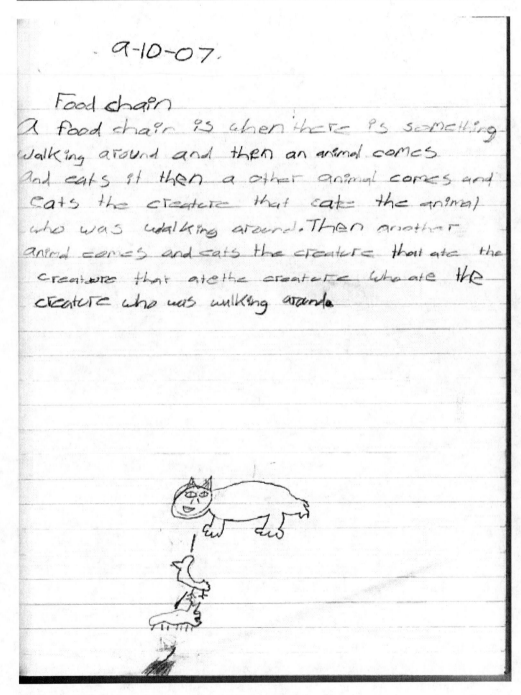

Figure 3. A Student's Picture of a Food Chain

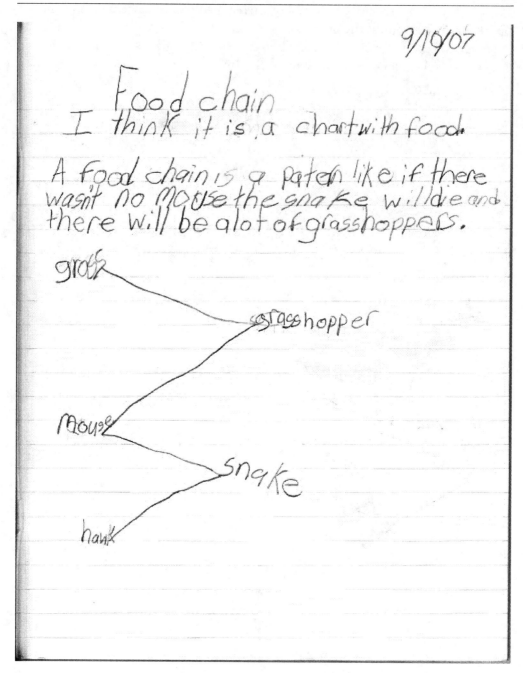

Figure 4. A Student's Diagram of a Food Chain

Overall, there is remarkable growth from the beginning entry to the last entry in students' notebooks. They no longer think a food chain is a chart or chain, but demonstrate understanding of the basic concepts in both their verbal and non-verbal communication of the content. The ELLs in the class, rather than being passive participants, have had the opportunity to actively participate in the process of creating meaning, of "doing science" and demonstrating the extent to which they have met intended lesson objectives.

REFLECTIONS

In this lesson, Mr. Hoose and Ms. Fulton identify the pertinent state science content and process standards (Table 1) and explore the TESOL (2006) English language proficiency standards at different developmental levels (Table 2). These standards are all addressed as part of the lesson plan objectives and are all linked to the assessments.

Guided inquiry is an effective teaching model that is student centered and can easily incorporate effective learning strategies in science for ELLs. Mr. Hoose and Ms. Fulton begin with a simple song to introduce the content and then guide students to discover the relationships that comprise a food chain and web. The students did not have a choice in the subject of the lesson, but they are led to discover the content objectives of the relationships among organisms in a food chain, giving them ownership in discovering new creatures and concepts.

Two keys to guided inquiry for ELLs are scaffolding and sequencing. Scaffolding for vocabulary, as illustrated in the modified text of "There Once Was a Daisy" (see the Appendix), allows ELLs to make sense of terminology relevant to the lesson and, along with the additional activities, provides for context-embedded language that is easier to understand. Mr. Hoose and Ms. Fulton allow students to experience and understand the context of food chains and webs, and then as key words come up in the lesson they are reinforced formally, discussed in groups, and added to a word wall for both immediate and future reference.

The sequence of the lesson is based on Karplus's learning cycle (Fuller, 2002),

Table 1. Nevada Standards Addressed in the Lesson

Content Standard: Life Science (Grade Band 3–5)	
L.5.C Students understand that there are a variety of ecosystems on Earth and organisms interact within their ecosystems.	• Students know the organization of simple food webs. • Students know organisms interact with each other and with the nonliving parts of their ecosystem. • Students know changes to an environment can be beneficial or detrimental to different organisms. • Students know all organisms, including humans, can cause changes in their environments.
Process Standard: Nature of Science (Grade Band 3–5)	
N.5.A Students understand that science involves asking and answering questions and comparing the answers to what scientists know about the world.	• Students know scientific progress is made by conducting careful investigations, recording data, and communicating the results in an accurate method. • Students know observable patterns can be used to organize items and ideas.

Source: Nevada Department of Education, 2008.

Table 2. TESOL Standard Addressed in the Lesson

Standard 4: ELLs communicate information, ideas, and concepts necessary for academic success in Science (Grade Level 3–4; TESOL, 2006) Topic: Life Science/Living Things	
Listening	
Level 1	Match words with diagrams with oral commands
Level 2	Select examples of organisms from magazines from oral directions
Level 3	Create a display of food web using visuals based on oral descriptions
Level 4	Organize information about food chains and webs on poster from teacher explanations
Level 5	Evaluate poster on levels of food chain: producer, consumer
Speaking	
Level 1	Name organisms from pictures: producer, consumer
Level 2	Describe which organisms consume other organisms from pictures
Level 3	Identify producers and consumers in the right tertiary order
Level 4	Describe and give examples of organisms in a food web
Level 5	Explain relationships of organisms within and between food chains and webs
Reading	
Level 1	Find examples of organisms in magazines
Level 2	Sequence organisms into food webs
Level 3	Follow directions to construct a food chain or web on a poster with labels
Level 4	Interpret information from your poster and others as to accuracy of food chains and webs
Level 5	Infer about other possible food chains in other ecological environments
Writing	
Level 1	Replicate a food chain from the class activity in your notebook
Level 2	Collect observations and record thoughts (pictures and words) from food web activity
Level 3	Compare food chains from other groups to yours; record similarities and differences
Level 4	Maintain illustrated notes from the food web activity, including your thoughts in your notebook
Level 5	Explain about producers and consumers in your notebook using examples from your food web

which has three main phases: exploration, concept/term development, and application. Also known as the *activity before content* (ABC) model of instruction, it aligns with the ESOL strategy of teaching the text backwards, which provides a rich contextual learning experience, such as a science investigation, and is followed by support reading material. Karplus's original cycle has been modified in several formats. Roger Bybee designed what is now referred to as the 5E model (Bybee, 2002b; Bybee & Landes, 1990; Trowbridge & Bybee, 1996), which proposes that a lesson contain five parts:

1. *Engagement:* Get students interested, and engage background knowledge.

2. *Exploration:* This is the main portion of the lesson that is hands-on and during which students make discoveries about the content being presented.

3. *Explanation:* The content is labeled and key vocabulary is reinforced.

4. *Elaboration:* This extension of the activity allows for further understanding of the content.

5. *Evaluation:* There should be both formative and summative assessment.

When adapted for guided inquiry investigations and language development for ELLs, the 5E learning cycle gives structure to the learning process, promotes student inquiry, and emphasizes all four communication modes of listening, speaking, reading, and writing. It also helps students develop thinking and problem-solving skills. The remainder of this chapter uses the 5E framework to explain the lesson on food chains and webs and explicitly show where science and language strategies are used to reinforce content and allow for language development.

Engagement

The first step of the lesson encourages students to write or draw in their science notebooks their current ideas of what a food chain and food web are. This activates background knowledge for the students, lets the teachers get ideas of what the students know about the topic, and is used as a preassessment for the lesson. Students also sing a song that models the food chain on a prairie, which reinforces correct knowledge and begins the process of learning the new content vocabulary and correcting misconceptions.

Cooperative learning allows for multiple uses of communication and cooperation when implemented appropriately. It also allows for pairing emerging ELLs with more proficient ELLs who may do some interpretation for them. Cooperative learning requires low-stakes use of social language and immediate applications of specific academic language, thus reinforcing Krashen's (1981) concept of affective filter for ELLs by reducing the anxiety level (lower stress) of learning for students. Through cooperative learning structures, ELLs have the opportunity to practice and get feedback on new words and structures in English. Large- as well as small-group cooperative learning opportunities are present in the lesson on food chains and webs.

Exploration

During this portion of the lesson, students receive a 3 x 5 card with both a picture and a label of the organism that they will represent as a link in the food chain. Then they throw the ball of yarn to the person representing the organism that would consume them and actually create a physical chain (kinesthetic learning). After the first chain is made, additional chains are added when students discover the connections between food chains and a food web. This portion of the lesson concludes with a scenario about the impact of humans on the food chain and web or ecosystem. This activity is guided by the teachers, and the students are led to make discoveries about the content (through both scaffolding and guided inquiry) by using some of the listening and speaking skills that are a part of the lesson.

The science terms *food chain, food web, consumer,* and *producer* are introduced in context during this portion of the lesson (contextualized vocabulary introduction). However, the terminology is not formalized in the learning yet, demonstrating a blended model of vocabulary instruction (20% front loading and 80% contextual), which allows optimum learning of vocabulary for ELLs (Wallstrum & Crowther, 2009). This portion of the lesson also enables students to go back to their notebooks to record their thoughts and ideas from the activity, thus affording opportunities to practice writing and reading skills.

The more that visuals and real objects (realia) can be used in science instruction, the better ELLs will be able to understand what is being taught and make connections to the real world. In the example lesson, pictures of the organisms, graphic organizers, and grids allow students to organize and understand material in multiple learning modes. This strategy is demonstrated in the example lesson through modeling, whiteboard diagrams, word walls for vocabulary, and science notebook entries.

Explanation

Mr. Hoose and Ms. Fulton begin the class discussion by going to the whiteboard and, with students' help, re-creating the food chain that they all just experienced. Through discussion, students learn about the different organisms and their roles in the food chain and web. Science terminology is formalized at this time by labeling the diagram on the board and adding the vocabulary to the science word wall, and then it is practiced again in the reconstruction of the food chain and web made of yarn. Lectures are not used; rather, partner, small-group, and large-class discussions provide students with time to think and respond to questions and scenarios, and this approach reinforces speaking and listening modalities.

Students are given plenty of time to respond orally and in writing, thus taking into account different processing times required for both comprehension and production by ELLs.

Elaboration

This portion of Mr. Hoose and Ms. Fulton's lesson lets students take the content that they learned and apply it to a new situation or task that demonstrates their conceptual understanding. While the children are constructing their posters utilizing pictures from *National Geographic* magazines (realia in a print format), the teachers are able to monitor and observe the progress. During the observations, as some misconceptions and confusion become evident, these are rectified through small-group discussions.

Evaluation

Good lesson planning takes into consideration the fact that evaluation happens both during the lesson (formative) and at the end of the lesson (summative). Although the last of the 5Es may seem out of place for formative assessment, having it in the lesson structure reminds teachers of the value and importance of evaluation and assessment. In the example lesson, Mr. Hoose and Ms. Fulton collect anecdotal information by monitoring students as they work, making observations about written work as well as participation in activities, and questioning students throughout the lesson, which allows for immediate modifications and accommodations in both teaching and learning.

Summative assessment lets students demonstrate their conceptual understanding. Mr. Hoose and Ms. Fulton's modifications of traditional summative assessment included having students create a poster in a group setting and complete individual science notebook entries that utilized pictures, diagrams, and words to communicate students' knowledge of food chains and webs rather than their level of command of the English language. (For further reading on effective assessment for ELLs in science, see Katz & Olson, 2006.)

Mr. Hoose and Ms. Fulton follow the 5E model as advocated by Bybee (2002b) fairly closely; however, they also make some modifications and use specific strategies to support ELLs. (For further information on modifying the learning cycle into more of a guided or scaffolded inquiry and how this impacts student learning, see Vanosdall, Klentschy, Hedges, & Weisbaum, 2007).

The *National Science Education Standards* (National Research Council, 1996) state that "science is something that children should do, not something that is done to them" (p. 20). This idea supports the importance of using inquiry-based instruction rather than direct instruction as a teaching method in science classrooms. Appropriate science instruction that provides opportunities for active construction of science content while integrating strategies for reading, writing, speaking, listening, thinking, and problem solving is greatly needed in the diverse classrooms of U.S. schools. The integration of language skills and the centrality of purpose in all likelihood offer the perception of authenticity and relevance, which is intrinsically motivating for ELLs.

In guided inquiry, the rich context and meaningful language and activities allow for better understanding of the concepts while promoting increased participation and student involvement regardless of learners' proficiency levels (Brown, 2007). Moreover, research-based science instruction that uses guided inquiry and incorporates language skills improves standardized test scores not only in science, but in mathematics and literacy as well (Amaral, Garrison, & Klentschy, 2002; Vanosdall et al., 2007).

The ELLs in Mr. Hoose and Ms. Fulton's class are clearly able to process directions, understand text and new vocabulary, share information with other learners, collect data, draw inferences, and explain relationships between concepts. By exploring the theme of a food chain and then moving on to that of a food web, learners are able to draw from context-embedded information to make sense of academic language (Cummins, 2000). Language and content standards are addressed through context-rich activities, collaborative techniques, and specific writing and reading tasks suited for varying proficiency levels.

Guided inquiry provides abundant opportunities for ELLs to engage in hands-on exploration of the subject and to listen, read, and write about a topic that is relevant and meaningful to them. Built on successful learning models and best practices to integrate language and content area instruction (Brown, 2007), the lesson described in this chapter provides abundant opportunities to use language in a meaningful context centered on subject matter that is of clear interest to all students. This, in turn, enables ELLs to receive the full benefit of a learning experience that is context embedded and facilitates understanding (Herrera & Murry, 2005).

David T. Crowther is a professor of science education at the University of Nevada, Reno, in the United States. In addition to teaching at the university level, he has taught elementary school as well. He is the coeditor of, and a contributor to, Science for English Language Learners *(NSTA Press, 2006). His research interests focus on effective instruction in elementary and middle school science.*

Lori Fulton is a science mentor at Jay W. Jeffers Elementary School, in Las Vegas, Nevada, in the United States, where she taught the lesson described in this chapter with Eric Hoose. She has 15 years of experience teaching adults as well as young children. She is currently working on a PhD in teacher education with an emphasis in science. She coauthored Science Notebooks: Writing About Inquiry *(Heinemann, 2003).*

Joaquín S. Vilá has a PhD in linguistics from Michigan State University and has taught ESL in Grades 7–12. For more than 25 years, he has worked in the development and delivery of teacher preparation programs. Currently he serves as a Specialty Program Area reviewer in TESOL and on the Board of Examiners of the National Council for Accreditation of Teacher Education.

Eric Hoose has been teaching for 7 years. His passion lies in teaching math and science through inquiry. With Lori Fulton, he taught the lesson described in this chapter to his fourth-grade class at Jay W. Jeffers Elementary School, in Las Vegas, Nevada, in the United States.

APPENDIX: "THERE ONCE WAS A DAISY"

(modification of song)

Daisy team:	There once was a daisy that grew on a plain, Where the sun helped it grow and so did the rain— Links on a food chain.
Bug team:	There once was a bug who nibbled on flowers, Nibbled on flowers for hours and hours—
Daisy team:	The bug ate the daisy that grew on the plain, Where the sun helped it grow and so did the rain—
All:	Links in a food chain.
Wren team:	There once was a wren, who gobbled up bugs, And creepies and crawlies and slimies and slugs.
Bug team:	The wren ate the bug, who nibbled on flowers, Nibbled on flowers for hours and hours—
Daisy team:	The bug ate the daisy that grew on the plain, Where the sun helped it grow and so did the rain—
All:	Links in a food chain.
Snake team:	There once was a snake, who often grabbed birds, And swallowed them whole, or so I have heard.
Wren team:	The snake ate the wren, who gobbled up bugs, And creepies and crawlies and slimies and slugs.
Bug team:	The wren ate the bug, who nibbled on flowers, Nibbled on flowers for hours and hours—
Daisy team:	The bug ate the daisy that grew on the plain, Where the sun helped it grow and so did the rain—
All:	Links in a food chain.
Fox team:	There once was a fox, and I'll make a bet: He'd eat anything he could possibly get.

Snake team: The fox ate the snake, who often grabbed birds,
And swallowed them whole, or so I have heard.

Wren team: The snake ate the wren, who gobbled up bugs,
And creepies and crawlies and slimies and slugs.

Bug team: The wren ate the bug, who nibbled on flowers,
Nibbled on flowers for hours and hours—

Daisy team: The bug ate the daisy that grew on the plain,
Where the sun helped it grow, and so did the rain—

All: Links in a food chain.

Fox team: The fox, he grew older and died one spring day,
But he made the soil rich when he rotted away.
A new daisy grew where he died on the plain.
The sun helped it grow, and so did the rain—

All: Links in a food chain.

CHAPTER 10

Building Bridges Between Language and Content in Religious Education

Rosie Tanner and Lorna Dunn

> I was used to teaching English *in English*; the challenge seemed to be doubled when I started teaching Religious Education through English. (Lorna)

How can teachers teach a subject "through English" to 12- and 13-year-old beginning-level learners? Lorna has been teaching English for 38 years and Religious Education for 3, and 2 years ago she started teaching in the new bilingual stream at Dr. Moller College, in Waalwijk, a small town in the Netherlands. In addition to Religious Education, she teaches extra English to the new bilingual learners to help them with their fluency. Teaching *in* English, teachers focus on language only, but teaching *through* English means both teaching your subject and being aware that learners are also learning language at the same time.

Lorna's classes are mixed ability in terms of English proficiency. Students are mostly "false beginners" with a level of English as low as A1 on the *Common European Framework of References for Languages* (Council of Europe, 2001). Their receptive vocabulary is relatively good (they frequently watch television and play computer games in English), but their knowledge of religious concepts related to different religions is next to nothing. In the first few weeks of class, the course book (C. Thomas & Thomas, 2005) covers unfamiliar and abstract ideas such as denomination, community, commitment, and Sikhism. Lorna had this to say about the book:

> Simply translating the words into Dutch is not enough for them to get to grips with the concepts. And I had chosen this book and the topic without realizing how difficult it would be for the children! Now I suddenly had to teach unfamiliar and typically British concepts such as the Salvation Army, a church school, a chapel or a carol service, to these near beginners. How could I possibly help them learn about alien concepts in a foreign language as well as motivate them to learn some religious education?

In this chapter, we discuss the context of bilingual education in the Netherlands, describe some ways in which Lorna worked on her problem, and analyze why her actions constituted good content and language integrated learning (CLIL) practice.

CONTEXT

The first bilingual schools in the Netherlands opened in 1989. They were actually bilingual streams within large, comprehensive-style secondary schools. These schools are also known as "CLIL schools," referring to the approach that they use. Many classes in higher education are already carried out in English, and the ability to function in English globally is seen as important, but CLIL schools have additional status. The number of schools starting a bilingual stream is increasing every year, and out of about 650 secondary schools in the Netherlands, nearly 100 have a bilingual department. To qualify as a junior CLIL school (a school with a bilingual stream), a school must offer at least 50% of lessons in English during the first 3 years, in any subject the school chooses (with the exception of languages other than English itself). Typically, these subjects are mathematics, biology, history, geography, art or drama, and physical education. (The CLIL school qualification must be granted within the first 5 years by the European Platform[1] [Europees Platform, 2008] through inspection visits.)

The school where Lorna works serves more than 1,000 students ranging in age from 12 to 18. The school began its CLIL stream in autumn 2006. In 2008 it had 170 bilingual learners, divided among two first-year classes, three second-year classes, and two third-year classes. School-leaving examinations in Dutch are compulsory, so bilingual schools offer a more limited number of subjects after the third year in English. Many bilingual learners opt to take some Cambridge examinations (First Certificate in English, Cambridge Advanced English, Cambridge Proficiency in English) and the International Baccalaureate A2 examination in English.

The Learners

Learners choose to go to a bilingual school in the Netherlands for various reasons. They like learning languages, and bilingual education is a modern alternative to the traditional grammar schools that emphasize Latin and Greek. For children who have been to international primary schools, it is an opportunity for them to continue learning in English; furthermore, a bilingual school is seen as having an extra challenge for gifted and talented children.

English has a unique place in Dutch culture and trade; much of the media is in

---

[1] The mandate of the European Platform for Dutch education is to increase the quality of education through internationalization.

English, and many people read in English. Dutch people benefit from the mastery of a lingua franca in order to communicate during work and holidays: Bilingual schools organize school visits or exchanges abroad so that pupils' horizons are expanded. Moreover, a high level of English is becoming more of a prerequisite to future career or study success: A growing number of higher education courses are taught partly or purely in English, and many academic textbooks are in English.

The Teachers

Teachers choose to teach in the bilingual stream for a number of reasons: They have links with British or U.S. culture (family, friends, a hobby, work or study experience); they have a good mastery of English; they thrive on new challenges and are open to new ideas, including about (language) learning; some even consider teaching in the bilingual stream to be an easy option because the pupils are mainly bright and interested. Teachers go through an internal selection procedure whereby their English is tested and they discuss their reasons for wanting to work in the bilingual stream. Once chosen, they attend in-service CLIL training courses in the Netherlands or the United Kingdom and are expected to achieve a certain level of English (Cambridge Proficiency Exam within 5 years) in order to teach in the CLIL stream. Beginning CLIL teachers attend English language courses; as they become more used to teaching in English, they take CLIL methodology courses dealing with issues such as self-confidence when teaching in a foreign language, children's language learning, and teaching subject matter while taking language learning into account.

In terms of what she has learned from these CLIL courses, Lorna has the following to say:

> Teaching according to CLIL concepts has made me aware of the potential for authentic use of English and language acquisition among learners of roughly 12 years of age. They absorb many structures and words without a great deal of effort. By comparison, I feel that there is a lot of wasted effort in regular classes on rules and tests, which are useful in themselves but are surely only a means to an end. CLIL allows us to work directly towards the goal.

Challenges in Bilingual Education

Lorna's problem is one shared by many subject teachers at bilingual schools in the Netherlands, who are working with near-beginning-level learners of English with course book materials written for native-English-speaking teenagers, usually in a British context. Her challenges are complex:

- She works with a mixed-ability group in terms of English: English is compulsory at primary school, but standards at secondary school entry vary considerably.

- The students are mostly academically strong (they must attain a certain score in their primary school examination to enter the bilingual stream), so they need to be challenged intellectually.

- All the pupils are fluent in Dutch, so they can communicate easily with each other in their native tongue. However, they are not used to communicating—in speaking or writing—in English.

- The brief for Dutch teachers of Religious Education (or *levensbeschouwing*, translated as philosophy of life) is to encourage pupils to reflect on major ethical and personal questions. The abstract concepts needed for reflection are hard to grasp for learners younger than 13 or 14 years old (Evans, 1973), and even more so in a foreign language.

- A major issue in Dutch education is a conflict of ideas between traditional and progressive teachers about whether knowledge or skills should predominate. How can a balance be achieved?

- Many concepts in the course book are culturally specific; a translation often cannot help.

CURRICULUM, TASKS, MATERIALS

In this section, we discuss and illustrate some strategies and tasks that worked for Lorna during her first 3 months as a teacher of Religious Education in the bilingual stream and then describe two longer activities that illustrate good CLIL practice.

Building Confidence

In the initial weeks, students in the bilingual stream need to become confident in using English. They are, after all, in an unfamiliar social context with new classmates, with the added difficulty that most lessons are in English. Lorna encouraged confidence by complimenting students who were trying hard to be creative with their English. For example, she encouraged the near-native learners to help with other students' language problems; if a learner was trying but had become stuck, she would stop briefly and ask, "Does someone know the word for . . . ?"

Using the First Language

In order to understand each other, learners and teachers need to do some switching in the beginning between their first language and English. During the first month, Lorna selected some activities from the book to do in Dutch and other, simpler ones to do in English. She asked questions in English, sometimes paraphrasing in Dutch. If students asked questions in Dutch or were stuck on a phrase, she rephrased in English. She encouraged them to speak to her and to each other in English as much as possible. By the autumn holiday, which occurred after about 8 weeks of English, most of the teaching was in English.

Tolerance of Errors

Accuracy in writing and speaking was definitely not a priority in the first few months. The emphasis was on fluency, on getting students to use the language. In written assignments and tests, Dutch was acceptable if a student wanted to get across a specific idea and could not express it adequately in English. Lorna's ultimate aim was for pupils to get used to putting their thoughts into English as naturally as possible, but at the initial stages it seemed unreasonable to expect pupils to discuss and argue in English, because they shared a common first language. Lorna thus tolerated discussions in Dutch in group work as long as pupils reported back to the whole group in English.

Building Vocabulary

The most important aspect of the first stages of learning was that students needed to learn and use new vocabulary as well as activate their receptive or latent vocabulary in order to communicate. They were not only learning new words related to the subject, but doing so in a foreign language, so emphasis on language at this stage was vital. Lorna's main strategy was to recycle new, important concepts several times through different learning activities so that students used the language in different contexts. The first unit, *Personal Identity,* started with the themes "Who Am I?" and "Where Do I Belong?" in which these new concepts were important: community, experiences, parents, religion, culture, teachers, media, friends, family, customs, practices. Some were easy to learn (family is *familie* in Dutch, and most learners knew the English words *friend* and *teacher*); others took more time.

Lorna used various strategies for building vocabulary:

- Recap the key words at the beginning of each lesson.

- Repeat words initially in context by using short, simple phrases. Learners had some difficulty with the word *community*, so Lorna illustrated the concept with sentences such as "You are all part of a community," "You are all part of the community of Waalwijk," and "At home you are part of the family community."

- Match words to definitions in simple English, and Dutch words to English ones.

- Match words to pictures in the book. This was also a thinking skills activity because the matching was not self-evident and required some cognitive ability. Students needed to think and discuss which picture matched which word, thus repeating the words and deepening their understanding of them.

Personal Idiom File

Each learner in a bilingual stream keeps a personal idiom file (PIF), an individualized vocabulary notebook where the learner keeps a record of new words and their definitions. The term *personal* is perhaps a misnomer because initially words are suggested by the teacher. The PIF helps pupils store important words or concepts and boosts their confidence, because pupils may use their PIF in tests for reference. During the first few weeks of Lorna's class, pupils found it hard to get used to using their PIFs, though these gradually became part of the learning process.

Teaching New Concepts and the PIF

One of Lorna's problems was that concepts occurred in her book that were totally alien to the pupils she taught—concepts such as church schools or the difference between church and chapel—and pupils felt uncomfortable because they did not understand them. She asked them to write "typically British" beside such a term or description in their PIFs, which helped them feel more comfortable about not fully understanding a concept.

Visualization

Visualization helped with retention of words and concepts. Lorna selected a course book that contained many photographs and visual activities, and she often used them to support pupils' learning. Pupils made spider diagrams, or mind maps, to help them activate vocabulary and expand on their own, individual vocabulary (see Figure 1).

Once the learners knew, or half-knew, some important concepts, Lorna introduced the Diamond Nine visual in which a list of nine important vocabulary items is rearranged in order of priority (see Figure 2). It is a cognitively demanding activity that works on vocabulary recycling and thinking skills, but even a less fluent English language learner can carry it out with success. This activity effectively helped learners retain vocabulary more easily.

Good Practice in CLIL 1: Sikhism Storyboard

Sikhism is a well-established and visible faith in the United Kingdom, but it was unfamiliar to Lorna's Dutch learners. After about 8 weeks of bilingual education, Lorna used a storyboard activity to introduce a topic from the course book about joining the Sikh community, or *Khalsa,* by means of the Amrit Ceremony. The unit reinforced the familiar concepts of community, ceremony, commitment, and rules, and included colorful illustrations of the Sikh turban, bracelet, comb, sword, and short pants. Lorna found a simplified version of the story about the founder of Sikhism and the founding ceremony in 1699 in a resource book (Myers, 2001). She read this aloud twice, checking for understanding as she went along. She then split the class into small groups; each group's task was to

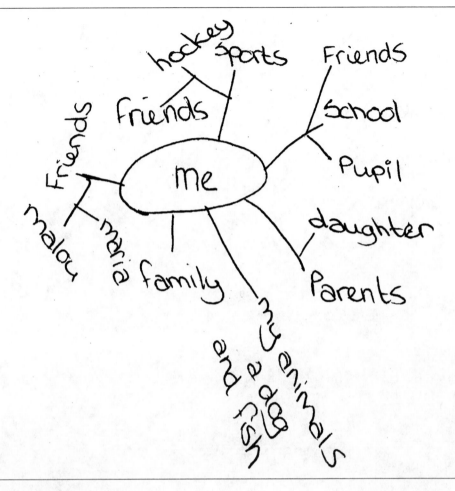

Figure 1. Student-Made Spider Diagram

create a dramatic "freeze frame" of a different scene from the story. These images would later be put together into a storyboard about the ceremony. All the group members had to appear in their tableau and were encouraged to make it visually interesting by means of gesture or height. The activity appealed to the pupils; many quickly improvised props such as paper turbans or swords. Figures 3–5 show the pupils hard at work.

In the next lesson, Lorna provided each group with a copy of their photograph. Their task was now to add a speech bubble for each of the characters in the scene, describing the emotions at that particular time in the story. Each group also wrote two or three sentences describing their scene and its place in the ceremony. This experience of working in a group to build a complete storyboard that reproduced the story proved to be a valuable way of learning and recycling the required concepts and vocabulary. Figure 6 shows the results of this activity.

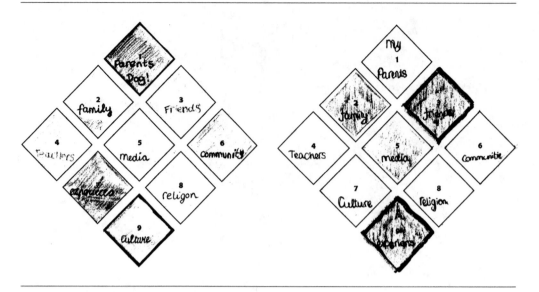

Figure 2. Two Completed Diamond Nines

Figure 3. Sikh Ceremony Freeze Frame Depicting the first Amrit Ceremony in the 17th Century

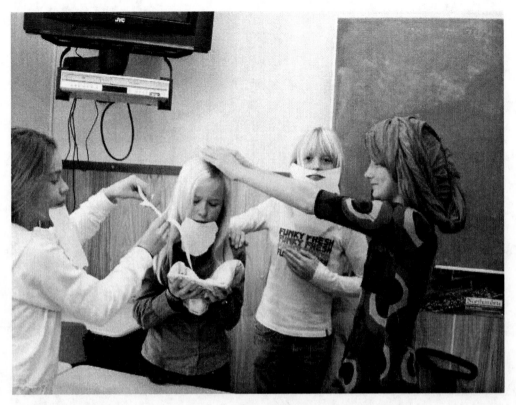

*Figure 4. Pupils Preparing for a Freeze Frame by Making and Putting on
Props and Headgear*

Assessment

The storyboard work was assessed on the basis of effectiveness of the scene (the
extent to which each group understood the part of the ceremony depicted in their
freeze frame), the involvement of the whole group in the scene (group process),
and the dramatic effect (the message). Lorna decided to focus on fluency at this
stage. As long as the group was able to get their point across, they had achieved
the object. When stuck, they were still allowed to use the occasional Dutch word.

Why Is This Good CLIL Practice?

This series of lessons is a clear example of good CLIL teaching. First, the storyboard tasks served as motivating and authentic communicative language activities.
The language and concepts were recycled by using three language skills: listening to the story, talking about the scene and the storyboard, and writing the
speech bubbles. Learners used their academic English authentically to refine their
understanding of lesson content, interacting in authentic ways to produce a real
product (the storyboard) and through the various tasks gradually refined their
understanding of the topic in a foreign language.

Figure 5. Sikh Ceremony Freeze Frame Depicting the Miraculous Return of a Volunteer Unharmed

Second, Lorna appealed to learner differences by addressing a variety of multiple intelligences (Gardner, 1993). Learners were given the opportunity to take up information in various ways through different channels. They used interpersonal intelligence to do the group work, intrapersonal intelligence in listening to the story, visual-spatial and bodily-kinesthetic intelligences in building up the tableaux and the storyboard, and linguistic intelligence in writing the speech bubbles and in discussions. The more intelligences that are incorporated into CLIL lessons, the more likely that learners will successfully take up the learning opportunities.

Third, learners could use drama to express their understanding of the concepts. This worked well because their productive language skills were as yet inadequate to express their ideas through language alone. Getting the message across through dramatic expression—thus demonstrating their understanding of content—was more important at this stage than flawless language. Filling in a speech bubble and writing a short description of the scene proved to be manageable language writing tasks, especially with the support of a group.

Finally, these lessons are a good example of cooperative learning. Pupils were dependent on each other to succeed (in completing first the scene in the

Figure 6. A Sikh Ceremony Storyboard Freeze Frame With Speech Bubbles

photograph and later the storyboard). Without effective scenes, the whole ceremony would have been unclear. Each person had a role in his or her group's scene and in the writing task. Everyone was involved. Learners were assessed as a group, so all needed to participate simultaneously and help each other create an effective scene.

Good Practice in CLIL 2: Hot Seating for Mary Magdalene and Doubting Thomas

When Lorna first tried out the drama activity of "hot seating," it proved over-ambitious and ill timed. Separate groups read three biblical stories. After reading their story, one group member was put into a hot seat to play someone in the story and be questioned by the other group members about their feelings. The activity proved too difficult, both cognitively and linguistically. Learners were not ready for the difficult concepts, the text was too hard for them, and they could not yet produce the language to create questions about emotions. Lorna realized that the task was too complex and decided to scaffold the learning more in order to help learners succeed (Wallace, 2007). She did this in several ways.

Texts and Tasks

First, Lorna selected the two easier texts out of the three suggested in her course book: one about Mary Magdalene meeting Jesus at his tomb (Text A) and one about doubting Thomas (Text B). Both relate to central Christian beliefs. She then formed random groups of four, with half the groups reading Text A and the other half reading Text B, ensuring that more learners had the same material to work on and could support each other. The groups were given a task sheet about their texts to complete, which scaffolded their learning (see Appendix A).

After taking turns to read the passage aloud, group members worked together to write their answers on the task sheet questions about who, when, where, and what, thus checking understanding of the material they had read. They then prepared a number of questions together that they might ask Mary Magdalene or Thomas in person.

Interviews

Next, Lorna formed new groups of four, each containing two pupils who had prepared questions related to Text A and two who had prepared questions for Text B, ensuring that two learners per group had the information for the interview. The groups now received a new task sheet (see Appendix B) that instructed them to read their texts to each other; two members with knowledge of the same story asked questions of each other as if they were the person in the story (i.e., Mary Magdalene or Thomas). In other words: hot seating. The other two group members made note of the questions and answers related to the unfamiliar story. This time, hot seating proved to be a manageable task. By the end of the lesson, learners had read and understood a text, asked questions, and answered them, all while putting themselves in the shoes of one of the characters.

Why Is This Good CLIL Practice?

This series of lessons is another example of good CLIL teaching. First, Lorna again worked on content through several different language skills. Students read a text, communicated with (spoke and listened to) each other about question formulation, spoke during the interviews, and practiced writing on the task sheets.

Second, by concentrating on the two easier texts from the course book, Lorna selected texts that learners could just understand (comprehensible input; Krashen & Terrell, 1983).

Third, she scaffolded (Vygotsky, 1978) learning effectively by designing special task sheets to help students understand the material. This sort of framework helps language learners grasp texts and concepts. Moreover, the task sheets were clear and written in simple language, the aim of which was to help learners understand the stories, not to develop their English. Ultimately, learners did the reading in a number of easy stages, were assigned tasks to help understanding, and helped each other with comprehension. They focused on answering questions to break down the text and also formulated questions about the feelings and thoughts of the character involved.

Furthermore, when creating the questions for the interviews, learners discussed both content and language (What shall we ask about? How shall we formulate a question in good English?). Working together to create questions helped them rehearse the language they needed later for an interview and think about concepts they needed to learn.

REFLECTIONS

After approximately 3 months of these lessons, Lorna felt that the pupils were really progressing in English and finally understanding more concepts related to Religious Education. This barely noticeable process developed gradually as a result of immersion in English, as Lorna describes:

> Today, the thought occurred to me that the Religious Education lessons are coming together at last. Initially, everything is chaotic, because students are new and have to get used to everything anyway. Sometimes it is hard to know if they are stumped by the English or by the content in the early stages. Today I felt that they were getting used to the English and also to the circumstances.

Through analyzing some of Lorna's first CLIL lessons, we conclude with a number of suggestions for CLIL subject teachers to help learners both understand content and work on language.

- Allow some use of the first language during the first months until learners are more confident in English.

- Gradually introduce English, using paraphrasing or translating into and from the first language when necessary.

- Encourage creativity with the language, and ignore language mistakes. Fluency is more important than accuracy at the beginning stages of learning.

- Select or create colorful materials with a strong visual component.

- Build vocabulary first, and help learners retain vocabulary in a (personal) notebook.

- Recycle vocabulary, using the same words in different activity types. Include a gradually longer time frame between recycling tasks.

- Work with the easier texts and tasks in your course book to help learners understand concepts. Omit overly difficult ones.

- Carry out a variety of activities, and recycle language through different language skills: listening or watching, reading, speaking, and (simple) writing.

- Break down complex tasks into simpler, shorter ones.

- Mix activity types to allow uptake through different learning channels. For example, use a mixture of tasks appealing to different intelligences in order to introduce and recycle concepts and ideas.

- Scaffold learning, for example, through the use of task sheets in simple English to help learners develop understanding of subject concepts.

- Use pair and group work to encourage maximum communication among learners.

- Use drama or photography to help learners understand concepts.

- Implement cooperative learning to include everyone at all stages of learning.

Rosie Tanner is an educational consultant at the IVLOS Institute of Education at Utrecht University, in the Netherlands. She works with in-service teachers at bilingual schools on integrating English and subject teaching. Some of her areas of expertise are language and general teaching methodology, active learning, multiple intelligence theory, video coaching, and content and integrated language learning.

Lorna Dunn is a teacher who has worked in mainstream education in the Netherlands since 1972. At present, she teaches English and Religious Studies in the bilingual stream at Dr. Moller College, in Waalwijk. Her background is in Scandinavian studies, and she will soon complete an MA in comparative religion at Tilburg University.

APPENDIX A: TASK SHEETS 1 AND 2

Task Sheet 1 (for Text A)

Number yourselves one to four, and read John 20: 11–18. Jesus appears to Mary Magdalene.

Take turns reading aloud. Answer the following questions:

Who is it about?

_____

What happens?

_____

When does it happen?

_____

Where are they?

_____

What are Mary Magdalene's feelings in the story, and how do they change?

_____

In your group, think of four questions you could ask Mary if she were here now about what she felt, saw, heard, or thought.

1. _____

2. _____

3. _____

4. _____

Task Sheet 2 (for Text B)

Number yourselves one to four, and read John 20: 23–29. Jesus and Thomas.

Thomas is sometimes called "doubting Thomas" in English. Do you know why?

Take turns reading your story aloud to each other. Answer the following questions:

Who is it about?

_____

Where are they?

_____

When does it happen?

_____

What happens?

_____

In your group, think of four questions you could ask Thomas about how he felt, what he saw, and what he heard.

1. _____
2. _____
3. _____
4. _____

What emotions do you think Thomas was feeling at the time?

_____

_____

APPENDIX B: TASK SHEET 3 (FOR TEXT A OR B)

You are now in a new group. Student 1 will read the story aloud. Then he or she will ask Student 2 the questions that their group wrote down, and Student 2 will answer. Students 3 and 4 will write down the questions and answers.

Next, Students 3 and 4 will do the same with their text, and Students 1 and 2 will write down those questions and answers.

Story: _____

Questions	Answers
1.	1.
2.	2.
3.	3.
4.	4.

Which story do you like best? Why?

_____

_____

Why do you think these are important stories in Christianity?

_____

_____

How Do Teachers Evaluate Language and Content Learning?

CHAPTER 11

Big Ideas in Little Pieces: Science Activities for Multilevel Classes

Ann K. Fathman and Patricia A. Nelson

> My middle school science classes contain English learners from more than 10 coun-
> tries as well as native English speakers. In these mixed-ethnicity and -ability classes,
> my goals must include the development of skills in language as well as science. I have
> found that students at all levels can learn the big ideas in science if the content is
> divided into small pieces and assessment allows students to express their understand-
> ing in a variety of ways. (Patricia, science teacher)

One of the biggest challenges facing teachers in sheltered, mainstream, and content area classes is designing activities that benefit students at different ability and
language proficiency levels. Hands-on experiences in science can help English language learners (ELLs) at all levels learn about science while developing language
and literacy skills (Fathman & Crowther, 2006). Research suggests that instruction that integrates science and language development objectives and experiences
can meet the unique needs of ELLs (Echevarria, Vogt, & Short, 2008).

   In this chapter, we give suggestions for planning, presenting, and assessing
thematic science lessons for ELLs in multilevel classes. We focus on a standards-
based physical science unit and describe sample activities from it. These hands-on
activities incorporate strategies for scaffolding for language and inquiry at different proficiency levels. Multiple assessments provide clear feedback and allow
students flexibility in demonstrating their understanding.

CONTEXT

This inquiry-based unit has been successfully used in teaching science concepts
and developing language skills for ELLs in a middle school setting. The theme of
the unit, a rocket-building activity, is commonly a part of science curricula. But
the focus given to language development activities and assessment in this unit

makes it appropriate for sheltered science as well as language development classes and for students at all proficiency levels.

Science lessons focusing on themes, or big ideas, can engage students irrespective of language ability or background. Inquiry-oriented science activities provide countless opportunities for students to develop academic language, oral communication, and literacy skills. In inquiry-based science, students regularly do the following:

- read and follow instructions on data sheets

- listen to, understand, and interpret information given orally

- participate in cooperative learning groups in which information is shared

- speak to explain their point of view about a subject

- write journal entries, reports, and narratives related to their science investigations (Thier, 2002)

In this unit, students use all of these language skills as they plan, participate, and report their findings. Science content can be adapted for all levels of proficiency using strategies that focus on connecting with students, encouraging collaborative learning, and scaffolding for science and language (Carr, Sexton, & Lagunoff, 2007; Dobb, 2004; Douglas, Klentschy, Worth, & Binder, 2006). In this unit, activities are organized according to the 5E instructional model: engage, explore, explain, elaborate, evaluate (Bybee, 2002a). Students are encouraged to observe, question, gather data, propose explanations, and communicate results—activities that provide opportunities for developing language and literacy skills.

CURRICULUM, TASKS, MATERIALS

The entire unit described here takes a number of weeks, but we describe only a few of the activities and strategies that have been especially beneficial for ELLs. All activities require students to use new language for the unit (scientific vocabulary, sentence patterns, language functions), both orally and in writing, through class and group discussions, planning sessions, investigations, and reporting.

For the main activity, students experience Newton's Laws of Motion through constructing and launching bottle rockets (water rockets). It is easy for all students to see that an object at rest stays at rest when the rocket remains on the launcher until a force is applied to move it. By physically pumping air into the bottle rocket, students can feel when the pressure is high inside the bottle and see that the rockets travel higher when they achieve greater air pressure on the gauge.

Language development is a key objective in the unit. Key academic language is introduced in a variety of ways. Students describe rockets and stages in notebooks; then they write their ideas, impressions, and conclusions on the whiteboard; and finally they take formal notes on the three laws. A preview-review strategy is used daily by introducing vocabulary and content in context using support materials (e.g., realia, visuals) and reviewing and explaining the language and content at the end of the lesson using the support materials.

Curriculum

The curriculum is based on the *Science Content Standards for California Public Schools* (California Department of Education, 2003) for Grade 8. The language objectives are adapted from Standard 4 of the *PreK–12 English Language Proficiency Standards* (TESOL, 2006), which address goals for students at all grade levels. These standards outline behaviors that ELLs should attain in reading, writing, speaking, and listening. Figure 1 displays some sample science and language standards for this unit. We integrated the science content standards for the unit with the language behaviors for Grades 6–8 (ages 11–14) in order to create language objectives.

Science Standards ***Science Content Standards for California Public Schools*, Grade 8** **(California Department of Education, 2003)**		
Science Process Skills Students have the necessary abilities to do scientific inquiry.	*Science Content Standards*	
	Motion 1. The velocity of an object is the rate of change of its position.	Forces 2. Unbalanced forces cause changes in velocity.
English Language Standards ***PreK–12 English Language Proficiency Standards*** **(TESOL, 2006)**		
English language learners communicate information, ideas, and concepts necessary for academic success in the area of science.		
	Speaking	*Writing*
Level 1	Students can describe and show how their group constructed a rocket.	Students can draw and label parts of a rocket.
Level 3	Students can compare the results of their group with partners from another group.	Students can describe Newton's Laws using information from multiple sources.
Level 5	Students can explain how the bottle rocket demonstrated Newton's Laws of Motion.	Students can interpret results and describe how they relate to Newton's Laws as described in the text.

Figure 1. Sample Science and Language Standards for the Rocket Unit

Classroom Organization

Lab group–oriented science activities facilitate the development of skills in language as well as science. Grouping decisions may vary depending on students and activities, but for this activity multilevel lab groups are successful and give ELLs daily opportunities to develop social and academic language with the help and modeling of students who are more proficient in English. Lab group photographs and interesting facts about students are put up as a bulletin board display. Students enjoy looking at their pictures, and this is an important show of respect for each student and a way for everyone to learn about each other's backgrounds.

Members of lab groups are given specific responsibilities to encourage cooperation and individual accountability.

- The principal investigator is responsible for knowing the protocol, making sure all jobs get done, and reporting to the class.

- The recorder is responsible for writing all data accurately and writing group observations.

- The timer watches the clock and makes sure the experiment is completed in a timely fashion.

- The materials manager gathers and puts away all of the supplies.

Lab responsibilities alternate between members of the group each week so that everyone has a chance at each post.

Tasks and Materials

This unit is divided into five stages based on the 5E model (Bybee, 2002a). Each stage encourages participation by all students and supports ELLs in learning both language and content:

- *Engage:* The teacher starts by creating interest, encouraging student questions.

- *Explore:* The students work together, ask questions, observe, record, test predictions.

- *Explain:* The teacher guides the students in explaining concepts.

- *Elaborate:* The teacher guides the students in applying concepts and skills in new situations.

- *Evaluate:* Teacher and students assess learning.

Engage

During the engagement stage, students' prior knowledge (of both language and science) is determined through questioning and key vocabulary and concepts are introduced. The following is a sampling of engagement activities that are effective in leading up to the main rocket activity.

Questioning. Each class begins with a starter question or short instruction (bell work) written on the front board, which students copy and answer in their lab notebooks. To begin this unit, the starter is "Define *motion* without using the word *move.*" Students share their answers, which are written on the overhead. Depending on level of English proficiency, either the teacher or students can write the answers. Students are encouraged to talk through their ideas until they understand the concept of change of position. This then brings them to the next discussion topic: "How can you tell if position has changed?" Students are now being introduced to the concept of a reference point. They are encouraged to ask their own questions, using sentence frames such as "What is the reason . . ." and "How can you tell . . ." which are displayed on wall charts.

Video. Videos provide an excellent introduction to this unit. The film *The Incredibles* (Lasseter & Bird, 2004) offers an especially good view of motion in action. In the beginning, a passenger train is moving around a curve headed toward broken tracks. Mr. Incredible stops the train, and the passengers fall back within the train car (Newton's First Law of Motion). From the video, students can "see" examples of major vocabulary words from the unit.

Vocabulary. After a video clip, as a class the students list action words they observed. Surprisingly, their list often includes most of the vocabulary they will define in the following days. Some words, such as *opposite* and *propel,* are academic vocabulary that must be understood if scientific terms are to be learned. Vocabulary is presented in pieces and repeated in various contexts in before, during, and after activities.

Individual whiteboards are used to get working definitions of vocabulary from students' own thoughts and experiences before doing formal introduction of scientific definitions. Students write down some idea in words or pictures and then hold it up for the teacher to see. Each student participates, and it is possible to assess what each student knows or has learned at a glance. Ideas are shared on the overhead to get the class's working definition to use initially. Students then record words in the vocabulary section of their notebooks, and these words are added to the classroom word wall.

Explore

The exploration stage provides many opportunities for ELL oral language development as students work together in groups following directions, discussing observations, expressing ideas, and recording results. Task-based lab group investigations provide a setting for peer interaction, teacher guidance, and class presentations. In addition, students are able to use language for a wide variety of functions as they take on different responsibilities in their group.

In this unit students explore by building bottle rockets (and there are numerous resources describing how to do so, e.g., Al-Garni, n.d.; Hayhurst, 2004).

They make the rockets using 2-liter soda bottles, manila folders, and duct tape. Anything else is optional, including using different-sized bottles. One soda bottle has the bottom cut off and is taped to the bottom end of a second bottle. Fins are cut from manila folders and taped to the side. A circle is cut from a folder, twisted to form a cone, and taped to the top of assembly. Figure 2 shows the progression of these steps. Students then enjoy decorating and personalizing their rockets. Some sort of launcher is also needed and can be purchased from various online sources (e.g., Amazon, Edmund Scientific, WARD's Natural Science).

This hands-on activity is a demonstration of guided inquiry and is especially effective for ELLs because there is structure but also flexibility. Students are guided in posing research questions and given directions for building the rockets, but groups are allowed to modify the suggested plan and ask their own questions.

Explain

Language use in the explanation stage focuses on student groups presenting their investigation results, which is followed by a discussion of key concepts and terms. Students talk about their observations of the rocket and its launching within their groups and report to others using key vocabulary.

Explaining results. After the activity is completed, students use large-group whiteboards to facilitate discussions and arrive at scientific explanations of their observations. Groups discuss, record, present, and compare their observations. A popular debate topic, and a subject of variability, between groups is the amount of water to put in the bottle. Students explain their results to the class and compare their results with other groups.

Focusing on scientific terms. Students form their own working definitions for terms first on their whiteboards, and the teacher provides "scientific" definitions

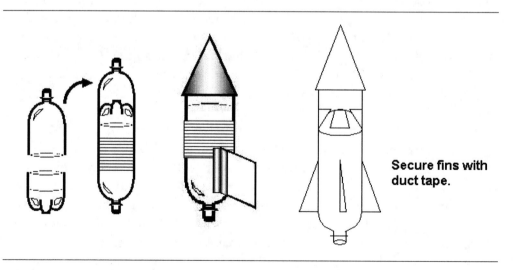

Secure fins with duct tape.

Figure 2. Bottle Rocket Construction

later as part of a lecture. Examples of scientific terms for this unit are *force, mass, motion,* and *velocity.* The lecture focuses on an outline that can be used as a reading guide for texts and expands on the same vocabulary that was introduced in the engagement stage.

Elaborate

In this part of the unit, Newton's Laws are explained and related to the bottle rocket experiment. Scaffolding of language for ELLs is accomplished through input from multiple sources, and the teacher guides students to better understand the more abstract laws.

Presenting Newton's Three Laws of Motion. The laws can be summarized orally using an overhead while students record them in notebooks:

1. An object at rest remains at rest and an object in motion remains in motion unless acted on by an unbalanced force.

2. The acceleration of an object depends on the mass of the object and the amount of force applied.

3. Whenever one object exerts a force on a second object, the second object exerts an equal and opposite force on the first. For every action, there is an opposite and equal reaction.

Lower level ELLs might copy the laws while others fill in words in a cloze exercise and more proficient students take notes from the lecture. The language of the laws should be familiar to students for it has already been used in teacher demonstrations, during the group investigations, and in lecture and readings.

Relating the bottle rocket experience to Newton's Laws. Each group chooses one of Newton's Three Laws of Motion and explains and diagrams how their rocket demonstrated that principle. For example, for Newton's First Law of Motion, students might note that the rocket stays on the launch pad until a force is applied to move it. For the Second Law of Motion, students might explain that the amount of force depends on how much air you pump inside the rocket. You can increase the force further by adding a small amount of water to the rocket.

By breaking down what is happening to the rocket during the experiment and describing the ideas aloud and in writing, key concepts and language are presented in bits. Language skills are enhanced through the repetition of content using scientific language in the context of what students have just experienced in the rocket activity, and Newton's Laws should be comprehensible to all students.

Evaluate

Students are evaluated based on their class participation in discussions and cooperation in building the rockets in their small groups. The group with the best rocket (i.e., the one that flies the highest and elicits the biggest reaction from the crowd) gets a few bonus points, but all of the students' rockets fly, and the students are boisterously excited. Groups are evaluated on their understanding of science concepts as they present their whiteboards and share what they have learned.

Language skills are evaluated on a daily basis in preview-review sessions and during activities at each stage of the unit. In the engagement stage, initial language proficiency is assessed. In the exploration stage, communication skills are evaluated during student–student interaction. In the explanation phase, students' ability to explain results orally and in writing is evaluated. In the elaboration stage, assessment focuses on students' ability to understand and use scientific language related to Newton's Laws.

The language proficiency of ELLs is taken into consideration in assessing skills in language and science, as demonstrated in the unit objectives (see Figure 1). For example, in the area of writing, Level 1 students would give labeled drawings to explain their rocket results, and Level 5 students would give interpretations of results. In the area of speaking, Level 3 students would be evaluated on their ability to compare results with others, and Level 5 students would be asked to discuss how the rocket results relate to Newton's Laws.

Student lab notebooks are a key means for evaluating individual students at all stages. For the summary lab report, words are listed that should be included in the report (*force, motion, mass, velocity, acceleration*). In addition, a writing scaffold using sentence frames, such as the following, is provided for lower level students:

- *I think that . . . because . . .*

- *I have observed that . . . . I have also observed that . . .*

- *My data provide evidence that . . .*

- *Therefore, at this time, I think . . .*

Many of the ELLs and a few of the proficient English speakers choose to use the scaffold instead of writing entirely in their own words. From what they write in their summary and how they use the key vocabulary words, the teacher can assess student writing skills and understanding of science concepts.

REFLECTIONS

In this unit, students learn both science content and academic language through discussions, films, demonstrations, experiments, whiteboards, lectures, kits and texts, science notebooks, and word walls. They learn by participating in groups in hands-on experiences, and individuals are held accountable irrespective of level.

This unit is successful because students are involved, are interested, and discover for themselves. Remembering any specific detail is not as important as for students to grasp the themes and to think back and say, "That was fun. I understand. I really like science." A key aspect of dividing the science into little pieces is to proceed from whole to parts. The important concepts, or big ideas, are observed during inquiry, but an understanding of these ideas is facilitated by examining the parts in a variety of ways.

Through scientific inquiry, students use English in various functions to express themselves while making observations, posing questions, planning investigations, gathering data, and communicating results. Students learn not only academic vocabulary related to the theme, but also sentence patterns for scientific discourse. Content is made comprehensible and academic language skills improve for students at all proficiency levels.

The *PreK–12 English Language Proficiency Standards* (TESOL, 2006) offer a valuable model for planning and assessing students for content and language teachers alike. The standards provide a method for integrating language and content as well as adapting assessment for different proficiency levels. During this unit, students at the lowest level (Level 1) are able to communicate information by identifying objects in pictures and models, repeating definitions, and drawing and labeling diagrams. Students tend to vary in terms of progress after the unit, but many attain a higher level of English proficiency. These students are able to convey information at a more advanced level in future work, for example, by "describing orally and in writing features, objects, functions, occurrences" (TESOL, 2006, pp. 84–85). Students are able to complete more complex language tasks as they gain proficiency.

The success of this unit can be attributed to the integration of science and language objectives as well as methodologies for teaching science and language. The best practices for both are closely related. Collaboration between teachers is important irrespective of whether the activities are used in a science or language class. The language teacher can provide methodologies for teaching language skills at different levels, ways of scaffolding content for language learning, and means of assessing language and content. The science teacher can provide science content and lesson plans, develop activities that are inquiry based, and ensure that assessment reflects science standards.

The success of this unit on Newton's Laws demonstrates that all students are capable of understanding the big ideas. If they are engaged and provided with small understandable pieces of information in a variety of ways, they can successfully learn science content while developing language and literacy skills.

Ann K. Fathman is professor of English at Notre Dame de Namur University, in California, in the United States, where she directs English language and teacher training programs. She received her PhD from Stanford University. Her publications on content area instruction include numerous articles as well as Science for English Language Learners *(with David Crowther; NSTA Press, 2006).*

Patricia A. Nelson received her PhD in biology from the University of California, San Diego. She has worked in the biotechnology industry for 20 years and published extensively in the field of immunology. She has recently been teaching science to English language learners at Kennedy Middle School, in Redwood City, California, in the United States.

CHAPTER 12

Exploration: One Journey of Integrating Content and Language Objectives

Kate Mastruserio Reynolds

English language teaching professionals and mainstream teachers who attempt to implement content-based courses frequently discuss the challenge of maintaining a dual focus in their courses and lessons (M. A. Snow, 2007). "There is just too much information to cover!" exclaim many teachers. This supports Castro, Sercu, and Garcia's (2004) finding that teachers "experience conflicts when having to prioritize language teaching and culture [i.e., content] teaching objectives" (p. 91). Stoller (2002) also highlights this challenge, which confirms my experience from working with hundreds of veteran teachers.

Over the years, teachers have regularly told me that there is no need to write objectives for lesson plans anymore, due to limited time and their claims that the objectives are "in their heads." They admit, however, that they lose track of either the content or language focus of the lessons while teaching. These comments reinforce for me the need for teachers, even highly experienced ones, to articulate their lesson and unit objectives in writing in order to ensure that they are achieving content as well as language instructional expectations.

The revised TESOL (2006) standards should facilitate for teachers the process of creating linked, learner-focused, and measurable language and content objectives. These standards focus on social language and appropriacy, and place a strong emphasis on academic language use within core content areas (language arts/literacy, math, social studies/history, and the sciences).

In this chapter, I provide a rationale for thoughtful interrelated objectives, describe my experience creating an English as a second language (ESL) standards-based content and language unit, and outline the challenges teachers often experience with objectives. To give guidance on how to develop interlinked content and language objectives, I provide practical suggestions for analyzing content and language standards, materials, and learners' needs based on learners' proficiency levels. Further, I discuss the interaction of objectives and assessment because a clear understanding of educational objectives is vital to being able to gauge students' learning.

Making appropriate educational choices concerning objectives that narrow the unlimited range of possibilities is a difficult challenge in teaching content-based language courses. When teachers interweave content and language objectives, they can explore subject matter in depth while simultaneously creating a solid linguistic lesson on concepts intrinsic to the material. Vague or divergent objectives are the harbinger of less effective teaching that may send unclear or contradictory messages to language learners. If teachers do not know specifically what they want learners to accomplish, instruction is likely to devolve into disconnected activities. When teachers sharpen their instructional focus and write better content and language lessons and units, they can save instructional time, create more cohesive and powerful lessons, and connect more effectively with students.

CONTEXT

I taught an ESL/geography class in the fall of 2006. My class of eight 6th-grade Hmong students born in the United States had relatively well-developed social language abilities in English (advanced low, per the American Council on the Teaching of Foreign Languages [ACTFL] proficiency levels; Breiner-Sanders, Lowe, Miles, & Swender, 2000), but their academic language, literacy skills, and study skills (beginner mid, ACTFL) needed improvement. In this context, it was important to clarify students' abilities according to Cummins's (1980) social language and academic language distinction. These learners also needed a great deal of literacy development because their oral language was far advanced in comparison to their writing skills. They were more comfortable doing work orally and struggled in their writing. Finally, their study skills, including how to read and use a textbook and how to take notes, needed significant development.

The class was Social Studies and Geography, which happily coincided with the middle school's yearlong theme, World Geography. All content areas were united by this theme, so math courses might calculate distances between countries or population growth, while history courses would focus on different countries' histories and science courses focused on Earth's physical aspects. This theme allowed for myriad choices, connections, and unlimited cultural exploration, and I felt I could work with it easily and knowledgeably. However, my challenge was to develop intertwined content and language objectives that would support the theme and focus on learners' needs.

CURRICULUM, TASKS, MATERIALS

I developed an East Asian geography unit from the *World Studies: Asia and the Pacific* (2005) textbook, which included content concepts such as mapping, identifying landforms and water forms, as well as general information about Asia. I derived the language objectives from the linguistic demands of the textbook and the grade-level Wisconsin state content standards.

I began planning the unit by analyzing the various linguistic aspects found in the textbook material as well as in the content standards. I looked at vocabulary, grammatical patterns common throughout each passage, and other linguistic constructions usually overlooked by teachers (e.g., language functions, passage sequencing).

Textbook Vocabulary Analysis

In order to select the appropriate vocabulary to preteach, I conducted a vocabulary analysis of the chapter I would be using. Ideally, an analysis of vocabulary goes beyond the glossary or the highlighted words in a text. I find that a useful tool is Bernier's (1997) categorization of types of vocabulary that challenge English language learners (ELLs). This framework is helpful for visualizing the language needs of learners. The first category is content terms that are not being highlighted in the text yet may be new to the students, or as Bernier describes them, content terms that "routinely occur in lectures and textbooks as 'common knowledge' references to course material within the discipline" (p. 96). According to Bernier, examples include

> "regular" history terms or historical jargon, archaic language (e.g., flappers, yeoman, draft animals, dowry), non-history terms or terms borrowed from other fields (e.g., overproduction, recession, cattle prod), obscure acronyms (e.g., FBI, CIA, WPA, V-J Day), and non-English vocabulary (e.g., elite, suffrage, bourgeoisie, laissez-faire). (p. 98)

For instance, in the unit I was going to teach, we had "regular" geography vocabulary, such as *climate, landform, border, region,* and *hemisphere,* as well as terms such as *migrations, investigate, colonial border, wet rice paddies, moored, plum rain, nomadic herding,* and *subsistence farming.*

The second of Bernier's (1997) categories consists of language terms such as metaphors (e.g., *offering an olive branch*), colloquial usages (e.g., *fell on deaf ears*), class-based constructions (e.g., *client, stocks, bonds*), and cultural idioms (e.g., *power trip, gossip monger,* fiction allusions from "classics"). Some of the terms employed in one unit of my text were *Slave Coast, Gold Coast, towering mountains, low-lying plains,* and *have had enough of winter.*

Bernier's (1997) third category, language-masking content terms, includes the fluid boundaries between the two previous categories. These are terms appropriated by teachers and scholars that hide content due to variant or multiple meanings (e.g., *class, high, right*), unfamiliar metaphors (e.g., *8-hour day, 24-hour day*), and oxymorons (e.g., *military intelligence, arms race*). For example, I had to teach the content vocabulary word *strait*. This is a language-masking content term if the students hear it orally and think "straight." So I explicitly taught *strait* with a visual and noted how the geographic feature is roughly straight. I overtly highlighted the spelling differences and told students that the spelling difference is a key to understanding the kind of straight/strait being discussed.

Textbook Grammar Analysis

The next step was to analyze materials for grammar both at the sentence level (e.g., tense, preposition use) and discourse level (e.g., format, cohesion, main idea, details; for information on communicative competencies, see Savignon, 2001). For example, is the passage employing many imperatives? If so, a brief deductive grammatical explanation could be taught with a series of controlled input activities (Crookes & Chaudron, 2001) so that learners understand the form prior to the reading. Are prepositions of location essential to learners' comprehension of the material? If so, then a game with total physical response (TPR), in which learners are directed by oral commands to perform an action, like Simon Says, using the locations *above, next to, below,* and *adjacent to,* can be taught or reviewed. With prepositions of location, the TPR activity might involve moving an object above, under, behind, and so on. When approaching a grammatical analysis, I ask myself, what forms do students need in order to understand this reading?

The final part of the content and standard analysis focuses on other linguistic constructions that are typically overlooked. I analyzed the materials for constructs such as language functions (e.g., agreeing/disagreeing), genre features (e.g., fairy tales—*once upon a time*), sequencing and chronology, and rhetorical structure (i.e., expository, descriptive, narrative, persuasive). An example is the passage describing the life of a peasant in the feudal system. With a descriptive passage, bringing the reading to life via adjectives and manipulatives is key. However, with a passage such as an excerpt from U.S. President John Adams's diary about the second Constitutional Congress, one could focus on the narrative format.

At the end of this analytical process, I typically compile a long list of potential linguistic material to be covered, but the solution is to choose from the list what each proficiency level needs. When I generate a list of linguistic material inherent in the standards and textbook, I notice that there are items that are needed by various proficiency levels. I can then specifically choose those items with learners' proficiency levels and skills in the forefront of my mind. For example, I could have beginning-level learners do "station work" (i.e., a lesson designed with various activities arranged at different locations in the classroom, where students do relatively independent work) focusing on prepositions of location while intermediate-level learners focus on the conditional and advanced-level learners practice their use of past conditional. All too often teachers can recognize the content or language needs of individual students, but they struggle with the mixed proficiency abilities of the whole group and so tend to focus on the middle level of proficiency. This approach enables teachers to design objectives to reach all levels.

Figure 1 shows an initial lesson plan on mapping skills, integrating language and content, from my ESL world geography unit. The Wisconsin state standards are listed first, followed by the TESOL (2006) standards, which were based on the WIDA Consortium (2007) standards. Wisconsin Standard A.8.2 states that learners should be able to "construct mental maps of selected locales, regions, states, and countries and draw maps from memory, representing relative location, direction, size, and shape" (Wisconsin Department of Public Instruction, n.d.). The language items inherent in this standard that could be taught, depending on learners' proficiency levels and needs, include cardinal and ordinal directions, size comparatives, and words for various shapes. Because this was an initial lesson, I started with shapes. I figured that students already had oral language for ordinal directions.

Because the learners needed literacy work, I decided to integrate language and content by using a fictional story, "Mapping Penny's World" (Leedy, 2000), that had mapping skill activities. The resulting content objective focused on teaching the mapping skills in the story ("Students will be able to identify labels and parts of maps in the story").

While the language objectives focused on comprehension of the story, skills objectives related to (a) identifying main ideas and activities in the story accurately (speaking), but in their own words, (b) listing several places where Penny visited (writing), (c) telling how the story ended (writing), and (d) retelling the story to a friend in a written letter. These objectives were considered mastered when students could complete the tasks with accuracy 80% of the time. Because this was one of my first meetings with students, I used the narrative format to gauge their reading comprehension and writing abilities as well as to introduce the concept of mapping. The follow-up assignment was for students to map their homes (see Figure 2).

A couple of weeks into the class, the language and content objectives were becoming more complex and detailed (see Figure 3). Although we were still working on the content objective about geographic representations depicting real places, students were also writing the names of important landforms and countries on a map (spelling work and copying for the lowest level proficiency students). We then did a skimming activity for new vocabulary (all proficiency levels—different levels would identify different words) and discussed the new concepts (see language objective #3 in Figure 3) followed by a teacher-led think-aloud reading about the countries included in Asia.

Standards

Content

Wisconsin Standards for Social Studies/Geography (Wisconsin Department of Public Instruction, n.d.)

A.8.1. Use a variety of geographic representations, such as political, physical, and topographic maps, a globe, aerial photographs, and satellite images, to gather and compare information about a place.

A.8.2. Construct mental maps of selected locales, regions, states, and countries and draw maps from memory, representing relative location, direction, size, and shape.

Language

TESOL (2006) Standard 5

English language learners communicate information, ideas, and concepts necessary for academic success in the content area of Social Studies.

Instructional Objectives (stated in terms of learning outcomes)

Content

1. Students will recognize that maps, globes, and other geographic representations depict real places and environments, and they will demonstrate this knowledge by mapping their home environment.

2. Students will be able to identify labels and parts of maps in the story "Mapping Penny's World," by Loreen Leedy (2003).

Language

1. From the story "Mapping Penny's World," students will be able to
    a. identify main ideas and activities in the story (speaking),
    b. list several places where Penny visited (writing),
    c. tell how the story ended (writing),
    d. retell the story to a friend in a letter (writing).

2. Students will be able to read, identify, and match the proper landform or water form definition to the term.

3. Students will be able to identify landform and water form vocabulary terms, place them in alphabetical order, and write a definition in their own words.

4. Students will be able to use descriptive words for shape (e.g., *round, flat, jagged*) and direction (e.g., *horizontal, vertical*) in oral descriptions.

These objectives are considered mastered when students can complete the tasks with accuracy 80% of the time.

Learning Strategy

1. Students will be able to use the strategies of reading, drawing, and labeling on personal maps.

2. Students will be able to draw a visual to coincide with their definitions of new vocabulary terms.

Figure 1. Initial World Geography Lesson Objectives

Traditional language constructs, such as parts of speech, were not overlooked in this lesson, nor were higher level thinking skills. Because all the students needed to work on both writing and understanding readings with rich descriptions, the students identified descriptive words from their readings and entered them in their adjective journals. We then discussed new vocabulary words' mean-

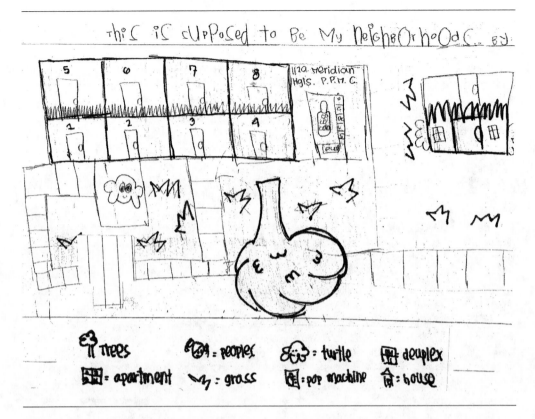

Figure 2. One Student's Home Map

ings and related them to words students already knew, which they also added to their adjective journals. I explained that there are many words in English to describe things specifically and that English speakers prize the use of specific words as well as creativity and originality in their word choices.

As a summary (which served as a performance assessment of language and a content knowledge check), students wrote a letter to a friend about an outdoor adventure that they would like to take in Asia and why they would like to take it, using two or more descriptive adjectives. The focus was not the informal format common when writing to friends (this became part of a later lesson). They wrote about where they wanted to visit, what they wanted to do there, and why, and they used descriptive adjectives. Although they did not necessarily use the ones that they had most recently learned, they did use adjectives they employed in their daily conversations. The difference was that the adjectives were finally present in their writing (see Figures 4 and 5); prior to that, they had just written simple sentences with no elaboration.

Throughout the unit we continued to work on developing vocabulary and using descriptive adjectives. At this point, the content and language objectives had merged closer together to form integrated literacy objectives that utilized

Instructional Objectives (stated in terms of learning outcomes)

Content

1. Students will recognize that maps, globes, and other geographic representations depict real places and environments, and they will demonstrate this knowledge by outlining the countries in Asia on a map.

2. Students will identify and describe important landforms and water forms present in Asia (e.g., Gobi Desert, Tibetan Plateau, steppes, archipelago, volcanoes, rivers, Indian Peninsula).

Language

1. Students will watch and listen to a video clip about the countries in Asia. They will outline on a map the countries in Asia. They will write the names of the major landforms and water forms on their map when they are identified in the video.

2. Students will identify, discuss, and write new vocabulary related to a reading on the physical geography of Asia (e.g., *elevation, altitude, plateau, basin, plain, desert, mount = mountain, fertile, vegetation, natural forces, volcano, rugged landscape, highlands, surrounded, dominates, coastal areas*).

3. Students will read silently to identify countries included in the Asian continent and complete a graphic organizer to demonstrate their understanding.

4. Students will identify from their reading adjectives used to describe natural phenomena in the passage (e.g., *highest* mountain or peak, *high* altitude, *spectacular* landforms, *steep* slopes or cliffs, *wide* plains, *narrow* plains, *powerful* nature forces, *rugged* landscape, *powerful* natural forces, *huge* highland area, *dry* region, *deepest* rivers). They will write the new words with a corresponding synonym in their adjective journals.

5. Students will listen and discuss with the teacher the role of descriptive adjectives and using diverse adjectives in writing to make their writing interesting.

6. Students will write a letter to a friend about one outdoor adventure they would like to do in Asia (hiking on Mount Fuji or trekking across the Gobi Desert) and why, using two or more descriptive adjectives.

Learning Strategy

1. Students will learn strategies of reading, drawing, and labeling on maps.

These objectives are considered mastered when students can complete the tasks with accuracy 80% of the time.

Figure 3. World Geography Lesson Objectives, Later in the Term

aspects of language arts (poetry), science (five senses and gathering data), and geography and history (explorers).

To recap, in creating a richly integrated lesson, I examine the standards and materials to determine the extent to which the four skills are present, what corresponding practice opportunities are needed, and which vocabulary and grammar points are skills that are needed based on learners' proficiency and that facilitate learning of the content information. I always list these skills so I can choose which are appropriate for which learners in the class. The following is my process for writing the objectives to integrate content and language:

1. I belive that one day I will get to go to korean and meet the actor and why I want to go there is because there place there are very pretty so I want to go.

2. I Think that one day I will get to go to china and meet cute actress.

3. I feel about going to japan and be a famous movie star.

Figure 4. Student Letter A

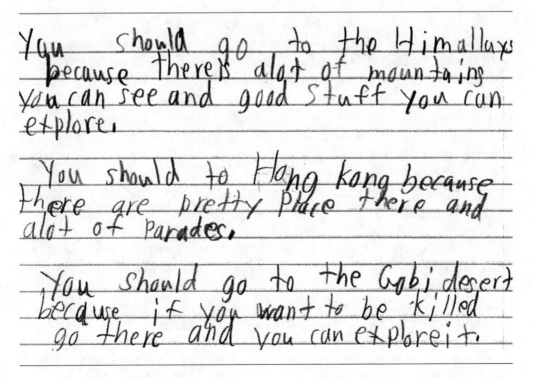

You should go to the Himallaxs because there is alot of mountains you can see and good stuff you can explore.

You should to Hong kong because there are pretty Place there and alot of parades.

You should go to the Gabi desert because if you want to be killed go there and you can explore it.

Figure 5. Student Letter B

1. Evaluate the content item.

2. Address the mode (speaking, listening, reading, or writing).

3. Remember the structure (grammar, vocabulary, and pronunciation points needed by this group of learners).

4. Choose interactive activities in which the content, mode, and structures can be utilized.

5. Determine target conditions (e.g., when, where, how).

   and/or

6. Determine the degree of mastery (e.g., mastery generally ranges from 50% to 80% accuracy; this range is flexible depending on the proficiency level and grammatical complexity).

I think of the content and language objectives as an omelet: a whole entity with distinguishable parts that together form a greater whole.

REFLECTIONS

Challenges

One challenge is that teachers feel burdened with too much material and make separate content objectives and language objectives that do not necessarily connect in obvious ways. For example, I observed a 50-minute lesson in a secondary-level, content-based ESL classroom for newcomers that comprised "daily oral language" (i.e., activities to develop social language), U.S. climate zones, and past tense regular verbs. These topics were too broad and essentially had no connective tissue. The lesson was difficult for the ELLs because the material lacked depth, the duration of work on the topic was short, and there was no cohesion to enhance their understanding.

An example solution, keeping with the topic of U.S. climate zones, would be to link the concept to descriptive adjectives (e.g., *dry, humid, moist, damp, frigid, icy*) and possibly the names of regions (e.g., *northeast, southwest*) or types of landforms that are typically found in the climate zones (e.g., *swamps, forests, plains*). Manipulatives such as sand, a damp sponge, or tactile items to represent the temperatures and textures would support the lesson. In addition, mapping skills would provide a foundation for learning the concept and the language necessary to describe the regions. One of the first steps to creating this kind of lesson is identifying enabling skills, the kinds that are required in the task but not necessarily taught. It is like assumed background knowledge. For instance, if you are teaching about the American Revolution and students do not understand taxes, they may not understand why the colonists rebelled. The enabling knowledge here is an understanding of taxes, and it could come in the form of a skill such as being able to do fractions when working in algebra. The next logical step is to analyze the chapter's vocabulary (not necessarily its bolded vocabulary words). Consider the vocabulary that would present a comprehension challenge for students, such as *Great Plains* in a chapter about the westward expansion. *Plains* would not necessarily be defined by the textbook's author or publisher, because it is not a high-priority content term such as *Manifest Destiny* or is not recognized as potentially problematic. If students do not notice the capitalization and pluralization as differentiating it from *plane* or *plain,* they may misunderstand it. Identifying enabling skills and vocabulary can be done by text analysis.

In my unit, cohesion was provided through the focused thematic approach and by choosing or developing materials on the grammar points needed using the topic at hand.

Another challenge may be that course and lesson objectives are neither fully developed nor articulated in a meaningful manner. Teachers are always short of time, but when it comes to the thorny task of integrating content and language teaching, taking the time to write down objectives is essential to separating critical material from the extraneous. If the objectives are loosely conceived or poorly thought out, classes can be too heavily focused in one area. I observed a middle school science lesson and lab that illustrates this point. The teacher had prepared a science lab about applying a litmus strip to identify acidic and alkaline solutions. This lesson was focused only on the science concept of identifying the two types of solutions using the litmus test; no language skills were being taught, nor was English required. The students in this class employed only their native language in their experiment teams, and the teacher did not interact with them at all.

A solution could have been to ask students to write out their predictions per chemical solution and then write a description of what happened on a graphic organizer. In addition, the teacher could have engaged in instructional conversation (Vygotsky, 1934/1962) with students about the experiment or, depending on proficiency level, taught them how to construct *if-then* clauses to predict what would happen on the litmus strips (e.g., Teacher: "What do you think is going to happen to the next strip? If this one is pink, then the next one will be what?" Student: "I think it will be the same, because the liquid is the same color in both." Teacher: "That's a good guess. Let's see what happens."). A better set of objectives would involve having students discuss their predictions with the teacher prior to the lesson, use social language to describe orally what they observed during the experiment, write down their observations on a graphic organizer, and write a five-paragraph essay about the results of the experiment.

For my unit, I chose to spend the time needed in order to develop the objectives thoroughly. I figured that if I did it properly and thoroughly once, I could always build on this foundation in future instruction and revise as necessary. Through the process, too, I became so much more adept at analysis and integrated objective development that it became second nature.

A third challenge for teachers is to design content and language objectives that are intertwined, appropriate for the proficiency levels and needs of the learners, and measurable. Teachers have a tendency to be vague in their objectives by not specifying how they will measure whether the objectives have been met. I saw an elementary school lesson with this objective: "Learners will be able to read the textbook." There is nothing here that explains how the teacher would measure whether students were able to read the textbook. A better example is "Learners will be able to read X passage in the X textbook for the three main ideas listed and will complete a written outline using them."

One solution, according to Heinich, Molenda, Russell, and Smaldino (2002), is to design objectives following the ABCD formula, specifying four main parts:

1. *Audience:* Who? Who is this aimed at?

2. *Behavior:* What? What do you expect them to be able to do? This should be an overt, observable behavior, even if the actual behavior is covert or mental in nature. If you can't see it, hear it, touch it, taste it, or smell it, you can't be sure that students really learned it.

3. *Condition:* How? Under what circumstances will the learning occur? What will students be given or already be expected to know in order to accomplish the learning?

4. *Degree:* How much? Must a specific set of criteria be met? For instance, do you want total mastery (100%); do you want them to respond correctly 80% of the time? (A general rule of thumb is accuracy 80% of the time.)

The *degree* aspect of the ABCD formula (i.e., setting measurable language objectives) is perhaps the most difficult component. Content objectives tend to be much easier to measure than language objectives. For example, to assess a content objective, a teacher can ask if students know who the first explorer to sail around the world was and if they can state the importance of this feat. This fact can be measured quickly and easily with any type of traditional test item type (e.g., multiple choice, true/false, fill in the blank) to see whether students mastered the concept with accuracy 100% of the time.

Measuring mastery of language objectives is much trickier because language is more complex. When teaching a grammar point such as the conditional, teachers may follow Larsen-Freeman's (2001, 2003) "grammaring" framework, in which forms, meanings, and uses of grammar should be taught together. In order to do that, teachers should ask themselves an array of questions about the students' understanding of the grammatical point. For example, do students understand the conjugation forms of the conditional? Do they understand when to use the conditional? Do they understand what the conditional implies to the native speaker? Do they employ the conditional form correctly for the social situation? Sure, teachers can teach the form and ask themselves the first question, but that does not mean 100% mastery of the language form for all contexts. Instead, teachers should develop a performance pretest and a series of instructional tasks that address each of these questions and then a performance posttest, all the while making the conditional congruent with the content topic. This is how students' understanding and use of grammar can be measured.

Teachers could intertwine content and language objectives by placing the conditional into history, teaching students to consider what they could, would, or should do if they were in the position of a famous ruler such as Cleopatra. The use of the conditional also links to issues of going to war (e.g., Vietnam, Iraq), giving individuals the right to vote (e.g., Civil Rights and Suffrage Movements), and reconstruction (e.g., U.S. Civil War). For example, students could be asked, "Who should have the right to vote? Why?" or "How could and should reconstruction occur? What would need to be rebuilt, and who should do it? What groups of people should be responsible for infrastructure reconstruction?" Measurement would be tied to students' written or spoken performance, which could be gauged using the *Student Oral Language Observation Matrix* (n.d.) or *Speaking and Writing Rubrics of the WIDA Consortium* (n.d.).

In my unit, I wanted to develop learners' abilities to write more complex sentences and descriptions using adjectives, so I assessed this through performance assessment tasks that required writing. They were the same tasks that I would assign as activities in the classroom, but modified slightly so as to avoid redundancy. I assessed the learners' writing on a regular basis to see the incremental and long-term development of their writing skills and use of adjectives.

Analysis

The big question is, was all this mental effort and time worth it? The answer is a resounding yes. The outcomes of this process exceeded expectations of success for the learners and for me. I know this according to their pre- and postunit performance assessments and the class's overall improvement on the ACCESS for ELLs test (Board of Regents of the University of Wisconsin-Madison, 2007). The ACCESS test is a new language and content exam for ELLs, which was developed to gauge nonnative speakers' progress in language acquisition in the content areas.

I felt that the greatest achievements were primarily in reaching learners at their own proficiency levels and helping them learn the language necessary to achieve in the classroom while at the same time not being overwhelmed by the material. Secondarily, it was rewarding to design a well-planned unit and implement it in a way that was empowering and effective for learners.

By the end of the unit, learners mastered the language and content objectives, but the learning went far beyond what was written as objectives on paper. Learners were inspired and motivated by the material and began to engage cognitively with the future material as active classroom participants and generators of knowledge.

An observer's perspective is also important in determining whether teachers should bother to articulate and integrate content and language objectives through a close analysis of the material. From the outside, when observing this kind of cohesive lesson, one sees students making powerful connections and developing deeper understanding. When teachers commit to this level of professional engagement, they imbue the material with coherence and enrich the learners' understanding of the world. They nourish learners in the instructional process by teaching it in a tough but thorough way, by offering them integrated objectives.

Kate Mastruserio Reynolds is the TESOL coordinator at the University of Wisconsin– Eau Claire, in the United States, and holds degrees in French and TESOL/literacy from the University of Cincinnati. A licensed language teacher, her instructional experiences span K–16 ESL, EFL, and French settings, and she specializes in language teacher training.

CHAPTER 13

Blending Digital Media and Web 2.0 in an English Advertising Class

Aiden Yeh

> To me, in advertising course, ideas and creativity are the most important things. Then, how to express our ideas in a fun way, and how to catch the attention of our audience comes the importance of using proper language skills. So every assignment we have done is useful in different ways in enhancing our English ability. (student feedback)

In the English Advertising class, students are taught the basics of advertising, from conceptualization to creative execution of commercials. For English as a foreign language (EFL) students, the fundamental concepts behind the required readings can be challenging. In addition to in-class discussions, students need practical tasks to hone their creative skills. This chapter addresses the following questions: How can such activities be implemented to achieve meaningful learning? How does assessment take place when the activities are experiential? What is the role of digital media and Web 2.0 tools (also known as interactive tools) in such tasks, and how can they be effectively integrated into the curriculum? In this chapter, I describe the collaborative task process that students use when creating advertising projects. Using examples from their public service announcement project, I discuss the various language goals of the task and how digital media and Web 2.0 tools are blended into the task process.

CONTEXT

English Advertising is a 2-credit elective course that I teach at a private college of languages in southern Taiwan. The semester-long (18-week) course is for third-year English majors who enroll in the continuing education program. English is the language of instruction. In this once-a-week class that lasts for 100 minutes, there are roughly 32 students (ages vary from 25 to over 30). Many of them have been studying English as a foreign language since they were in elementary school and have already acquired a satisfactory level of competency. Almost all of the students maintain daytime jobs, and pursuing a college degree is a challenge. They have shown particular interest in advertising because they see its practical application in their existing professions (e.g., international trading, marketing, sales, business administration). The focus of the course is threefold:

1. learn basic advertising concepts

2. use the skills required in producing print, radio, and television commercials

3. enhance English language skills

The design of the English Advertising curriculum is based on the pedagogical constructs of the sheltered instruction model of content-based instruction (CBI). With CBI, the learning of language is integrated with the learning of a particular subject matter (Larsen-Freeman, 2000). Brinton, Snow, and Wesche (1989) propose three models for CBI: theme-based courses, sheltered content-based courses, and adjunct courses. The sheltered content-based model is commonly used in second language environments (Edwards, Wesche, Krashen, Clement, & Kruidenier, 1984; Gaffield-Vile, 1996); however, this model is also applied in various foreign language settings (see Stryker & Leaver, 1997). Brinton et al. describe a sheltered content-based course as one that is "taught in a second language by a content specialist to a group of learners who have been segregated or 'sheltered' from native speakers" (p. 15). Although the teaching approach is the salient aspect of sheltered classes, the separation of language learners from native speakers of the target language is, in a way, sheltering course content to accommodate students' learning needs (Reppy & Adames, 2000). However, because of the nature of the English Advertising course, which is situated in an EFL setting, the students are already separated from native speakers.

Stryker and Leaver (1997) suggest that another way of sheltering content is by making it accessible and comprehensible to students. Thus the language instructor, also a content specialist, makes the necessary adjustments in his or her instructional delivery and adapts various strategies to present the course materials in a meaningful and interesting way (Carrasquillo & Rodriguez, 2002; M. A. Snow, 2005). This strategy is more feasible in my context. Additionally, my academic background in mass communications and marketing management as well as English language teaching management, and professional experience in advertising and public relations as well as teaching EFL, certainly helped boost my confidence in designing the syllabus and teaching the subject from the point of view of both a teacher and a practitioner. A teacher's content knowledge is, therefore, crucial in selecting and teaching topics that are highly useful, practical, and challenging (see Tsui, 2003).

The pedagogical approach and course content are based on the required textbook, *Contemporary Advertising* (Arens, 2004). The course content (see Appendix A) is based on what students needed to learn by the end of the course. The course begins by looking at the theoretical and pedagogical frameworks of advertising. Students then examine the role of advertising agencies and fundamental concepts of marketing. They learn how to plan, write, and report advertising analysis and marketing research. Students move on to work on developing creative strategies and effective advertising campaigns using various media platforms. They learn the basics of copywriting (for print, radio, television, and web-based media), layout, audio and video recording and editing, and the skills necessary for creating their own advertisements. The design and organization of the lessons and activities are structured from the ground up, building a strong foundation in terms of acquiring the knowledge and skills needed to meet the requirements of this course. Because the course is also intended to enhance students' English language abilities, class activities, homework, and projects highlight the four language skills (speaking, listening, reading, and writing). Table 1 shows the kind of learning activities students engage in to enhance their use and acquisition of English.

Integrating Digital Media and Web 2.0 Tools

I introduce a blended learning environment (both face-to-face and online instruction) even before the course starts, which allows me to integrate multimedia and web 2.0 tools into the curriculum. I first create a group using *Yahoo!*

Table 1. English Advertising Learning Activities

Language Skills	Learning Activities
Reading	Students read lecture materials such as chapters from the textbook, authentic advertising and promotional materials (print and web based), print ads, and radio and television scripts. They identify the main ideas and concepts presented in the academic texts and ad materials.
Writing	Students engage in copywriting and writing radio and television scripts, which are necessary for the production of commercials. They also prepare a report paper and take written examinations.
Listening	Students listen to academic lectures, have in-class discussions in which they exchange ideas, and listen to or watch authentic radio and television commercials in which they need to catch the main message and other details to analyze the commercials' creative concepts.
Speaking	Students give oral presentations using visual aids to showcase the outcome of their projects (e.g., print ads, radio and television commercials) and web portfolios. During the presentations, they defend their work and answer questions, making use of their discourse strategies.

Groups (Yahoo!, 2008), which serves as an online learning environment where discussions and communications via an e-mail-based messaging system enhance student–student and student–teacher rapport. It also serves as an archive for syllabi and other learning materials. Additionally, I create a class blog using *Blogger* (Google, 1999–2009), which I use for publishing learning materials that students use in and outside the classroom. Our class blog also serves as an online archive of students' work that exhibits their skills; it is effectively an online portfolio that showcases everything they accomplish in the course. Visual aids used during students' presentations and Microsoft PowerPoint lecture materials are uploaded online using *SlideShare* (SlideShare, 2009) or *Google Docs* (Google, 2009), which I then post on the class blog. The same process is used for Microsoft Word documents or written reports, provided that I upload them to a web server that hosts or archives documents, such as *ThinkFree* (Haansoft, 2009). I also create an account with online video services, such as *Blip.tv* (Blip Networks, 2009) and *YouTube* (YouTube, 2009), which I use to store student-produced commercials and share these videos with students by embedding them on our class blog. By adding the *Yahoo! Group* e-mail address to our blog's BlogSendAddress feature, I enable students to automatically receive updates on blog publications. All of these Web 2.0 tools provide a virtual extension of the classroom where students can learn and showcase their creativity to the rest of the world (Yeh, 2007).

Digital media such as digital audio and video recording, media players, editing programs, and other multimedia tools are necessary for creating radio and television commercials; the digital format makes it easy to transfer and share files swiftly from one platform to another and has a great impact on language learning, particularly in enhancing students' oral and communicative competence by producing authentic language in the form of digitally recorded materials.

Multiple Intelligences

I assign individual and collaborative tasks to gauge students' learning ability. In individual tasks, the level of difficulty is kept low to make sure that students can perform the activity alone. Such tasks include copywriting exercises and voiceover (VO) recording. Tasks such as radio and television commercial production require group work for successful completion. This collaborative approach provides the opportunity for collective learning to take place while students interact with each other and perform tasks (Brufee, 1984; Vygotsky, 1978). This type of social interaction is educationally beneficial because it allows students to work together in accomplishing the required tasks. Although students work in small groups, the tasks highlight the contribution of each member's prior knowledge and skills. This approach is in sync with Gardner's (1993) multiple intelligences theory, which suggests applying students' abilities according to the intelligence they could contribute to creating a product. For instance, VO narration—a prerecorded off-camera commentary—can be assigned to students with good oral or linguistic skills, and students with a strong musical bent could be responsible for music editing or sound effects. On the other hand, the rotation of roles and responsibilities gives students the opportunity to develop particular language skills that need enhancement, and students with stronger skills can act as mentors.

In collaborative tasks, students apply the skills that they have learned. As shown in Figure 1, the process begins with pretask activities whereby students participate in lectures and discussions of ad samples. It is also during this time that I inform students of language and learning objectives, task guidelines, requirements, and criteria for assessments (see Appendix B). In the second stage, students brainstorm, plan, and gather sufficient information to help them pin down their topic and task strategy. Then they implement the creative execution by engaging in copywriting, preparing a storyboard (a graphic illustration of what is written in the script; see Jenkins, 2005), producing the ad, and writing their report. In the third stage, they present their final projects. The final stage is the assessment, during which students are evaluated based on the quality of their presentation, report, and collaborative execution of their project. Throughout the entire process, students use English to learn content while learning how to use English to express their ideas.

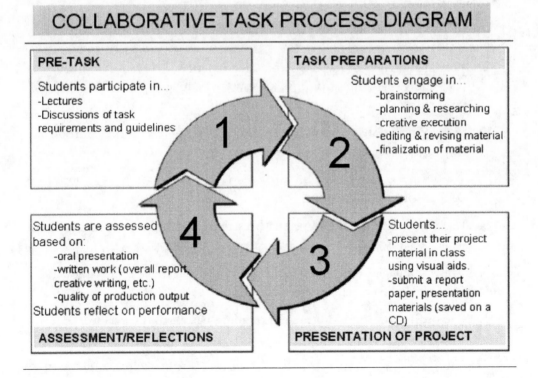

Figure 1. Collaborative Task Process Diagram

CURRICULUM, TASKS, MATERIALS

> By doing the class projects, we have more time to think about and discuss the ideas
> in our minds. After brainstorming the concepts, we start to write the projects. In this
> step, it's useful to improving our English language skill—when you want to express
> the words (in your mind), you will find out ways to accomplish it. (student feedback)

In this section, I discuss in detail how the collaborative task process was implemented, how the language and learning objectives were chosen and presented to students, and how digital media and Web 2.0 tools are integrated into the process via a public service announcement (PSA) project.

A PSA is a 30- to 60-second commercial for a nonprofit organization. The objective is to disseminate information that has social overtones (see Govoni, 2004). Similar to news releases, PSAs includes facts that answer the five Ws— who, what, where, when, why—as well as how. Like in product advertisements, the goal of PSAs is to persuade people. So in addition to having a conversational tone, the language used in the VO and the approach in sending the message must be simple and soft but direct, and it must be able to catch the audience's interest. For visuals, students use items such as slides, static pictures and graphics, and short videos.

In this class project, objectives focus on two main areas: content and skills, and language. The following are the content and skills objectives:

1. Study what makes a persuasive argument by critically analyzing different PSAs.

2. Learn to search for questions embedded in a PSA's creative approach, text, and visuals (question-finding strategy) and apply them to a topic of your choice.

3. Practice persuasive writing by creating PSA scripts using the appropriate language forms and structures (see language objectives).

4. Use a variety of media techniques to enhance what you have written in your scripts, and create and edit video PSAs.

5. Use video techniques and persuasive writing strategies you learned about while creating your PSAs to evaluate those of your peers.

The following language objectives were chosen based on the specific language requirements needed to create a persuasive PSA:

1. Use present tense to indicate the ongoing nature of the event or situation.

2. Use specific words that have emotional appeal to make the target audience feel compassion, guilt, sympathy, and so on.

3. Use action words to say exactly what viewers have to do and how to do it.

4. Use vocal variety and appropriate pacing when delivering the VO.

Pretask Activities

The pedagogical rationale for using PSAs, as well as their social relevance, is discussed in the classroom to help students establish a meaningful connection between what they are expected to do (the task) and real-life issues. Examples of professionally executed PSAs (linked from the class blog) and student-produced PSAs (see Appendix C) are also shown and analyzed in class to frame the language and content goals that students need to accomplish by the end of the task. The visual materials enable students to easily understand the nature of the task. For instance, after showing a selected PSA, I ask the following questions to encourage use of critical thinking skills and generate discussion that highlights both the language (form, structure, and use) and content (social relevance of the material):

1. If you were to meet the creative director, what question(s) would you ask regarding the PSA's creative approach?

2. What is the social issue (problem) behind the selected PSA?

3. Did the PSA explicitly or implicitly talk about or show the gravity of the problem? If yes, how? If no, what do you think should have been done about it?

4. If you were the advertiser, what would you do to show the seriousness of this dilemma?

5. What was the call for action? What words, phrases, and sentence structures were used to persuade people to act?

6. What words and phrases were used to indicate emotional appeal?

7. In your opinion, was it a good PSA? Why or why not?

Questions 4–7 focus on the language goals of this task. I use them to present to students various language forms and structures, and how to use them to persuade the target audience. I conduct a brief exercise to review what students have learned and to assess their readiness for the task. The discussion and analysis of PSA samples provides students with ideas to give them a head start in doing this project.

In addition, a workshop is conducted so that students can learn the ropes of digital video production (creating storyboards, using a digital camera, editing, integrating graphics and pictures using PowerPoint slides, producing the final video using Windows Movie Maker). Then I show students the assessment rubric (Appendix B), and we discuss it in class so that students are aware of the various grading criteria for the project (e.g., language, content, execution). With the task criteria clearly stated in the rubric, students know what they need to do in order to meet the requirements. The rubric also provides objective information for me to use in evaluating students' skills and serves as a checklist for them to use while producing their PSAs.

Lecture materials, task guidelines and requirements, the rubric, links to online PSA samples and video instructions for creating PSAs, and all other relevant materials that students need to successfully meet the requirements of this task are uploaded to the class Yahoo! Group, giving students the opportunity to access the files anytime.

Task Preparation

The students brainstorm and hold discussions in and outside the classroom before settling on one storyline for their PSAs. After deciding on a theme, students are required to post their chosen topic to the class Yahoo! Group in order to ensure that topics are not presented twice. Once topics have been settled, students proceed to creating the storyboard. They present to me a sketch of their storyboard to discuss the feasibility of their plans (e.g., scouting models or actors and shooting locations, use of images, researching for background information). Group members proceed with the PSA production as soon as they reach consensus on what their creative plan is and how and when they will execute it.

Once the final PSA is ready for presentation, each group prepares its report, which is a written discussion of the PSA theme as well as the group's creative approach and reflection on the production process. Students are given questions that should be answered based on their past experience or real events that took place while producing their PSAs (e.g., What are the visual effects that you used, and why did you use them? What message do you want your PSA to express to viewers?). This is a group task, but members can add individual comments or self-assessments on either language or content. In addition to the written component, the report displays the storyboard and script. Lastly, a report is incomplete without a job listing—a description of each group member's roles and responsibilities (see Appendix D).

Project Presentation

Students are expected to present their PSAs in class, and for assessment purposes I require them to hand in their work (report, audio/video materials, etc. saved on a CD) on the day of presentation. Aside from using a scoring rubric (Appendix B), I also write down my observations about the presentations. Each group is given 15 minutes to present, discussing the storyline, message, and social relevance of their PSA as well as production details. Once all the groups have presented and students have seen what other groups have created, they briefly assess how they have performed in comparison to other groups. Students discuss which group they think did a better job and share their opinions about the changes that they would implement if they were given the chance to do the project again.

Assessment

Assessment is done based on students' reports, audio/video materials, the scoring rubric, and notes taken during the presentations. The feedback I provide is based on the criteria stipulated on the scoring rubric, how successfully students met the task requirements (both technical and language), and the overall quality of their PSAs.

Figure 2 shows the storyboard of a group that successfully achieved the main objectives for the project. The PSA begins with a loud, screeching sound of a car crash. While this background sound immediately invokes intense fear, the black background—in its stark simplicity—strongly delivers the PSA's message: Drunk-driving accidents cause death. In Taiwanese culture, the color black is associated with death, and using this local belief quickly gets the message across. The images shown are of various fatal car accidents in Taiwan that students found

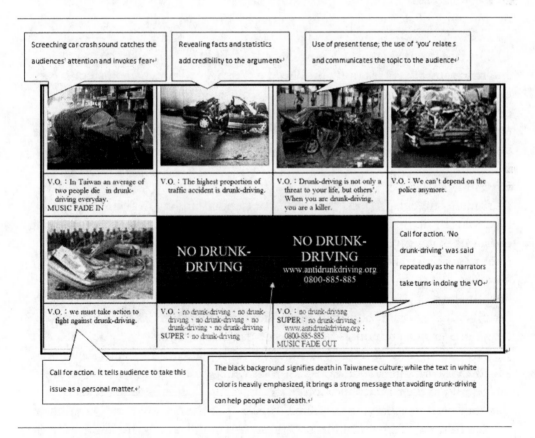

Figure 2. Public Service Announcement Storyboard

on the Internet. The first VO narration does not describe the obvious, but rather makes a factual statement ("In Taiwan an average of two people die in drunk-driving every day") that provides background information about the seriousness of the problem.

The language structure reveals the present condition, starting with the first sentence: "An average of two people die . . . every day" connotes a regularly occurring action. The same is true with the second sentence: "The highest proportion of traffic accidents is drunk-driving." In the third bit of VO ("Drunk-driving is not only a threat to your life, but others'. When you are drunk driving, you are a killer."), the creative strategy is to speak to the audience through the use of direct address in the second person. The next sentence ("We can't depend on the police anymore") uses the first person pronoun *we,* which suggests a shift in the manner of speaking; the narrator talks not just to the audience, but with them. The message is thus personalized. The message "We must take action" calls for the viewers and creators of the PSA to unite in the effort to stop drunk driving. The last two visuals show this call to action: a superimposition of the text "No drunk-driving." The students take turns saying this phrase in the VO, which adds a collaborative touch to persuading people that by avoiding driving under the influence of alcohol they can save not only the driver's life but other people's lives as well.

The audio and video projects uploaded on the class blog allow me to play back and review how well or poorly produced each PSA is. I watch and listen to each one two to three times, occasionally using the pause button to review specific details. These materials not only provide strong evidence of how much time, effort, and skill went into producing the PSAs, but also help me justify my own assessments of the work.

Reports

By reading students' reports, I have a better understanding of the process that they went through in creating and producing their PSAs. Using the seven guide questions that I gave them, students briefly discuss their PSA's thematic and creative approach. For instance, Question 1 asks students to share the information they found that made them choose their topic. Question 2 intends to reveal how the project changed their opinion about their topic. Question 3 asks them to describe their storyline and transitions and explain why they used them. Figure 3 shows one group's responses to Questions 1–3.

Question 4 deals with the creative effects that students used and how they added to the meaning. Question 5 looks at what students think about the language used in their PSA. Question 6 asks students to discuss the PSA message that they wish to express to the audience. Most of the responses to Questions 4–6 are descriptions of the visual imagery presented in the storyboard and explanations of the language used in the script. Figure 4 shows the script for the drunk-driving PSA and the corresponding points related to Questions 4–6.

1. Describe your planning process. What questions led you to your topic?

   Water is very important to humans. It is needed every day. However, there are many people using too much water without any consideration. Water restriction does happen in Taiwan. So water conservation is considered to be a social issue.

2. How did creating a public service announcement (PSA) change your opinion about the topic it was about?

   Saving water is not a hard thing to do. Some easy actions can make a big difference.

3. Describe the transitions you used, and explain why you chose them.

   In the beginning, the PSA informs the fact that only 2% of water is used as fresh water even though 70% of the earth is covered in water and then shows two pictures of the dry land and dead trees as prediction when water runs out. Finally, the PSA teachers some easy ways to save water in daily life. We would like to warn people that water wasting problem is a big issue and should be concerned. However, worrying doesn't help. So the PSA also tells some ways to save water and encourage people to do these actions.

Figure 3. Water Conservation Group's Response to Questions 1–3

Question 7 asks students what they learned about technology by participating in this project. Most students comment on learning how to produce a PSA and how easy it is to learn how to use Windows Movie Maker.

Language Goals

In meeting the language goals set for this task, students needed to use their language skills to successfully produce the desired outcomes. Having good pronunciation and articulation of English words is highly valuable for creating jingles and doing VO narration. Correct grammar usage is likely to influence a PSA's credibility and the audience's perceptions about the production quality. Although the students' level of English competency is considered to be upper intermediate, errors in word choice, usage, and grammar still exist. Such errors are minimized

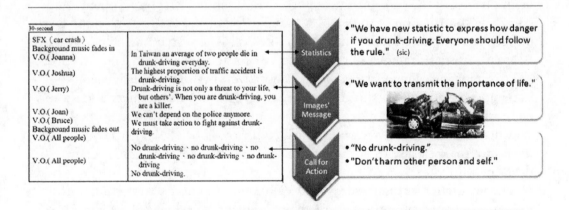

Figure 4. Script for a Drunk-Driving Public Service Announcement

when students present their draft script and storyboard to me during the task preparation stage for final review. The learning of basic English language structure is not the main focus of this course, but students still need to compose appropriate English phrases, sentences, and paragraphs when writing their copy, scripts, and reports. As one student put it, "by practicing to be a good voiceover, we can enhance our fluency of speaking. By writing scripts for TV and radio commercial, we can enhance our writing skills and creativeness."

Publishing the PSAs Online

With students' permission, I upload the PSAs to the class blog. First, I upload and archive the videos on a video server such as *Blip.tv* (Blip Networks, 2009) or *YouTube* (YouTube, 2009). Next, I link or embed these videos on the blog. Because the uploaded files have an accompanying embed code (html), it only takes a few seconds to copy that code and paste it on the class blog (in edit mode). Video files can be viewed either from the blog or from the server. Figure 5 is a screenshot of the class blog with PSAs that are available for viewing.

Once they are published on the blog, students' PSAs can be shared with other students and colleagues from around the globe. Figure 6 shows some of the comments that these viewers have posted on the blog.

Such comments and feedback inspire students to work harder in producing creative advertisements and make students feel proud of their achievements, thus motivating them to become confident speakers of English. Figure 7 shows a student's reaction to a brief write-up about the class blog and the PSAs that was posted by Nik Peachey (learning technology consultant and manager of the British Council's English language teaching web sites) and linked from his wiki project, *ELT Course Book* (n.d.).

REFLECTIONS

The outcomes of the PSA project described in this chapter prove that the collaborative nature of this task greatly supports the learning of language, content, and skills. The contribution of students' knowledge, skills, and use of English played a major role in the successful completion of the task. The storyboards, reports, and PSAs are concrete examples of the products of collaborative effort. The recorded VO narration also demonstrates how collaborative work supports language learning. The job list that students submitted as part of the assessment also shows how tasks were divided and shared. But most important, this project enabled students to gain deeper awareness of their culture and society, and it provided them with the exposure to understand social issues that have direct impact on their lives.

The integration of digital media and Web 2.0 tools into a traditional face-to-face course created an optimal learning environment for language learning. Aside

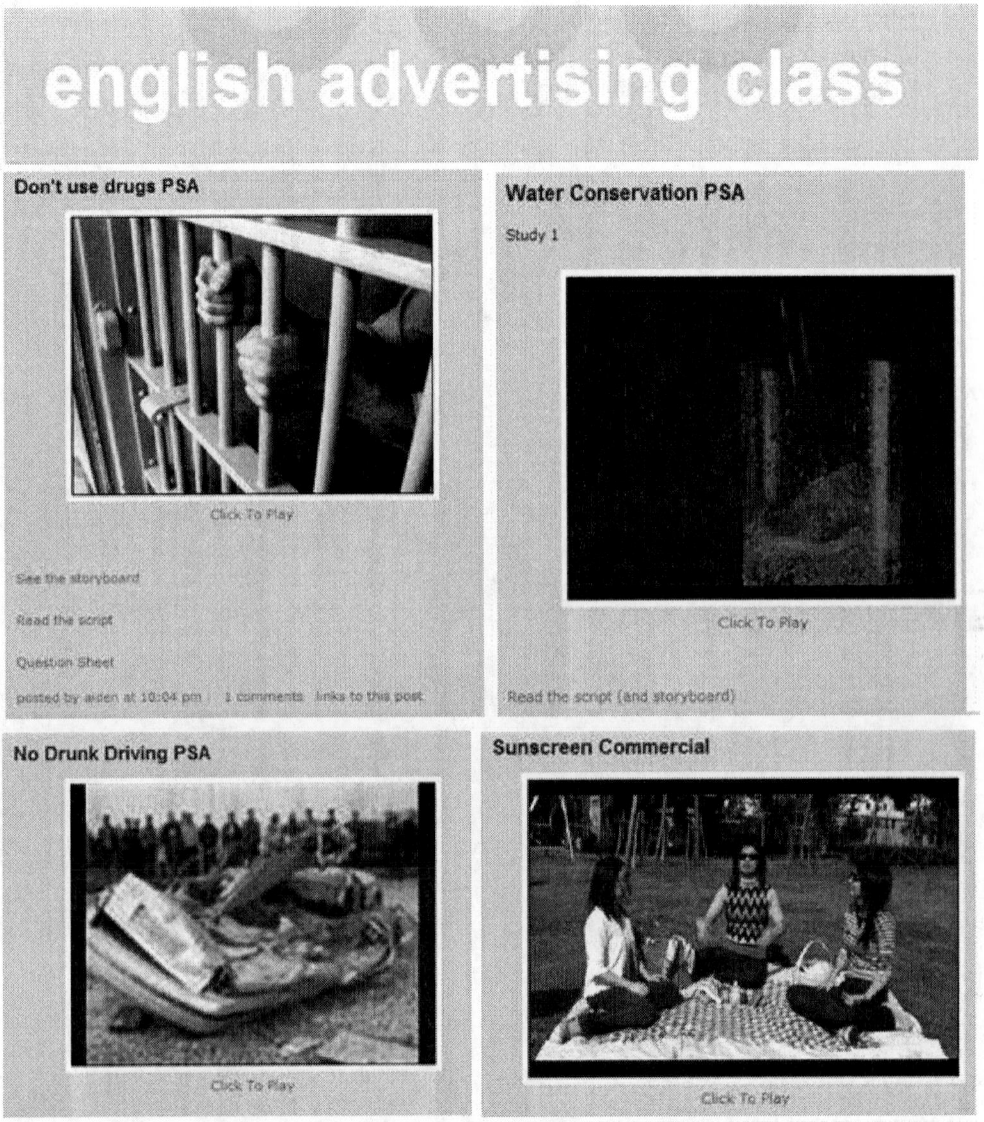

Figure 5. Public Service Announcements Published on the Class Blog

from developing computer literacy, students were continuously engaged in collaborative work, spending a great deal of time writing their plans, scripts, storyboards, and final reports. The oral language produced in the form of recorded speech or VO narrations was disseminated on the Internet using digital audio/video formats. When written text, speech, photos, music and sound effects, and video were blended in digital forms and embedded in interactive web interfaces (e.g., blogs, social networking sites), they transformed the conditions for learning,

"No Drunk Driving PSA"

4 Comments - <u>Show Original Post</u>

<u>Collapse comments</u>

 michael said...

Well done team! I especially like your point that you can't rely on the police. It is everyone's responsibility.

11:09 PM

 barbara dieu said...

A much needed ad and message. Well-done! Here in Brazil, a law was recently passed that you cannot drink a drop of alcohol before driving. What is the law in Taiwan?

3:55 AM

 christine bauer-ramazani said...

Great job, class. Your message comes through loud and clear. I especially liked the way you first said "No drunk driving" individually and then in chorus. Very effective. I also looked at your process plans -- well thought-out! You are clearly passionate about this important topic. Great job, team!

5:08 AM

susanacanelo said...

Good job !!! Very impressive images!. I could heard you clearly. What a good ad !
Last year in Argentina there was a terrible accident. A group of students who were coming back from a social task (helping a poor school in a far away province), were killed by a drunk lorry driver. They were travelling by bus when the accident happened. Their parents are working hard in campaigns to prevent accidents, especially caused by alcohol consumption...but they aren't going to have their kids back any more.

7:44 AM

Figure 6. Blog Comments About Students' Public Service Announcements

---

The blog hosts a remarkable collection of advertisements made by students of English as a fonegn language. The topics of the advertisements vary greatly and many of them are like public service broadcasts, but they are great examples of student creativity using various digital mediums.

I also really like that many of them include the 'storyboards' that the students used to plan and design the advertisements.

Take 1

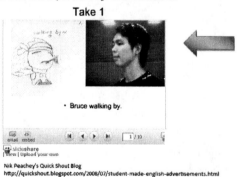

- Bruce walking by.

slideshare
View | Upload your own

Nik Peachey's Quick Shout Blog
http://quickshout.blogspot.com/2008/07/student-made-english-advertisements.html

Messages

Message # [ ] [Go] dvanced   [ ]   [Search]

What a surprise! That's unbelievable!

Reply | Forward | Delete

I'm so excited that our works became the teaching materials of the wiki project on the website. Now more people on the planet will pay a visit to our advertising blog. I'm so proud of my group team, and so proud of our instructor, Ms.Yeh.

By the way, I like demanding. Lots demanding. Because the demanding make me better and progressive.

Good luck to all.

Bruce

Posted by a student to the class Yahoo! Group where the announcement of the write-up was made.

Class Yahoo Group: http://groups.yahoo.com/group/english_ad/message/178
Class Blog: http://english-ad.blogspot.com/

Figure 7. Student Reaction to a Viewer's Write-Up

inevitably enhancing language ability. Publishing and sharing students' creative work on the Internet visually articulated their learning experience. Comments and feedback posted by a real audience motivated them to excel, giving them the driving force to believe in themselves, use English confidently, think of and create advertising ideas, and make their concepts come to life. In the end, students developed better creative thinking processes and enhanced their English abilities, which was crucial for achieving their personal career goals. This collaborative task-based PSA project was a practical example of how CBI can be used effectively to motivate students to use English for a meaningful purpose.

Aiden Yeh is a doctoral student at the University of Birmingham. She is the head coordinator of the TESOL Computer-Assisted Language Learning Interest Section's Electronic Village Online and the 2009–2010 chair of the Nonnative English Speakers in TESOL Interest Section. Her research interests include blended learning, integration of technology in EFL teaching and learning, and teacher professional development. She teaches in Taiwan.

APPENDIX A: ENGLISH ADVERTISING COURSE CONTENT

上課日期 **Date**	課程內容 **Course Content and Progress**	授課方式 **Instructional Approaches**	作業、報告、 考試或其他 **Assignment**	備註 **Remarks**
Week 1	Introduction Chapter 1: What Is Advertising Today?	Lecture/Q & A	Read chapter on Role of Advertising	
Week 2	Chapter 5: Marketing and Consumer Behavior	Lecture/ discussion class activities	Assign. 1, p. 26, #11 The Advertising Experience	
Week 3	Chapter 4: The Ad Agency	Lecture/ discussion class activities	P. 53, #2 Advertising History	Discussion for Group Project 1
Week 4	Group presentations: Ad history		Forming your own ad agency	Discussion for Group Project 2
Week 5	Chapter 6: Marketing Mix, Ad Plan, p. 249 (Ch. 8)	Lecture/ discussion class activities	Quiz	
Week 6	Group presentations: Ad agency			

Week 7	Chapter 9: Media
	Creating advertisements and
	  commercials
	Creative execution: Writing
	  headlines, subheads,
	  body, and slogans
	Lay-outing
		Lecture/discussion class activities		

Week 8	Midterm exam week	Draw lots re: products/services, create print ads		
Week 9	Create print and radio ad studies	Lecture/ discussion class activities		

Week 10	Writing radio and TV
	  commercials scripts for
	  product ads
	Using audio/video editing
	  software workshop
			Doing voiceover narration
			Brainstorming/discussion ideas
			for radio commercial	

Week 11	Radio commercial project preparations			
Week 12	Radio commercial project presentations			

Week 13	Lecture: Public service
	  announcements/nonprofit
	  organizations Ch. 3, p. 346
		Lecture/
		discussion class
		activities
			Draw lots re: government public
			service/nonprofit organizations
			and needs	

Week 14	PSA project preparation			
Week 15	PSA project presentations			
Week 16	TV commercial storyboard review			
Week 17	TV commercial preparations			
Week 18	TV commercial project presentations			

APPENDIX B: PUBLIC SERVICE ANNOUNCEMENT SCORING RUBRIC

Group Members: _____

PSA Theme: _____

PSA length: _____

Criteria	Y/N			Comments		
Provided two studies						
Provided public service announcement (PSA) script						
Meeting Language Goals E=Excellent, VG= Very Good, G= Good, A= Average, P= Poor	E	VG	G	A		P
Use present tense to indicate the ongoing nature of the event/situation						
Use specific words that have emotional appeals to make the target audience feel compassion, guilt, sympathy, etc.						
Use action words to say exactly what the viewers have to do and how to do it						
Use vocal variety and appropriate pacing when delivering the VO						
PSA Content						
Clearly identified the "who"						
Clearly identified the "what"						
Clearly identified the "where"						
Clearly identified the "when"						
Clearly identified the "why"						
Clearly identified the "how"						
Level of PSA Persuasiveness						
Creative Skills						
PSA concept						
PSA message						
Creative execution						
Technical Skills						
VO quality						
Choice of background music						
Sound effects						
Talents/actors (if applicable)						
Transitions of visual images						
Collaborative Tasks						
Provided job listings for individual contributions						

Group Grade: _____

APPENDIX C: SAMPLE STUDENT-PRODUCED PUBLIC SERVICE ANNOUNCEMENT

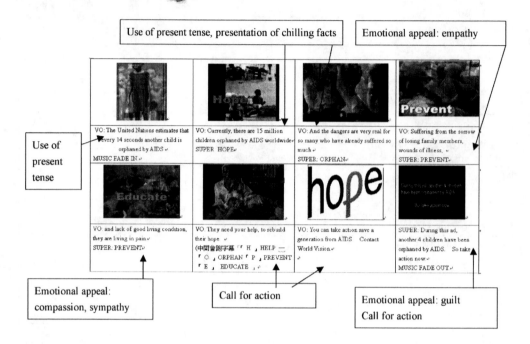

APPENDIX D: SAMPLE JOB LISTING

Joshua	1. Do the voiceover. 2. Operate the "Movie Make" to combine all the photos and sounds. 3. Come up with the script. 4. Come up with the idea of drunk driving.
Joan	1. Do the voiceover. 2. Make the "Reflections on the Process" and "Evaluating the Products." 3. Search the photos. 4. Make the form of the script.
Joanna	1. Do the voiceover. 2. Come up with the idea of drunk driving. 3. Come up with the script. 4. Make the "Reflecting on the Process" and "Evaluating the Product."

CHAPTER 14

Developing Language Skills While Studying Cultural Identity

Pavel V. Sysoyev and Stephanie R. Funderburg-Foreman

> I think all people participate in cultural oppression. By keeping silence, by observing, by doing what everyone does. That is the reason why there is racism, classism, sexism, ableism, homophobia and other "-isms." Many people understand that that is bad, but do not do anything to stop oppression. So am I. I understand that homophobia is bad. But I just laugh, when my friends make jokes. (Journal reflection, student in the American Studies course)

This chapter describes an American Studies course in a teaching English as a foreign language (TEFL) program in Russia whose aim was to integrate three components: language, culture, and identity. This integration included the teaching and assessment of content and skills in these three areas. The defining characteristic of the course was its cultural identity component, the development of which was the impetus for the new curriculum.

CONTEXT

During the past decade, special attention in foreign language pedagogy has been given to the development of learners' critical thinking skills and self-awareness as members of particular social and cultural groups. Several studies have proved that foreign language teaching can contribute to the development of learners' social identity (belonging to a particular social class; Norton, 2000) and ethnic identity (belonging to a particular racial or ethnic group; Leung, Harris, & Rampton, 1997).

A recent study examined the extent to which teaching a foreign language and its culture can contribute to the development of a student's cultural identity (Sysoyev, 2003). It was found that a foreign language plays an important role in learners' secondary socialization. Through the content of the course and the method of teaching, educators can either restrict learners' sociocultural space and

193

make them see themselves as outside of a global community or, conversely, extend the sociocultural space and help learners see themselves as an inseparable part of the global community, with common interests, beliefs, problems, and solutions.

Cultural identity is defined as "learners' realization of their own multiple group membership[s] and actions to be associated with their cultural groups based on ethnicity, gender, social class, location, sexual orientation, language, etc." (Sysoyev, 2003, p. 39). According to Sysoyev, the development of learners' cultural identity includes fostering the following abilities:

- understand culture as a theoretical construct (characteristics and borders)

- identify one's multiple group memberships

- extend the borders of one's group beyond the political borders of one's country

- take an active part in actions against cultural aggression, cultural vandalism, and cultural discrimination

- act as a representative of one's culture

Eighty second-year university students participated in the course described here. They were enrolled in the TEFL program at Tambov State University, in Russia. Their EFL level was from high-intermediate to advanced, according to American Council on the Teaching of Foreign Languages (ACTFL) proficiency guidelines. The EFL curriculum consisted of the following language courses: Basic English Skills (with prime focus on speaking and reading, 8 hours per week), English Grammar (2 hours per week), Morphology (2 hours per week), and American Cultural Studies. American Cultural Studies was a new semester-long course designed specifically to integrate language and culture. Students met for 90-minute sessions once a week for 9 weeks, and at each class they were expected to do the following:

- read the materials on each topic, and complete tasks (comprehension questions, inferences, synthesis)

- discuss the readings

- respond to the reflective journal assignment (in writing)

CURRICULUM, TASKS, MATERIALS

Course Content

The American Cultural Studies course curriculum included the following topics:

- *Cultural diversity and identity:* Students learned about racial, ethnic, gender, social, religious, and ability versus disability diversity in the modern United States and about the concept of cultural identity.

- *Frameworks of diversity and oppression:* Learners studied types of relationships between cultures in the modern multicultural world, using the United States as an example, and the privileges that certain groups receive based on every facet of identity: ethnicity, gender, social class, ability versus disability, territory, and so on.

- *Stereotypes and the media:* Learners studied how certain stereotypes, images, and standards are imposed on society by the media as well as their purpose and danger.

- *Race and ethnicity:* This theme addressed racial and ethnic diversity in modern U.S. society, their stereotypes, and the cultural conflicts between them.

- *Social class and classism:* This topic focused on the socioeconomic diversity in the United States. Learners discussed the myth of the American Dream, social stratification in the United States, social class mobility, and the media.

- *Disabilities and ableism:* Learners studied major stereotypes about people with disabilities, privileges of "temporally able bodies" in modern U.S. and Russian societies, legislation aimed at eliminating discrimination against people with disabilities, special programs for people with disabilities in the United States, and the integration of people with disabilities into the "abled" mainstream world.

- *Gender and sexism, sexuality, and homophobia*: This topic focuses on the differences between biological sex and gender (as a socially constructed phenomena), gender roles, and gender stereotypes in modern Russian and U.S. societies; myths versus realities about homosexuality; and the origin of feminism.

- *Languages and cultures:* This theme addressed such issues as linguistic diversity in the United States, reflection of culture in language, debates about English as the official language in the United States, U.S. and Russian language politics, language as the reflection of one's cultural identity, and discourse analysis.

In this course, the English language was both the objective and the medium. Instruction was in English, and three basic skills were addressed explicitly: reading, writing, and speaking. No specific attention was paid to the development of listening skills because listening was an integral part of the course's communication in a foreign language. Students were aware that communicative English skills and cultural content were being taught and assessed.

Reading: Academic Papers and Literature

For each class, students were asked to read scholarly papers and excerpts from literary works on the target issue. Table 1 shows the reading list for each topic.

Table 1. Course Topics and Readings

Topic	Readings
Cultural diversity and identity	Crystal, 1997
Frameworks of diversity and oppression	Blumenfeld & Raymon, 2000; McIntosh, 2001; Tatum, 2000; Wildman & Davis, 2000
Stereotypes and the media	LeNoir, 1997; Morrison, 1994; Tatum, 1997
Race and ethnicity	Cofer, 2001; Silko, 2001; Martin Luther King, Jr.'s 1963 "I Have a Dream" speech
Social class and classism	Langston, 2001; Mantsios, 2000
Disabilities and ableism	Rauscher & McClintock, 1997
Gender and sexism, sexuality, and homophobia	hooks, 2001; Hubbard, 2001; Lorber, 1994
Languages and cultures	Sysoyev & Donelson, 2003; Zormeier & Samovar, 2009

Since students were involved in extensive reading, reading comprehension was tested globally—during further participation in group discussions and writing a reflective journal. The way students participated in speaking and writing reflected the level of their reading comprehension.

Writing: Reflective Journals

Based on the readings, learners were asked to complete reflective journal assignments, responding to the following questions, which were due at the beginning of each class:

- What have you learned so far in the class that has challenged what you thought previously about race and ethnicity issues in the United States and Russia?

- What questions do you have about race and ethnicity issues based on the readings and class discussions?

- What would you like to remember (information, feelings, and thoughts) about the activities you have completed in class?

- Think of situations in which you and your friends have expressed negative attitudes toward people of a different ethnic group. What would you do if this happened again? Do you think it is important to challenge racism and ethnocentrism every time you face it? Why?

- What can you personally do to stop racism?

Speaking: Student Collaboration

During each class, students were divided into groups of seven to discuss reading assignments and share reflective journal responses. On the first day of class, the instructor assigned roles to the students: leader, secretary, and spokesperson. In later classes, students took turns to make sure each of them played each role at least once. The primary language of the discussion was English; however, at times students chose to use their native language in small groups to discuss issues that were complex and difficult for them to understand. One example was the issue of privilege and oppression.

In addition to small-group work, students were also involved in whole-class discussions moderated by the instructor. They expressed their points of view and shared their examples voluntarily. English was the only language used during whole-class discussions.

Assessment

Before and after the course, students were given the TEFL program's standardized EFL test, which has a format similar to that of the Test of English as a Foreign Language and measures the development of learners' communicative competence in English. The results showed that over the period of the semester students improved greatly, but only in the development of speaking and writing skills.

During the course, through small-group discussions and presentations, the following speaking skills were assessed:

- identify and explain the major ideas and issues addressed
- categorize issues
- retell events in logical order
- express a point of view on the target issue
- develop arguments
- use specific new vocabulary introduced in class
- make requests for specific information

All of these skills were evaluated explicitly. For each lesson, the teacher gave students specific instructions about what to discuss or address in small groups after the readings. Students were then asked to explain the major ideas and issues addressed in the reading using the skills in the previous list. They had to explain the main idea of the reading in five sentences and use specific vocabulary, which proved that they had a good grasp of the material. Students were also asked to make requests for specific information, which showed verbal mastery of the content. They were required to formulate 10 specific questions about the content of the reading. Students were then rated on their proficiency on a scale of 1–5, addressing the areas in the previous list.

Some students also took part in informal interviews and said that by the end of the course they felt more confident speaking in English and would feel comfortable using it as a means of communication, as opposed to a language only used in the classroom.

Such great results in the development of speaking skills can be explained by several facts. First, during every class students were involved in small-group and whole-class discussions. Open-ended problem-solving assignments and discussion questions contributed to the development of authentic speaking skills. Second, the faculty of foreign languages selected students whose motivation to study languages and language proficiency was quite high (advanced level according to ACTFL proficiency guidelines). Most of those admitted to the program already possessed some communicative skills; however, they were not able to use them in authentic situations that required English to be used as the primary language. They had no mental system for using English accurately while simultaneously being able to synthesize information. For example, some students were able to retell the text and explain the general idea, but were not able to focus equally on the details; other students' presentations focused on one of the details without paying attention to the main idea of the story. This course allowed students to focus on the development of communicative skills as a system.

In addition to sharpening their speaking skills, over the course of the semester students developed the following writing skills:

- identify and explain major ideas and issues addressed in the reading
- categorize issues
- express a point of view on the target issue
- develop arguments

Students' writings became more structured and to the point and less watered down. They were instructed to answer questions specifically without introductions, which is a characteristic feature of Russian discourse.

Grammatical mistakes were corrected in the reflective journals; however, because the main focus was not grammar, mistakes did not affect students' final grades. The journal assignments emphasized fluency over accuracy. On the final assessment, students were graded on content and expression. (Other courses in the curriculum, such as English Grammar and Basic English Skills, specifically focus on grammar.)

At the end of the course, students took an oral comprehensive exam. This format of conducting final exams is typical of Russian institutions of higher education. Students picked up cards containing exam questions from a pile, and they were expected to give oral answers to the questions. Only content knowledge was assessed. Notes about students' grammatical inaccuracy were taken by the teacher during oral presentations and were explained to students afterward. Grammar errors were not taken into account when calculating their final grade.

Exam questions reflected major cultural issues addressed in the readings and in class. Some examples of the questions are as follows:

- *Card 1:* What events in world history led to the foundation and development of the United States as a multiethnic country? What major ethnic groups live in the United States, and what kind of relationships do they have with each other? What privileges based on race and ethnicity do some groups have over others?

- *Card 2:* What is ableism? What types of disabilities do you know about? What kinds of programs for people with disabilities exist in the United States? How do these programs help people with disabilities integrate into mainstream life?

- *Card 3:* What languages are spoken in the United States? What are the pros and cons of making English the official language in the United States? How are U.S. culture and its realities reflected in the varieties of English in the United States (dialects, sociolects, African American vernacular)?

Cultural Identity Research Tool

At the beginning and end of the semester, students were given a cultural identity test that focused on self-awareness and the development of critical thinking skills (see Figure 1). The test questions considered aspects that affect the development of cultural identity. The cultural identity information of individuals was examined for research purposes only and did not affect students' final grade.

An examination of students' responses to the questions before and after the course show that this integrated course contributed to the development of their cultural identity. Their answers indicated their growing awareness of the concept of cultural identity.

Most students were able to answer all of the questions by the end of the course. The remainder of this section explores excerpts from their responses, which display the positive gains of this content-based approach to EFL teaching. Studying about different cultural groups, their relationships with each other, and reflecting on their native culture helped learners get a better understanding of who they were. Another important outcome was students' understanding that group membership changes depending on time, place, and context for communication. Prior to the course, most students did not completely understand what culture was and what cultural groups coexisted within one country. The most typical example of this is shown in Excerpt 1.

Question		Students demonstrate their ability to...
1. If you are asked by someone to describe who you are, starting with "I am . . . ," what would you say?		see themselves as individuals with multiple group memberships based on ethnicity, social class, gender, religion, and so on
2. How many culture groups (cultures) do you belong to? What are they?		
3. Do you think that your (cultural) group membership will change in several hours? Days? Why?		understand that group membership may change over time and based on place
4. Do you think that your (cultural) group membership will change in several months? Years? Why?		
5. Do you agree or disagree with either of the following statements: • "Almost all people are the same." • "All people are different." Explain your point of view.		see multiculturality of the surrounding environment and perceive cultural diversity as a norm of cultural coexistence in a modern multicultural world
6. What is culture?		
7. How many and what cultures exist in your community? City?		
8. What does the phrase *cultural diversity* mean to you?		
9. Do you think it is good or bad to live in a diverse society? Why?		
10. Have you ever been oppressed? If yes, please explain how.		see cultural oppression and discrimination in the modern world
11. Have you ever oppressed others? If yes, please explain how.		
12. How would you compare yourself to others within your society in terms of privilege? Explain your point of view.		
13. How can discrimination and privilege be minimized and eliminated?		show readiness to take an active part in actions against cultural discrimination, cultural aggression, and cultural vandalism
14. What can you personally do to change a situation of cultural conflict?		

Figure 1. Cultural Identity Test

Excerpt 1

I belong to only one culture—Russian culture. I am not a hippy or anything like that.

By the end of the course, most students were able to demonstrate their understanding of their multiple group memberships, as shown in Excerpt 2.

Excerpt 2

I am a guy. I am 19 years old. I am a student. I am from Tambov, Russia. I like fishing and pop music. I am single.

Another result from the course was that learners developed understanding of the multiculturalism of their environment and of cultural diversity as a norm. Before the course, most students were able to define culture as a set of shared values, norms, and customs. They realized that Russia is a multicultural country, but this multiculturalism was seen only on the ethnic level. No one thought much about belonging to cultural groups based on gender, physical ability, social class, language, and so on. Also, cultural diversity was seen as a negative feature of the modern world. Excerpt 3 illustrates this idea.

Excerpt 3

Unfortunately there are diverse groups in our country such as fascists, punks, skinheads, and others. I don't think diversity is good, because people from other cultural groups do not understand us. It would be much easier, if we all belonged to one culture.

Excerpt 3 also illustrates the learner's hidden ethnocentrism and belief that only his or her culture is right. Cultural coexistence was not viewed as a positive factor of cultural development. Also, for most students, *diverse* had a negative connotation.

After the course, students' responses were just the opposite. They were able to define various cultural groups based on different facets of identity, and diversity was seen as reality, as shown in Excerpt 4.

Excerpt 4

There are many other cultures in our country. People are most commonly defined as other on the basis of race, ethnicity, gender, religion, sexual orientation, socioeconomic class, age, physical ability. All of these categories, which form otherness, can be made kinds of cultures. Within each kind there are also different cultures.

Also important was the fact that students developed an understanding of the cultural oppression and discrimination that exist in the modern world. Before the course, most learners were not able to see how they could be culturally oppressed; Excerpt 5 demonstrates that oppression was understood as gang violence and fights between teenagers.

Excerpt 5

I take karate lessons and I have a lot of friends, so I am not oppressed.

Excerpt 5 also illustrates that most learners had never thought about such issues as cultural oppression. There were, however, two exceptions; one student who had come from a village to study in the city (Excerpt 6), and another who had come from a different region (Chechnya; Excerpt 7).

Excerpt 6

Yes, [I have been oppressed] several times. One of them was when I was entering this university. I am from a different city and came to Tambov before the entrance exams. Many students from Tambov knew professors and teachers, who work here. Some of them had private teachers. Of course, for them it was easier to enter a university.

Excerpt 7

I often feel that I am oppressed, when police stops me on the streets and checks my passport every day, because I look dark. They think that I am a terrorist. They do not think that other people, who look white, may be terrorists. To my mind, other students never experienced the same.

It is obvious that for both of these students oppression was (Excerpt 6) and continued to be (Excerpt 7) visible and quite painful. That is why they were able to bring it up and write about it. For the rest of the students, oppression was not pivotal and, therefore, not apparent.

After the course, most learners looked at oppression as a problem stemming from the relationship between cultures within modern multicultural societies, as described in Excerpt 8.

Excerpt 8

I wrote you before and will write now that I am always oppressed for the color of my skin. Maybe I was oppressed differently in the past, but now I can think of only examples of racism.

Similarly, students looked at the oppression of others. Before the course, no one was thinking about oppression and privilege (as is obvious in Excerpt 9), which can be explained by the fact that most of the students who attend the Faculty of Modern Languages courses are from families with above-average socio-economic status. The term *privilege* was understood in the context of communist privileges, which none of the students had.

Excerpt 9

I have never oppressed others. Even if I did not like a person, I just tried to go away and not to have anything in common with him.

After learning about the types of relationships between cultures and types of discrimination such as racism, classism, sexism, ableism, and homophobia, most students admitted that they often consciously or subconsciously participated in cultural oppression and discrimination, which is obvious in Excerpt 10.

Excerpt 10

I think all people participate in cultural oppression. By keeping silence, by observing, by doing what everyone does. That is the reason why there is racism, classism, sexism, ableism, homophobia and other "-isms." Many people understand that that is bad, but do not do anything to stop oppression. So am I. I understand that homophobia is bad. But I just laugh, when my friends make jokes.

After the course, students were able to articulate their privileges—things that they took for granted as representatives of the mainstream culture (middle-class members of Russia's linguistic and ethnic majority). They even made up privilege lists based on their belonging to different cultural groups. It is important to note that in being able to point out their privileges based on various facets of identity, learners demonstrated their understanding of multicultural group belonging. The ability to openly name one's own privileges is the first step in taking action against cultural vandalism, cultural discrimination, and cultural aggression (see Figure 1, Questions 13 and 14).

Before the course, students understood (even on an ethnic level) cultural discrimination and inequity as things that were out of their hands. They felt that something should be changed to stop cultural inequity, discrimination, and oppression, but they sought for someone else to make that change. As Excerpt 11 makes clear, no one saw him- or herself as someone who could do so.

Excerpt 11

Only government or the president can make changes.

After the course, the answers were completely different. Excerpt 12 is a representative example.

Excerpt 12

We are citizens of this country. It is our country. If we want to change the situation, it is up to us to change it. No one will come and help us, if we don't try.

It is not possible to prove that most students now desired to take an active part in actions against cultural discrimination, cultural vandalism, and cultural aggression. It is also not possible to say whether they would choose to use their knowledge and skills in real life. But cultural learning is a lifelong journey, and through beginning to study cultural diversity in their first and second language societies, learners had an exclusive opportunity to think about the issues connected to the relationship between cultures in this modern multicultural world and about their own role in the global processes of cultural interaction.

Some learners' answers regarding the elimination of cultural inequity were quite naïve. At the same time, though, by completing the course assignments, learners came to a closer understanding of their own role, importance, and responsibility in today's world.

REFLECTIONS

The integration of language, content, and cultural identity in this American Cultural Studies course proved successful in several respects. First, the use of English for content-based teaching contributed to the development of students' speaking and writing skills. They had opportunities to communicate in an authentic environment, and the journal writing, reflections, and open-ended discussion questions required that students synthesize information. The fact that test results did not show any improvement in their listening and reading skills can be explained by the homogeneity of learners. All of them were highly motivated to study at the university, TEFL was their major, and they had to pass a competition to enter the program. By the time they took the course, their English proficiency in reading and listening was already on the level required by the program. In another teaching context, with a group of students with different levels of language proficiency and motivation to study, test results could show the improvement of learners' communicative skills. Second, students clearly demonstrated that they had learned the content of the course—aspects of U.S. culture and society. Third and most important, the course contributed to the development of learners' cultural identity; they developed a better understanding of who they were. By the end of the course students were able to do the following:

- understand culture as a theoretical construct

- identify their membership in multiple groups

- see different types of relationships between cultures in the modern world (dialogue between cultures and cultural oppression)

- realize their cultural privilege based on various facets of identity

- show readiness to take an active part in actions against cultural aggression, cultural vandalism, and cultural discrimination

The constant comparing of U.S. and Russian societies enabled learners to act as representatives of their own country and culture as well. The following are some reflections on what others might learn from this experience:

- *Role of the teacher during whole-group discussions:* The teacher should be a facilitator of all talks and discussions. His or her purpose is to keep the group discussion going and to quickly respond to aggressive, diminishing, or assaulting comments and reactions.

- *Role of the teacher during small-group discussions:* It is important that the teacher observe small-group discussions to make sure students are on task and speaking in an authentic communicative environment. In the American Cultural Studies course, students sometimes asked for vocabulary help or an explanation of peculiar cultural issues, which was given by the instructor. Small-group discussions also provide an opportunity for the teacher to observe the development of English speaking skills. In addition, through interacting with groups during these discussions, the teacher can elaborate on certain issues in more depth or for clarification.

- *Trust building:* In a course like this, it is essential to build trust. Students in American Cultural Studies already knew the instructor from a previous course. By the beginning of the American Cultural Studies course, the instructor and students had established a good relationship based on trust. As a result, students were not afraid to share personal information with the teacher.

- *Discussion of certain sensitive topics:* Experience shows that not all topics can be addressed equally. Sexuality and homophobia are issues that, if chosen, should be addressed especially carefully. Students tend to make homophobic comments and express prejudice, and discussions can easily devolve into jokes and laughter. This is not to say that minority students will not be willing to share. It is important to create a friendly climate and teach students to perceive diversity as a norm, but do not push them.

- *Class examples of diversity:* Most students in this course represented a White middle-class majority, and they took for granted much of the privilege they possessed. So it was quite beneficial to have one ethnic-minority student in the class who was willing to share his personal examples of ethnic discrimination and oppression. These real stories from someone they knew enabled learners to see many things that were previously invisible to them.

- *Use of the native language in class:* All of the small-group discussions were intended to take place in English. Though whole-class discussions were held in English only, in small groups some students preferred to discuss the subject matter in their native language, Russian. Because the teacher's role is not that of a watchdog, he or she can exert little control over the language students use in small-group conversations. With this in mind, groups were allowed to use any language they wanted, as long as they kept the discussion going. After granting students permission to do this, the teacher saw that motivation improved and fewer groups chose Russian as the language of discussion. Those who chose to use Russian explained that they wished to gain a better understanding of the subject matter by using their native language.

If preparing students for society is a main goal of education in the 21st century, then using content-based instruction in the language classroom is an effective way to motivate and practice a foreign language while focusing on important issues that promote critical thinking and evaluating one's self in the world today. Through integrated language and content, the students in this course gained a deeper understanding of their culture and how it impacts society, all while using a foreign language.

―――――――――――――

Pavel V. Sysoyev has a PhD in applied linguistics from Tambov State University and an EdD in foreign language pedagogy from Moscow State University. He is director of the Foreign Language Multicultural Education Research Laboratory and professor in the Institute of Foreign Languages at Tambov State University, in Russia. His research interests revolve around teaching foreign and second language culture.

Stephanie R. Funderburg-Foreman is senior English language specialist at the U.S. Embassy in Moscow, Russia. She has conducted numerous teacher training workshops on teaching American Studies and EFL throughout Russia.

How Do Teachers Collaborate to Integrate Language and Content?

CHAPTER 15

What Counts as Good Math Instruction for English Language Learners

Kimberly Hunt and Linda Walsleben

Nick uses ¼ cup of vinegar for every 1 cup of olive oil when making salad dressing. Using this recipe, how much vinegar would he need to make salad dressing with 12 cups of olive oil?

- 2½ cups
- 3 cups
- 5¼ cups
- 6 cups

If you're a middle school student in Vermont, in the United States, this is an example of the types of items you would find on the state's annual mathematics assessment. If you're an English language learner, this item represents the depth of math content knowledge you would be expected to learn while also learning English.

How can educators teach English language learners (ELLs) the math skills and knowledge they need while also helping them learn English? This chapter discusses how we, a math specialist and an English as a second language (ESL) specialist, collaboratively developed and taught a math class for middle-level ELLs in which students learned math and language concurrently. First we describe the context of our schooling situation, including the origin of our collaboration. Then we detail how we planned, delivered, and assessed instruction in light of the research on teaching ELLs. Finally, we discuss the outcomes of instruction and our reflections on the experience.

CONTEXT

The number of ELLs in U.S. classrooms is increasing. The U.S. Department of Education reports that whereas total K–12 enrollment increased by 2.59% from 1994 to 2005, the number of limited-English-proficient (LEP) students increased by 60.76% in the same time period (National Clearinghouse for English Language Acquisition and Language Instruction Educational Programs, n.d.). Vermont schools have also experienced increases in ELL enrollment. Refugees and immigrants have resettled in the Burlington area since the early 1980s; many families from Vietnam, Bosnia, Tibet, Russia, Congo, and Somalia now live in Burlington, and their children attend local schools. The Burlington School District has approximately 500 students receiving ELL services. This number represents approximately 13% of the total student population in the district (*Burlington School District Annual Report*, 2007).

With the increasing number of ELLs nationwide, an achievement gap persists. Analyses of national and state assessment data show that ELLs do not perform as well on tests of academic achievement as their non-ELL peers. A recent report using National Assessment of Educational Progress data found that 29% of ELLs tested at or above the basic achievement level in math, compared to 79% of White students (Fry, 2007). In a Government Accountability Office (2006) report, the achievement gap on state math assessments between ELLs and the total school population was reported to be more than 20 percentage points in more than half of the states. Reviews of students' scores on Vermont's annual math content assessment show similar gaps. Researchers cite various reasons for the achievement gap in math between ELLs and non-ELLs, including the impact of students' language backgrounds (Abedi, 2003), the linguistic complexity of the assessments (Abedi & Lord, 2001), the absence of meaningful and appropriate accommodations for test takers (Abedi, Courtney, Mirocha, Leon, & Goldberg, 2005), and testing bias (Solano-Flores & Trumbull, 2003).

The impact of students' language backgrounds on their academic achievement was a concern for us as we examined the education of Vermont's most recent immigrants. Recent refugees to be resettled in Burlington have come from various countries in Africa, including Somalia, Congo, Sudan, and Tanzania. Many of the students lived several years in refugee camps, where they may or may not have attended school. Teachers have found that, in addition to having limited English language proficiency, many students lack basic content knowledge and skills. Not only is language a barrier to accessing the regular curriculum, so is students' lack of basic numeracy skills.

To address students' limited language and numeracy skills, our school's principal asked us if we would coteach a sheltered math class. Students were chosen for this class based on their scores on the WIDA ACCESS for ELLs test, the English language proficiency assessment administered in Vermont, and their score on a math screening instrument developed by Kimberly. Students with composite scores of less than 2.0 on a 6-point scale on the ACCESS test and scores of 25% or less on the math screener were scheduled for the ESL math class.

We had both worked in the school for years but had only had a few short professional conversations with each other. A week before the class began, we met to discuss the scope and content of the class. Linda had worked on math with some of these students in an ESL class the previous year, and she described to Kimberly a lively class full of challenges, both academic and emotional. Students had struggled to be kind to one another and to understand simple concepts such as division.

We left our meeting both energized by the possibilities and nervous about the size of the task that lay before us. We decided that the class content would be organized around the areas of math defined by the grade expectations for the *Vermont Framework of Standards and Learning Opportunities*: numbers and operations, geometry and measurement, functions and algebra, and data and probability (State of Vermont Department of Education, 2008). We would begin with a topic that students hadn't studied at all during the previous year: geometry. This several-hour meeting, weeks before school began, was essential to the success of the collaboration. We openly discussed grading policies, discipline, and math teaching methods.

The scheduling and staffing of this ESL math class required considerable administrator support. The class consisted of approximately a dozen sixth-, seventh-, and eighth-grade students (class enrollment varied as students moved in and out of the district) and met for one mod (45 minutes) every day. An educational assistant was assigned to the class. Because the class was designed to address the learning needs of low-proficiency ELLs by combining the teaching of math with the teaching of the language of math, the teaming of two teachers was key to the implementation of this approach.

CURRICULUM, TASKS, MATERIALS

As we began to work with the students, we could see that, although most were many years behind their peers in math content knowledge and skill, the students were bright, capable, and eager to learn math. This would not be a class that learned just basic skills, but rather one in which instruction focused on developing the deep understanding of mathematical concepts and problem solving that all students deserve to learn (Secada, 1998).

We began with a hands-on unit on geometry. Students first learned the names of various shapes and the words with which to describe and distinguish between the shapes. The following vignette from Kimberly gives an example of how instruction unfolded:

> I began with shapes by showing examples of rectangles [Figure 1] and discussing its properties: "A rectangle has four sides. All of the angles are right angles. A

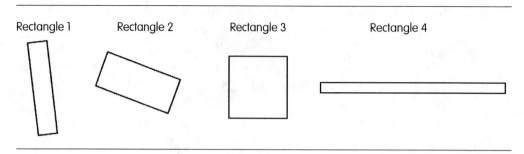

Figure 1. Examples of Rectangles

rectangle has two pairs of parallel sides. These sides have equal length. Here are four rectangles."

"Look at Rectangle 1. It has all the properties of a rectangle." I pointed to the sides. "It has four sides." I pointed to the angles. "It has all right angles." I pointed to the vertical sides and then the horizontal sides. "It has two pairs of parallel sides." I repeated this for each of the rectangles.

Now that students had seen different possibilities I asked them to show us what they knew. "Can you draw a rectangle?"

Linda and I walked around the room to see what students had produced. Their examples [Figure 2] showed so many misconceptions. Student 2 hadn't understood the idea of parallel. Student 3 hadn't understood that sides need to be straight. Most concerning was that Students 1, 4, and 5 hadn't understood that a rectangle must have four sides.

"Oh no," I said and ran back to the overhead. "The sides have to be straight, and there have to be four sides. Let's count the sides of this rectangle. One, two, three, four."

Thinking that I had now made things clear, I asked students to try again, but they continued to draw figures with three sides, curved sides, and unparallel sides.

"Ms. Hunt," Linda called from across the room. "Perhaps we should have a discussion about the language. Let's start with the word *side*."

Linda held up a pocket folder. "One way we use the word *side* is when we open a folder. A teacher might say to you, 'Put this piece of paper on the left side.'"

"Another way we use the word *side*," I added, "is when we talk about a table. Run your hand along the side of the table." I demonstrated with my hand, and students happily joined me.

"But in this case, we are looking at the straight lines. And we're looking at how many sides each shape has." We had students come forward and highlight a side of a rectangle on the overhead.

After class, Linda and I brainstormed all the words we were going to need for this unit and all the meanings each word can have: *straight, curve, line, corner, vertex, parallel, perpendicular, angle, right, right angle.*

This became a regular occurrence and made all the difference in students' learning. What seemed impossible for them to understand one minute became fluid the next. Our room became filled with word walls that helped students understand mathematical concepts.

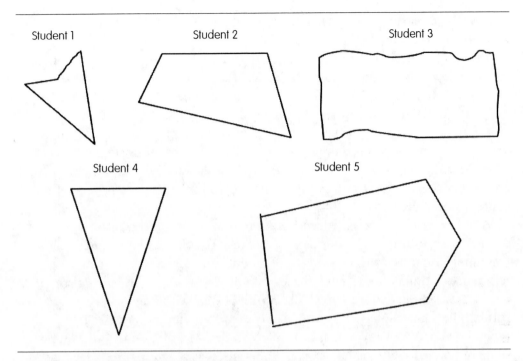

Student 1   Student 2   Student 3

Student 4   Student 5

Figure 2. Student-Produced "Rectangles"

As this vignette illustrates, this primarily physical activity promoted extensive use of and investigation into the language of math. This approach encouraged language acquisition while the focus remained on communicating about the math (Dale & Cuevas, 1995). Not only did student learning begin to improve, student behavior did as well.

Because Vermont is a member of the World-Class Instructional Design and Assessment (WIDA) Consortium, a group of 16 states with common English language proficiency (ELP) standards and a common assessment program, the WIDA standards served as a guide to the language we needed to teach, and could expect from, the ELP Level 1 and Level 2 students in our class. Specifically related to math, WIDA ELP Standard 3 states that "English language learners communicate information, ideas, and concepts necessary for academic success in the content area of mathematics" (WIDA Consortium, 2007, p. RG-10). This broad standard is supported by Model Performance Indicators (MPIs), or examples of tasks a teacher could expect students at the various levels of proficiency and in the four language domains to perform. The language functions or verbs that begin each MPI guided us in designing instruction and teaching the language of math. For example, *draw, match, show, label,* and *point* are typical language functions at ELP Level 1. *Describe, identify, compare,* and *respond to yes/no questions* are common language functions at ELP Level 2. Thus, we designed lessons in which students had to draw a circle, label the sides or vertices of a square, compare a triangle and a rectangle, or respond to the question, "Is it a square or a rectangle"?

Imagine the language students needed to compare shapes: adjectives (e.g., *round, straight, long*), comparative adjectives (e.g., *longer, shorter*), and math-specific vocabulary (e.g., *angle, vertex, side, equal, same, parallel, perpendicular*). Language functions also informed us of what not to expect. Students at ELP Levels 1 and 2 could not be expected to summarize, explain, predict, or interpret—at least not without significant scaffolding—because they simply did not yet have the language to do so. By using the WIDA standards' MPIs, we were better able to plan instruction by anticipating the linguistic challenge that the math content would present.

Another area of the regular curriculum that we spent quite a bit of time on was fractions, or learning about part–whole relationships. Using manipulatives commonly found in math classrooms (e.g., fraction bars, fraction circles, pattern blocks, number lines), students learned the terms *one whole, one-fourth, one-half, one-third, fourths, halves,* and *thirds.* Posters with graphics showing parts of the whole along with vocabulary words were hung on the wall. "Which is bigger, ⅓ or ¼?" we would ask. As many students learning fractions assume, some responded that ¼ is bigger than ⅓ because 4 is bigger than 3. Having the manipulatives before us, which students had just used to construct whole circles or bars from parts or pieces of the whole, enabled students to think deeply about this concept without having or needing a high level of English language proficiency. When one student could answer correctly, this answer was repeated by one of us, repeated in a choral response by the class, and written on the overhead to be copied by students into their notes.

To broaden and deepen students' understanding of fractions, we brought in bags of paper clips, erasers, and game pieces. Students were asked to find one-half, one-third, or one-fourth of the items in the bag. They then moved on to finding two-thirds or three-fourths.

Still, we weren't satisfied with students' understanding. We borrowed a produce scale from a local farmer's market and measured the weight of potatoes, onions, and apples to explore the idea of fractions and mixed numbers in a linear way. By exploring fractions in many different ways, students overcame their language difficulties and grew to have a deep understanding of fractions, their use, and their meaning.

All content areas have language specific to their fields, but mathematics has especially rich examples of academic language and vocabulary that all students must master to be successful in the subject. As we just discussed, students learned vocabulary words for the parts of a whole. They also practiced understanding and producing comparative structures such as *more than* or *bigger than*. We found teaching the syntactic or structural features of the language of math to be just as important as teaching vocabulary. Examples of syntactic features of the mathematics register are comparatives (e.g., *greater than, less than*) and prepositions (e.g., divided *into*, divided *by*, take away *from*; Spanos, Rhodes, Dale, & Crandall, 1988). The following vignette from Kimberly details an instructional exchange in which understanding the meaning of one preposition made all the difference.

> We had studied fractions for several weeks and had been pleased and excited about the progress students had made. One day I had several minutes left, and I wrote on the board, "How much is half of a half?"
>
> I knew this was a challenging question and was prepared to see blank faces when I turned around. Spinning on my heel and facing the class, I was shocked at the sight. Almost every hand in the room was reaching to the ceiling. Bright, proud, shining faces stared back at me.
>
> "What do you think, Hawa?"
>
> "It's a whole," she answered proudly.
>
> "Yeah, a whole," was murmured throughout the room.
>
> I sighed. They were so proud of themselves. And so wrong. I left class exasperated and defeated. Had they learned nothing about fractions?
>
> A quick conversation with Linda lifted my spirits.
>
> "You know they don't understand the word *of*," she pointed out.
>
> "Go on," I replied.
>
> "They thought you were asking about a half and a half," she continued. "That makes a whole."
>
> We began the next mod discussing *of* and *and*. This made a tremendous difference. A few days later, asking a similar fraction question with *of*, I found that more than half of the students got it correct.

A focus on vocabulary became important in the unit on numbers and operations, which required that students practice addition, subtraction, and multiplication word problems. Word problems do not contain the word *add* or *subtract* to tell students what operation is needed; they need to figure this out for themselves.

As students struggled to make meaning of word problems, we drew pictures, talked about vocabulary, and acted out simulations. As vocabulary was discussed, we kept track of important words using word charts that were hung on the wall. We began with easier problems like this one: "I have three apples. You have two apples. How many apples do we have together?" *Together* is an important vocabulary word for ELLs learning to understand word problems, so we put it on our chart as a common word that is seen in addition, subtraction, and multiplication. Later, as students worked on problems more independently, or when they wrote their own word problems, they were able to refer to the word charts we had constructed together.

Once students were able to identify addition, subtraction, multiplication, and division in extremely easy problems, we pushed their thinking again by creating word problems that implied an operation, such as this one:

> There are 18 tables in the cafeteria and eight seats at each table. How many students can sit at one time?

The word *groups* isn't in the problem, but in order to solve the problem, students needed to recognize that the tables formed groups of students. As they moved toward a deeper level of understanding, they moved from incorrectly answering the question as $18 + 8 = 26$ to correctly answering it as $18 \times 8 = 144$. (Alternatively, some students may have chosen to answer the question as $18 + 18 + 18 + 18 + 18 + 18 + 18 + 18 = 144$, which showed growth in their understanding of multiplication but lack of comfort with a multiplication algorithm.)

Interestingly, probably the hardest words to teach students were commonly known words that had a different meaning in math. For example, many lower-proficiency ELLs can give examples of *table*, *left*, and *change*. But are they using these words as native speakers use them in math? Probably not. Students needed to learn that a *table* is something they sit at as well as a graphic on the page with rows and columns. The same was true for *left* ("How many are left?") and *change* ("How much change do you have?" or "How much change do you get back?"). Spanos et al. (1988) cite natural language vocabulary with a different math meaning as one of the lexical items that can confound ELLs learning math.

The year ended with students learning about data and measurement, including measuring time and money. Manipulatives were key in this unit, with students using clocks they made themselves and bags full of real-looking fake bills and coins. As had been done throughout the year, examples or problems typically found at the first- or second-grade level were introduced first. As students mastered the concepts, scaffolded problems from higher grade levels were attempted. Students understood that this was a special math class and were quite motivated to try the math problems introduced as "middle school math." And with support, many students were able to find the right answers.

REFLECTIONS

Collaboration is not always easy. Both people in the collaboration must think carefully about the words they choose when giving advice to each other while at the same time being ready to learn about their own teaching. The following vignette from Kimberly highlights the ups and downs of our collaborative effort.

> As school began, Linda and I were granted some common planning time. Our principal makes sure that people working together have time to discuss and strategize. This strong administrative support is essential to our partnership. For the first few days of class, Linda and I reflected on the learning that had occurred and on the behavior we had seen that needed to change. Open and honest reflection on teaching isn't always easy, but it proved to be the single most important element of our collaboration.
>
> I had been the one up in front of the class giving directions for the majority of the time, and Linda would watch and make notes. We both worked with students individually. At our meetings, Linda would tell me I wasn't focusing enough on language for students to learn. At first I became defensive, but with time Linda opened my eyes to what she was saying using both of us as an example.

One day she plopped herself down next to me in the library and said, "I wish you were just more structured." Then she laughed. "We're both just so big-picture, but they need someone who gives them every little detail."

I wasn't sure, but I began to delve into assessing what students were learning, and then I began to understand. That's when I saw the kinds of mistakes students were making. They were not retaining the understanding of geometry concepts that I wanted them to. They confused squares with circles and triangles with rectangles and made many other mistakes, too.

By the end of the second week, I felt defeated. I was supposed to be a mathematics teaching coach, and my own class seemed to be miserably failing. How was I ever going to help other teachers in the building?

At that moment, I drew a deep breath and resolved to make it better.

I found Linda in the school library. "All right. Tell me about this thing with language."

Linda began taking notes every day, and we discussed them for 15 minutes after each class. She began to talk about the vocabulary during class. Through these conversations, we developed the methods of using word walls and stopping in the middle of math to discuss language.

I became more open to the idea of having my teaching critiqued, so Linda taped an entire class and wrote a transcript for me to analyze. I could see all the language I used that could be difficult for students.

Then Linda taped herself teaching and wrote a transcript of that. She compared the two transcripts and brought her results to one of our meetings.

"I don't ask questions the way you do."

"Oh?" I said.

"It just hit me, sitting there looking at the transcripts that you approach every problem as if it's problem solving. It's all thinking about the meaning of the math and making it make sense. That's what gets kids to the finish line."

"Yes," I said and smiled. And then I realized we were learning from each other. Linda now understood the importance of deep conceptual understanding, and I now had knowledge about the importance of language.

And now the students were really learning. Meeting with each other after class became fun and meaningful. We'd grab the markers and a huge sheet of paper, excited to think about the words we would discuss before the next unit began. The growth in students' learning really pushed us forward. By the end of the year, we decided that many of the students should try taking a mainstream math class.

Collaboration isn't always the easiest approach, but it can be the most effective.

Few middle schools are prepared to teach adolescents who are coming to school for the first time in their lives, learning in a new language and in another culture. This math class, however, succeeded in meeting the needs of such students. As teachers, we had significant time to collaborate and reflect on what happened in class every day.

There is no doubt that the needs of the students were great. We were offering a challenging curriculum in which students were expected to focus on instruction and participate in activities. So we needed two teachers and an educational assistant working in the class to support the struggling students and challenge the successful ones.

We can see that the students made considerable progress, but they have a long way yet to go. It will be a few years before what they learned in our class can be demonstrated on the state mathematics assessment. With students starting so many years behind their peers, they will need to make more than 1 year's progress in a year.

So we forge on together, the math department and the ESL teachers. Today, Kimberly teaches the class with the school ESL teacher; the principal has assigned this class as one of her regular teaching duties. And several ELLs have had success in mainstream math classes with the ESL math class as an additional support. We continue to learn from each other as we continue to watch this population of students learn and grow.

[*Authors' Note: At the time of publication, students in poverty at our school have met the requirements for annual yearly progress in the area of mathematics on the statewide assessment for the first time. Included in this group are all of the students who were originally in our ESL math class 2 years ago, which shows their remarkable growth in both mathematics and academic English.*]

Kimberly Hunt has taught mathematics in Grades 6–12 for the past 16 years in Vermont and holds a degree in secondary education mathematics from the University of Vermont. She is currently a mathematics coach at a middle school in Burlington, Vermont, in the United States. Recently, she won the Northern New England chapter of TESOL's Mainstream Teacher Award for her work with recently arrived refugees from Africa.

Linda Walsleben has taught ESL in K–12 schools for more than 20 years in Vermont and beyond. She has worked as an ESL content specialist and currently serves as the English language learner program coordinator for the Burlington (Vermont) School District, in the United States. She is also a doctoral student in the Education Leadership and Policy Studies Program at the University of Vermont.

CHAPTER 16

Sustained Content-Based Academic English Teaching Through Paired English and Philosophy Courses

Jerry Spring

Freshman English for academic purposes (EAP) courses are a clearly accepted feature of higher education in both English as a second language (ESL) and English as a foreign language (EFL) contexts. Less clear is whether and how such support should continue into the sophomore year and beyond. In this chapter, I share the experience of developing a sophomore EAP course in one EFL context (a private English-medium university in Turkey) to argue that this can be a worthwhile way to extend EAP support beyond the first year of college. I hope to show that it was the particular approach adopted that made this project successful.

The sophomore support works as follows: Students attend paired classes, one an EAP course and one a challenging course on political and social philosophy. The instructors for each class work together closely, using the same unabridged philosophy texts as teaching material so that the EAP course provides tailored support for the philosophy course. At the same time, the EAP course aims to develop students' general EAP skills beyond the freshman level. Its objectives include reading, thinking critically, and speaking about authentic academic texts and producing researched academic essays and term papers.

This curricular model can be described as a *sustained semiadjunct content-based instructional approach*: sustained because the course includes a limited and coherent set of topics investigated through an appropriate set of texts; adjunct because one of the EAP course's main roles is to support learning in the philosophy course; semiadjunct because the EAP course has its own objectives beyond supporting the philosophy course; and content-based because the course is organized around philosophy topics and texts, rather than linguistic objectives.

I was involved in this project in various ways: as teacher, course designer, course coordinator, and evaluator. This chapter draws on interviews I conducted with both sets of instructors and a number of students as part of an evaluation of the project. From my involvement, I see four main lessons to help colleagues who are considering how to extend EAP support further into their institutions. First, by presenting sophomore students with a new, significantly more difficult linguistic and intellectual challenge, it is possible to motivate them to develop their EAP skills further. Second, through closely linking an EAP course to an academic content course, it is possible to gain synergistic benefits in both courses. Third, these synergistic effects can benefit instructors and students alike as two rather different pedagogical cultures interact to produce new solutions to teaching and learning problems. Fourth, this project highlights important issues for content-based instruction regarding the development of academic thinking skills and academic English language skills.

CONTEXT

Origins of the Project

Originally, the university provided two forms of language support:

- preparatory EFL courses focusing on general as well as academic language skills for new students whose English language proficiency was insufficient to begin their academic studies

- compulsory EAP courses focusing on academic English language and thinking skills for all freshman students

Later, the university introduced a writing center, and some departments requested EAP tutorial support for sophomores preparing term papers. Later still, the university became aware that 4 years of English-medium education was not developing students' language as much as expected. In response, sophomore EAP courses were proposed, initially for students from the Faculty of Economic, Administrative, and Social Sciences. As part of a wider project to broaden these students' intellectual background knowledge and thinking skills, the courses were also required to expose students to unabridged seminal texts from the history of Western social and political philosophy.

Reasons for Pessimism . . .

The proposal appeared to face several challenges. First, the students were not majoring in philosophy, so they might resent devoting a significant proportion of their courses to philosophy. Second, they might have a sense of already having "done" EAP in freshman courses and thus resent doing the same thing yet again. Third, even if students accepted the need to study philosophy and improve in EAP, they might resent teachers' imposing long, difficult, antiquated texts as core course material. Finally, from a broader educational perspective, the new course might raise tensions in relation to surface and deep approaches to learning (Ramsden, 1992).

A surface approach to learning involves unreflectively memorizing material simply to meet course requirements without intrinsic interest in learning. Memorized material remains poorly integrated with other knowledge and is soon forgotten. A deep approach involves learning with intrinsic interest to understand and integrate new material with existing knowledge. Researchers see these approaches primarily as responses to current and previous learning environments (i.e., changeable) rather than traits in students (Trigwell, Prosser, & Waterhouse, 1999). Although memorization has its place in learning, the general view behind this research is that higher education should aim to encourage a deep approach.

The first possible tension arises from the fact that many Turkish students manage to reach university by adopting a surface approach to studying. Some university courses then reinforce this by continuing to reward rote memorization of course material. The new courses, however, would be designed to reward a deep approach, which might well be resented by those previously successful surface students. The second possible tension was that if the intellectual and linguistic difficulty of the course texts was too great, it could force many students toward a surface approach simply as a means of academic survival, which would contradict the project's aim of encouraging a deep approach to learning. In short, the courses would need to strike a careful balance in terms of approach to learning.

. . . and Optimism

At the same time, we hoped that the students' freshman EAP experiences might act as a buffer against these challenges. Over the past decade, the curricular approach of the university's two freshman courses has radically changed. Previously organized around teaching a sequence of itemized EAP objectives (e.g., skimming and scanning, topic and supporting sentences), the courses have moved toward sustained content-based instruction (SCBI; see Pally, 2000). Here, *sustained* means that each instructor's course follows one distinct relatively specific theme (e.g., crime and punishment, theatre of the absurd, social causes of health and illness), using texts from a variety of relevant academic disciplines and genres.

Now, although students achieve many of the same objectives as before, each course is structured around content (topics and texts). Instructors individually base course texts and tasks around the academic investigation of a single theme of their choosing. Students then choose their EAP class according to which theme they find most interesting. Through the academic exploration of this content, each instructor helps students meet common freshman EAP objectives through a mix of individual and common tasks and assessments. The objectives focus most on academic reading and writing skills, academic thinking and argumentation skills, and vocabulary development. Instructors meet regularly to standardize the operationalization and assessment of these common objectives, despite the unique thematic focus of each instructor's course.

The effect of these curricular developments has been mostly positive. The thematic approach has increased student interest and motivation, which has in turn allowed instructors to increase the intellectual and linguistic difficulty of texts and tasks, and raise expectations of student learning. Surprisingly, perhaps, these courses seem to improve students' academic language learning by teaching it less explicitly.

EAP writing skills have been particularly improved. The previous curriculum encouraged a formulaic approach to essay writing through explicit teaching and testing of rhetorical forms (e.g., cause-effect, compare-contrast). Faced with a new task, students tended to ask, "What type of essay is this?" If a task didn't follow a formula, some students tried to distort it in order to fit. SCBI moves instructors away from these formulae toward setting, within broad parameters, whatever tasks emerge naturally out of course readings and discussions. Students then have to solve the writing problem posed by this unique task.

In short, although there were some reasons to be pessimistic about the project's feasibility, the curricular developments in the freshman EAP program suggested reasons for optimism. In addition, whatever the challenges, the project needed to succeed because, like any country, Turkey needs its universities to develop well-read critical thinkers. The question for us was how best to contribute to achieving this goal through the design and implementation of the sophomore project.

CURRICULUM, TASKS, MATERIALS

Organizing a Paired Course Curriculum

Students attend two 3-hour courses: one on the history of social and political thought, taught by Philosophy Department instructors; the other an advanced EAP course, taught by selected instructors from the School of English. Exactly the same group of students meets in any pair of philosophy and English classes so that they can immediately and precisely apply their learning from one course to the other. Both courses draw from a common list of set texts, including Plato's (1992) *The Republic*, Hobbes's (1986) *Leviathan*, Kant's (1998) *Groundwork of the Metaphysics of Morals*, and Mill's (1978) *On Liberty*, and instructors reach agreement on how to use them to meet each course's distinct objectives. The university aims to cap class sizes at 20 students in order to foster a seminar- rather than lecture-based pedagogy in the philosophy course and to allow both sets of instructors to give students intensive support.

As mentioned earlier, an important feature is that the EAP course is not merely an adjunct of the academic course, but is rather semiadjunct, that is, although supporting the philosophy course is an important part of the EAP course, its syllabus also includes independent EAP objectives to raise students' general EAP capabilities beyond the freshman level. These include advanced academic reading and writing skills, and academic presentation and discussion skills. The managers of the project stressed this aspect of the relationship from the outset to ensure that both sets of instructors would accept the courses' equal educational status.

A Flexible Approach to Assessment

Each set of instructors agrees to design and weight assessment tasks within broad parameters, including essays, presentations and peer teaching, and discussions. The EAP instructors also design other language-focused assessments (e.g., reading comprehensions, vocabulary logs, error correction logs, argument summarizations). Instructors choose tasks according to their perception of students' needs and the priorities of their EAP-philosophy pairing. There is, therefore, a relatively high level of flexibility in the assessment system. This approach is appropriate because of the individuality of the course pairings. As in the freshman program, EAP instructors meet regularly to standardize essay marking according to common criteria and monitor and exchange ideas about essay prompts. The philosophy instructors have also moved toward standardizing marking, but rather less than their EAP colleagues. Some essay assessments are done in class (at least for the first draft), but neither course currently includes formal assessments in the shape of midterm or final exams. Rather, assessed tasks form part of the everyday fabric of each course, as class work or homework, which reflects our attempt to encourage a deep approach to learning. Students are not expected to memorize large chunks of material simply to regurgitate it in formal exams (and then forget it). Instead, as an integral component of exploring course topics, assessment tasks push students to develop their philosophical reasoning and academic language skills.

Tailored Tasks and Activities

EAP instructors are constrained by the common course objectives, but the tasks and activities they choose vary according to several factors: their own experience with the course and the texts, the particular challenges of various texts, their beliefs about how best to promote EAP learning, and the reading requirements of different philosophy instructors.

When the project started, guiding students through the set texts was quite challenging, particularly for instructors lacking a philosophy background, so it helped to organize lessons around reading comprehension questions (both for understanding and for responding to texts). Preparing questions forced instructors to study and annotate texts carefully and to know answers to questions beforehand. In addition, teaching became less threatening because students were working together through the questions, turning the focus away from the instructors. As instructors developed familiarity with the texts and confidence in helping students, preprepared comprehension questions became less important (though still useful). Instead, instructors could ask students to read, and then work through questions, with more flexibility and spontaneity, depending on how understanding and discussion developed. Instructors also became sufficiently familiar with the material to jump between various sections of a particular text (or between texts and authors) in order to help students make useful comparisons. However, the combination of experience and confidence carries the danger that EAP instructors become amateur philosophers, forgetting the need to keep EAP objectives in mind while teaching.

Each text presents particular problems that change the focus of tasks and activities. With Plato's (2002) dialogical writing, students need to learn to extract the steps in his argument from what is supposedly a conversation. With Hobbes (1986), they need help with antiquated spelling and punctuation. With Locke (Wooten, 1993) and Mill (1978), long complex sentences are one of the main challenges. With Kant (1998), incredibly dense argumentation needs to be unpacked.

Depending on the demands of a text and on each instructor's beliefs about EAP teaching, reading tasks vary in terms of how implicitly or explicitly they focus on EAP skills. For example, questions can focus directly on meaning, or they can directly ask students to find topic sentences (at least to the extent that philosophical writing uses these). Tasks vary also according to how much the philosophy instructor wants students to read. For example, tasks that are appropriate when students read a short extract will be unsuitable when instructors ask them to read a whole book.

A Variety of Collaborations

A crucial feature of the project is that, although instructors on each course share a common curriculum, they have freedom to adapt and experiment. This provides the flexibility needed to search for effective solutions to varied teaching challenges. The result has been a wide spectrum of collaborations, as I discovered through my evaluation interviews as well as my own teaching experiences.

At one (unfortunate) extreme, coordination has occasionally remained minimal—usually because the philosophy instructor maintains a traditional lecture-based approach, coupled with assessment that rewards basic knowledge of the texts. This undermines the EAP instructor, whose course appears pointless: If students simply listen to lectures rather than "do" philosophy, they understandably see little point in struggling through difficult tasks and activities in the EAP course.

Near the other extreme, EAP instructors participate in the philosophy classes to gain a closer understanding of what students are doing philosophically and how effective the EAP preparation has been. Some pairings have become team teachers, appearing together in most classes and contributing their particular expertise to supporting the students. For example, as the class discusses a text, the EAP instructor notices what hinders students' understanding linguistically while the philosophy instructor notices inaccurate text deconstruction or poor philosophical reasoning. Sometimes the two instructors disagree over the meaning of the text. This may be because the EAP instructor's interpretation, like the students', needs correction, which helps students realize that their EAP instructor is also an apprentice philosopher and open to criticism and learning. Alternatively, it may be because there is no one correct interpretation of the text. For Turkish students, who are often used to rather hierarchical student–teacher relations, these are both valuable experiences.

At this extreme, the borderlines between the two courses become almost invisible except in assessment. Although some students find this rather disconcerting, at least initially, they generally come to appreciate the intensity of learning that is possible through such collaborative teaching.

Most of the instructional pairings, however, lie toward the middle of the spectrum, where students prepare particular sections of text in each EAP class for the following philosophy class or the EAP course covers further text to complement the philosophy instructor's focus. Students may also first write for the EAP instructor and then extend that writing for the philosophy instructor (although students sometimes find the differing feedback of the two instructors confusing).

REFLECTIONS

Lesson 1: We Can Develop EAP Skills Beyond the Freshman Year

It is possible to raise students' academic English proficiency beyond the freshman level. Many students report a feeling of great achievement and satisfaction. They know that they have been doing something very difficult, and they are proud of this. Encouragingly, many students want more of this kind of learning, confirming research that suitable conditions can foster a deep approach to learning (Kember, 2004; Kember & Leung, 2006).

Regarding linguistic capabilities, students acquire valuable skills for parsing complex sentences and building mental models of complex arguments. Vocabulary knowledge develops in various ways. Through reading texts of contrasting eras and styles, students meet, and to some extent learn, a new range of formal vocabulary. Through writing, they expand their general academic and technical vocabulary. Through speaking, given sufficient preparatory support, many students learn to teach their peers quite effectively through presentations and discussions. In one version of the EAP course, with minimal instructor involvement, student groups lead 70- to 90-minute seminars based around essay prompts. Students then write in-class essays, with their success largely dependent on the quality of the preceding peer teaching and discussions.

Regarding thinking skills, students learn to analyze and criticize arguments with greater care and accuracy. One core activity—identifying a claim (conclusion) together with the chain of premises leading to it—has proved very valuable. By learning to work out argument structures, students are in a much better position to critique them (whether they belong to a fellow student, an instructor, a Turkish public figure, or a famous philosopher). In writing tasks, students learn to analyze complex essay prompts to prepare thoughtfully organized responses. Such essay tasks also drive them to develop more sophisticated and accurate use of ideas from reading texts.

Lesson 2: Paired Courses Have Synergistic Benefits for Students

Basing an advanced academic English course on philosophy (or, more exactly, philosophizing) has an unexpected benefit. The philosophy course's explicit focus on argumentation rather than factual knowledge switches many students' approach to learning compared to their other courses. From observing philosophy classes, I have learned that they work best when students become "apprentice intellectuals" whose views (even if unsound) are taken seriously by the philosophy instructor. This pretentiousness (in a positive sense) of the philosophy course helps the EAP instructor motivate students to struggle to improve their linguistic capabilities, across the four skills, in order to be part of this intellectual apprenticeship.

Students as well as philosophy instructors consistently report how the philosophizing can only succeed because of the EAP course. If the academic English class prepares students' reading well, then the philosophy instructor can proceed immediately to discussion. The widened vocabulary and heightened confidence that students develop in the academic English class allows them to benefit from a discussion rather than lecture format in the philosophy class. If students receive detailed support and feedback on essay preparation in the EAP class, they can meet the challenge of intellectually difficult philosophy essay tasks.

These synergistic benefits for students only occur, however, if instructors align their aims and approaches. As mentioned earlier, students are naturally more willing to struggle with difficult texts in academic English classes if they can immediately apply that learning in philosophy classes that also require close reading and discussion. Conversely, if they can remain passive in the philosophy classes and pass assessments without properly understanding the texts, then they see the challenge of the EAP course as unnecessary and they learn less.

Lesson 3: Paired Courses Have Synergistic Benefits for Instructors

This synergy does not only benefit students, though. By bringing together two rather different academic tribes (Becher, 1989), the project has valuable effects on both sets of instructors that feed back into enhanced teaching and learning. For all instructors, it is a chance to experiment with a wide range of solutions (and hear about other experiments) to the learning problems posed by the courses.

The interviews I conducted reveal that, in tandem with pushing students toward a deep approach to learning, the project has moved instructors away from what Ramsden (1992) terms *theory 1* teaching, whereby teaching is considered as a relatively straightforward and predictable transmission of knowledge from expert to nonexpert. Instead, teachers move to *theory 2* teaching, a "supervision process" of creating activities for students to learn, rather than simply engaging in knowledge transmission, or even *theory 3*, "a notion of teaching as a speculative and reflexive activity" (p. 115) whereby instructors can only hope to create the conditions within which students learn.

For the philosophy instructors, the project exposes them to a different approach to designing and implementing courses. They have to work with EAP instructors who want to define explicit objectives and course outlines, clearly define assessment tasks, and calibrate assessment criteria through regular standardization sessions. While the philosophy courses have not generally reached the same level of specification as the EAP courses, philosophy instructors report that they are now more rigorous in thinking about course design, teaching, and assessment. The EAP instructors have helped raise awareness in their partners about how, for linguistic reasons, students sometimes fail to read texts, give presentations, or write essays to the level expected. As a result, rather than frustratedly blaming students for their failings (symptomatic of a theory 1 teaching approach), philosophy instructors have more understanding of how to support students linguistically, or when to call for academic English support.

The EAP instructors have also benefited greatly. Interaction with philosophy instructors has pushed them to significantly develop their own skills in understanding, analyzing, and critiquing texts, which is essential for teaching and assessing the sophomore students. The EAP instructors' conceptions of essay writing are now more sophisticated, particularly regarding philosophical presentation and criticism of arguments. Interestingly, when these EAP instructors interact with colleagues in other EAP departments (who have not been involved in the sophomore project), it is clear that their views have noticeably changed. For example, they no longer conceptualize academic writing in terms of the simple rhetorical patterns (e.g., compare-contrast, cause-effect) that are still dominant in EAP courses. This experience has also fed back into the way the sophomore project instructors approach their freshman courses, particularly in terms of being more demanding of sound argument in student thinking, discussion, and essay writing.

Caveats

Before turning to the final lesson of the project, I want to list three caveats regarding the discussion so far. First, the sophomore courses do not benefit all students. Although some students improve enormously and become keen philosophers, and others make solid gains in both courses, a significant minority find the courses too challenging and only meet course requirements with great difficulty. More needs to be done to support these students, but their difficulties are also related to the problem that some students attempt to get through university with a surface approach. Although this strategy sometimes works, it leaves students floundering when courses (like the two in this project) demand a deep approach. Considering that such students have managed to complete every previous stage of their educational career through a surface approach, it is easy to imagine their helplessness and frustration when they find that the rules of the learning game have fundamentally changed.

A second caveat concerns instructor readiness. Not all the philosophy instructors are willing to adopt the project's pedagogy. When this happens, collaboration cannot work properly and students experience two disjointed courses. Some EAP instructors struggle with the difficulty of the texts and philosophical discussion and writing. For this project, instructors need relatively high general academic abilities and thinking skills, plus an ability to apply EAP pedagogy flexibly. Those involved have all had extensive experience of designing CBI freshman courses, which they have been able to apply to the sophomore project.

A third caveat is that a paired course design will be unlikely to work well unless the two groups of instructors can maintain a respectful and honest working relationship. In this project, primarily due to the way the equal status of both courses and instructors was emphasized at the outset, coupled with effective leadership and team working skills, the two groups have generally worked well together and there has been very little friction between teaching partners.

Lesson 4: There Are Two Issues for EAP Teaching

The final lesson of this project concerns two important issues in academic English teaching. The first relates to developing academic thinking skills and connects to a wider educational debate between generalists and "specificists" about the extent to which thinking skills learned in one course can be transferred to different contexts (e.g., Atkinson, 1997; Davies, 2006; Donald, 2002; Moore, 2004).

EAP teachers presumably want students to transfer the thinking skills learned in their classes to new situations. A question for SCBI, then, is, how transferable are the thinking skills students learn? It could be that the more the students study a subject in depth, the more specific and untransferable their thinking skills may become. For example, a great deal of critical thinking in this project revolves around first precisely identifying a philosophical argument's explicit and implicit steps and then evaluating them. These are rather specific skills, raising the question of whether students can generalize or adapt them to other situations within and beyond academia.

This suggests that perhaps we as educators need to consider more precisely what we mean by *sustained*. Does, or should, it refer to both the course topic and the academic discipline through which it is explored, or to only one or the other? The sophomore project is sustained in both topic and discipline, and we should be aware that, if the specificists are correct, this may limit the transferability of the thinking skills learned in the course.

The second issue concerns how best to help students develop academic English writing skills. Currently, a dominant approach to academic writing, despite its weaknesses (Davidson & Spring, 2008; Raimes, 1991), is to teach in terms of rhetorical forms (e.g., compare-contrast, cause-effect). However, this can encourage formulaic writing in several ways. It can lead instructors to create essay tasks in terms of these forms, rather than in terms of issues raised authentically by reading texts. It can also allow students to believe that simple essay templates (rhetorical forms) exist, into which you drop your ideas for the current writing. I think it is noteworthy that advice on philosophical writing written by philosophers makes no mention of such rhetorical forms (e.g., Fishman, 1989; Martinich, 1996).

The experience of instructors in the sophomore project is that this formulaic approach to academic writing (which they have experienced in other EAP courses) is seriously misguided. Instead, a problem-solving approach is needed, that is, instructors should derive essay tasks from course content, according to the academic problems raised by the texts (e.g., asking: What is wrong with Kant's argument in these pages?) without any regard to rhetorical form (e.g., not asking: Shall I give the students a problem-solution essay question?). The essay task should be a relatively distinctive problem for students to solve through their written response, such that they have to analyze and then solve it by flexibly applying relevant EAP skills. What they shouldn't (can't) do is distort the task so that it matches some rhetorical form.

Although this may make the learning task harder, or at least more ambiguous, it gives students the invaluable opportunity to develop the necessary analytical skills and the ability to select among them. However, they can do this only through repeated exposure to a range of different writing problems that cannot be solved by filling in the slots in a rhetorical template. This is not to argue that students do not need, for example, the compositional skill of comparing and contrasting, but rather that students learn something much more powerful when the need to compare and contrast is disguised within an essay prompt for them to discover through thoughtful analysis.

A further benefit of this approach to academic writing is that students are not making meaning artificially, whereby an activity is merely a way to practice some rhetorical form or writing skill that has been imposed on the task. Rather, meaning is authentic because the writing's primary focus is on making genuine arguments (arguments for their own sake), whatever rhetorical forms might be required. The sophomore project suggests that this content-based framework works even better when it is sustained. By following a coherent (if twisting) intellectual path throughout a course, rather than jumping between relatively disconnected topics or course objectives, students develop a more motivating sense of momentum and background knowledge to help them struggle with hard texts and arguments in their writing.

This problem-solving approach certainly creates challenges for instructors as well as students. Instructors must be able to diagnose the complex linguistic needs of students as they arise, often unpredictably, during individual tasks. It simply isn't possible to walk students through a tidily prearranged list of EAP skills and rhetorical forms. Students may experience frustration, particularly in writing, as instructors force them to deal metacognitively with each task as a unique problem, identifying new writing strategies (and thoughtfully adapting existing strategies). However, I believe it does students a great disservice to let them think there are easy solutions by, for example, choosing texts to neatly illustrate supposed rhetorical structures or choosing writing tasks to neatly fit templates of essay organization. The great beauty of a sustained content-based approach, at least in our experience with the sophomore project, is its power to create authentic and unpredictable EAP problems for students to solve. If, from repeated experiences of this nature, students develop a flexible ability to analyze problems, together with a range of skills and knowledge (whether learned explicitly or implicitly), then surely this approach is worthwhile.

ACKNOWLEDGMENTS

I would like to acknowledge the contributions of the colleagues and students who have helped make a success of the EAP philosophy course.

Jerry Spring has been working in university-level EAP teaching for more than 17 years as a teacher, curriculum and testing developer, teacher trainer, and manager. For most of this time, he worked in Ankara, Turkey. More recently he has been working in Dubai, in the United Arab Emirates.

CHAPTER 17

Motivating Students to Develop Their English Literacy Skills Through Science

Eilidh Hamilton

> My students are so much more interested in writing now that it has a real communicative purpose; they actually look forward to editing their work knowing it will be read by a student in the United Kingdom. (Fatima, secondary school teacher, Sana'a, Yemen)

Secondary school graduates in Yemen need a functional level of English across all of the four skills to access good opportunities for work or tertiary studies. However, many Yemeni students experience real difficulties with English literacy, which has a negative impact on their motivation. In a pilot project, I explored the use of content-based language learning to see if it could increase their engagement and deliver better results.

Children naturally engage with their environment and make observations based on their experiences in life. Using content from the world around young learners can give real purpose to literacy tasks in class and be more motivating than dealing solely with textbooks. Many of the published materials available to students in Yemen are quite Eurocentric and far from the students' experience of the world. Using language for a purpose needs to become the goal, rather than practising structures taught in the previous lesson. This occurs when teachers focus on providing the language needed to express specific ideas generated by the content. Learners' determination to share their thoughts and knowledge, in this case with a partner school in another country, helps motivate them to overcome difficulties with their writing skills.

In this chapter, I describe the context for my work in Yemen, outline lessons learned from my experience of integrating content into language learning, and show how those insights were implemented through a teacher training project. Finally, I hope to show how relevant content-based language learning can be to any teaching context and what positive benefits it offers to teachers and students.

CONTEXT

Traditional Education in Yemen

Yemen is a poor country that sits at 140th on the Human Development Index (United Nations Development Programme, n.d.). More than 40% of the population is under the age of 15, and life expectancy is quite low (Assaad & Roudi-Fahimi, 2007; United Nations Development Programme, n.d.). Many schools have especially challenging teaching circumstances. Class sizes of 80–120 students are common, and resources are limited. Rural schools lack electricity, and even in urban areas there is little technology. Only 65% of children in Yemen attend school, and of those, only slightly more than half finish basic primary education (at approximately age 11), with the main dropout year being Grade 3 (age 7 or 8), which means that less than 40% of Yemeni children complete primary education (World Bank, 2008). Currently, English language study begins in Grade 7, so very few children have the opportunity to gain this skill. However, reforms in the education system (including a British government–funded pilot project for introducing English in Grade 4) may improve access to English over the next 5 years.

Yemen's current need for English language instruction is exceptionally high. English language proficiency is the one skill that can quadruple a salary, and there is great demand for providing school graduates with a good level of instruction in the language.

As the English manager for the British Council in Yemen, my remit was to work with state school English teachers, providing training and workshops in collaboration with the Ministry of Education and Vocational Education to update teachers' methodology and give them ideas about how to encourage students to develop their level of English. Early discussions showed that there was great demand for cross-curricular studies because students, whether going into vocational education, tertiary sector studies, or the workplace, needed English and teachers found it difficult to develop English for specific purposes (ESP) materials that would help them with this. A science workshop by visiting consultants Keith Kelly and Lida Schoen (see *CLIL in Yemen*, n.d.) was extremely popular because it highlighted the possible integration of content and language in the classroom, and teachers requested more training in this approach.

Arabic-Speaking Learners of English

Native Arabic speakers often struggle with literacy issues in English, which can be explained in part by the different script, the fact that spoken dialects often differ greatly from the written form of the language, and the fact that in many Middle Eastern countries cultural traditions have valued oral storytelling over communicating through the written word. Another contributing factor may be traditional methods of teaching and decontextualised materials. The content and presentation of lessons have not been sufficiently engaging to motivate learners to work on their literacy skills; accuracy has traditionally been valued over fluency, and frequently there has not been any real-world application to writing tasks.

Background on Content and Language Integrated Learning

In previous teaching contexts, I saw the success of a focus on integrating other subjects into English classes, with teachers of young learners becoming interested in what we called *topic- and content-based learning.* I observed English language classes on a range of subjects, from geographical information about Mount Everest to looking at gravity in space. These lessons went beyond simple project work. The mental focus of the teachers had shifted; they wanted to communicate the content just as much as develop the language required to explore the subject, which had a positive effect on students' language learning motivation. Students' desire to express their ideas and ask questions about the content meant they sought more complex and sophisticated language in order to express themselves better.

This drew my attention to content and language integrated learning (CLIL), a term used to describe a range of ways in which language and subject content are united within the learning experience. For example, learners may be gaining geographical knowledge of Mount Everest, but they are also learning that content through English in an English language classroom. In a bilingual setting, this might be done by the main classroom teacher, but in my teaching contexts the content has been introduced in the English (i.e., foreign language) classes rather than vice versa. In this chapter, I use CLIL as shorthand to mean using content to drive the need for communication and provide the language required to complete a task effectively, rather than through a planned scheme of work.

CLIL in Yemen

Currently there is a project in Yemen, funded by the Dutch government, to reform the school science curriculum. This will radically change the breadth and scope of the content covered and necessitate a more practical and interactive teaching methodology, with students taking more responsibility for research and discovery. In preparation for this forthcoming change, some of the science teachers I met in Sana'a were particularly interested in finding out more about both *Science Across the World* (*SAW*; bit10, 2003; introduced in the workshop by Kelly and Schoen) and an integrated approach to content and language learning in order to enable students to use English to access this international project. *SAW* enables schools in different countries to work collaboratively on a science project by conducting research, completing an exchange form, and then reporting back to their class on the exchange forms received from schools around the world. The topics available through the *SAW* web site are designed to cover issues that most schools would, to a greater or lesser extent, have in their science curriculum, such as health and lifestyle choices, environmental issues, and genetics. Although there is an option to exchange in other languages, including Arabic, it was felt that using English would be a great opportunity to develop Yemeni students' language skills and give more options for exchanging ideas.

I consulted with the Ministry of Education's curriculum and teacher training departments, and they gave permission to conduct an experimental series of workshops introducing this approach to a small number of secondary school science and English teachers. Results and feedback would then be evaluated to see what potential the approach might have for Yemen on a broader scale.

When the project was introduced to the Yemeni English teachers, they had two main areas of concern. First, they wondered how they would balance this work of supporting subject teachers with the constraints of the state-produced syllabi for English, especially given the end-of-year exams. So we discussed the possibility of achieving the same language objectives through different approaches. Second, the teachers felt there was a need to brief their supervisors so they would understand and support the work being done, and I agreed to arrange this. The teachers were also keen to involve their colleagues from other departments in order to liaise over topics and gain better understanding of the content areas. In terms of benefit, they felt an integrated approach to teaching content and language would give them greater rapport with students because it would generate real interest in a relevant subject and they would experience real communication in the English classroom.

For the pilot, I identified a number of schools that were already involved with a British Council school links project. At these schools, the head teachers were familiar with and supportive of experimental projects, and all teachers had access to a computer with an Internet connection, making it easier to administer the *SAW* project (although exchange forms can be sent by post or fax when necessary). Many of the teachers from these schools had also attended the workshop with Kelly and Schoen, so were already interested in exploring a topic through *SAW*.

CURRICULUM, TASKS, MATERIALS

Teacher Competencies for Implementing CLIL

In preparing the teachers for this approach to language learning—their first CLIL experience—I identified areas of teaching competence that the English teachers would need to develop in order to work alongside the science teachers and support them in getting involved in the *SAW* project.

- the ability to be more flexible and deal with language as it is generated, rather than a "Today we're going to learn the present perfect" approach (Many English language teaching books stipulate a language level prerequisite before presenting a particular grammatical point, so introducing language as it is required by the learners can be quite a radical request.)

- confidence in reformulating students' language, because there is no teachers' book to help

- skills in drawing out language from texts and recognising useful patterns for students to work with

- awareness of genre in the target subject, such as discourse markers and standard organisation of a science report

- willingness to move away from a red-pen mentality and create space for students to communicate without fear of immediate correction

- willingness and ability to collaborate with colleagues in other departments (This is essential to make sure the content work is relevant and builds on the subject curriculum.)

We discussed and worked on developing these skills through workshops and team planning. None of these came easily at the beginning, but the teachers recognised they would be more successful with time.

Teacher Training Program

Initially I held three sessions just for the English teachers, looking at these areas of teaching competence and building a foundation for the work. They then chose a science colleague from their school with whom they felt they would be able to work. When the English teachers came to the next workshop, they were asked to select a science topic from the *SAW* web site that they wanted to work on together and that they felt would be accessible and relevant to students. Topics selected included domestic waste, drinking water, and global warming. The teachers then discussed the topic together to help them generate language that students might need to complete related tasks in English. This was the most time-consuming stage the first time they did it because they were not sure what content words their lower secondary school students (ages 12–16) might already know in English.

How Language Was Taught and Assessed

Once the teachers had identified key language, vocabulary, and structures, the next step was to implement it with students. For the initial classes, most of the teachers team-taught: The English teacher introduced the topic and some of the key vocabulary, and the science teacher took over, explaining the task in students' native language. For example, on the topic of domestic waste, students had to distinguish between different strategies for dealing with waste (reduce, reuse, recycle, energy recovery) and then classify waste materials as either natural or synthetic to help decide on the best disposal. Teachers allowed discussion in both English and Arabic initially, but made it clear that the exchange form and class presentation of students' findings would have to be completed in English. Students then undertook a waste audit in their homes to see what was being thrown out and in what quantity, which led into a project investigating options for recycling waste in the community. Their class presentation had to cover the findings of one of these studies. They were given a completed model report, which included sentence stems, collocations, and other language for ordering their findings.

Impact on Students

The English teachers commented on what a buzz there had been during the lessons and that students were immediately asking more questions about how to best express themselves in English. Although there was a fair amount of Arabic being used at the beginning, students soon switched to English as they began to think about writing their report. On students' completed exchange forms, the English teachers highlighted language errors only if they interfered with communication, and students were asked to try to self-correct in groups. Initially, the teachers decided to exchange with the U.K. school they already had a partnership with because there was not much time left before the end-of-year exam. They would build on that experience in the next academic year, using the more global forum that *SAW* provides.

I shared with the Yemeni English teachers how these outcomes clearly reflected my prior experiences with integrating science into language lessons for young learners (ages 7–14). It had been quite engaging for them to do simple experiments in class, such as predicting and then seeing whether objects could float or sink or were magnetic. Before conducting the experiments, they had tried to classify the items being used. They had become engrossed in the tasks and keen to share their findings with their peers—reading and writing significant chunks of text almost inadvertently. Their literacy skills had therefore been attended to in a motivating context and with a more holistic approach to learning.

We also discussed how these types of outcomes are particularly useful in an Arabic-speaking environment, where literacy skills tend to be far lower than oral communicative ability. I had been pleased with the outcomes in my class and initially focused more on students' communication through writing, reformulating their work where necessary. Once I had established that students were enjoying the approach, I decided that I needed to be a little more strategic about the language they were using and incorporated organisational structures and key collocations according to what they needed for their experiment. Nevertheless, my main focus had still been to develop their reading and writing skills and help them overcome their hesitance to work on these.

A strategic language focus was integrated to good effect in the Yemeni context in that the language element of the classes was planned from the outset. It was clear from the experiences of the teachers that the collaborative planning work between departments laid an excellent foundation for the lessons, and the students' motivation to use English in class significantly increased when engaging with a relevant topic.

REFLECTIONS

Teacher Development and Observations

This project is in its early stages in Yemen, but even from the initial work described here, it is clear that there will be positive benefits for learners and teachers. We have learned that it is not enough for the English teachers to do more task-based project work in their lessons to increase motivation. Ideally, in a secondary school context, they also need to have the necessary knowledge and ability to relate the language focus and choice of topic to what learners are covering in the broader school curriculum—making content work relevant and useful. This underlines the importance of teachers being able to communicate across subjects and willing to coplan and codeliver where logistically possible.

The Yemeni teachers appreciated having the chance to collaborate, but this collaboration was facilitated by them having chosen their partners and by team teaching. They were concerned about the level of additional preparation it might entail if they were to deliver the language and content components separately. However, a few teachers tried it that way, because their schedules did not permit codelivery, and found that once they got into the rhythm, it worked well as long as they maintained good communication, even in one instance when the science teacher had almost no knowledge of English.

In terms of motivation, teachers and learners alike seemed to benefit. The students were quite enthusiastic, which in turn motivated the teachers to continue. The most exciting thing was receiving the reports from the other schools and comparing the findings. Next year, the Yemeni teachers want to completely explore the project through *SAW* to maximise this input and enable student groups within the class to work on a range of topics. Teachers commented that learners wrote and read more text than in any other language context during the year and with far fewer grumbles.

Directions and Suggestions for Future Growth

Although this content was not directly assessed in the exams for either English or science, the language teachers felt that many students performed better on their English exams than on previous tests because they had been using English more and had become more confident in their use of the language for communication. The teachers recognised that to sustain this kind of project work in the future, they need to formulate assessment of student work in both language and content; otherwise, they may have issues maintaining momentum with students and administrators. Once the novelty wears off, students may lose some of their motivation to work hard on these tasks if they do not receive direct credit for their efforts. Also, without student assessment built into the project, it makes it difficult to evaluate the programme and monitor student learning, which are necessary to justify class time. Quantitative results would also provide more weight, when added to anecdotal evidence, in demonstrating the effectiveness of this approach and would encourage more schools to explore using it. However, one of the major achievements is that students as well as teachers are interested in continuing with such projects and feel that they benefitted from the CLIL approach.

For content and language integrated learning through collaborative projects to really have a future in this region, it needs to be integrated both into official systems and into teacher development programs so that teachers have the confidence to implement it. However, I believe that unless those of us with experience with CLIL start the ball rolling, explore the options, and gain momentum from classroom success, this cannot happen. It will be evidence of positive outcomes that will persuade the authorities to invest in the change process.

I believe that collaborative CLIL project work can be adapted for any environment to maximise the engagement of young learners in their language acquisition. The focus on content helps move students as well as teachers away from an obsession with accuracy in school and frees them to seek communicative competence as a goal. The structure of the lessons also helps deal with large mixed-ability classes because the language focus is driven by the content and addressed when necessary. Groups of students with different levels of language ability can work on the same materials more easily than when working from a textbook. As evidenced in Yemen, the motivational aspect of relevant and interesting contemporary topics helps students apply themselves even when struggling with literacy skills.

Eilidh Hamilton is currently the project manager for a client-funded content and language integrated learning project with the British Council in Qatar. She was previously the English manager for the British Council in Yemen. She has worked as an EFL teacher and teacher trainer in the Middle East since 1995 and with the British Council since 2004.

APPENDIX: RECOMMENDED RESOURCES

Cutler, M. (2004). Exploring science locally and sharing insights globally. *School Science Review, 86*(314), 33–41. Retrieved from http://www.scienceacross.org/

FACTworld: Forum for across the curriculum teaching. (2009). Retrieved from http://www.factworld.info/

Jappinen, A. K. (2005). Thinking and content learning of mathematics and science as cognitional development in content and language integrated learning (CLIL): Teaching through a foreign language in Finland. *Language and Education, 19,* 147–168. doi:10.1080/09500780508668671

References

Abedi, J. (2003). *Impact of student language background on content-based performance: Analyses of extant data*. Los Angeles: University of California, Los Angeles, National Center for Research on Evaluation, Standards, and Student Testing.

Abedi, J., Courtney, M., Mirocha, J., Leon, S., & Goldberg, J. (2005). *Language accommodations for English language learners in large-scale assessments: Bilingual dictionaries and linguistic modification*. Los Angeles: University of California, Los Angeles, National Center for Research on Evaluation, Standards, and Student Testing.

Abedi, J., & Lord, C. (2001). The language factor in mathematics tests. *Applied Measurement in Education, 14,* 219–234. doi:10.1207/S15324818AME1403_2

Al-Garni, A. Z. (n.d.). *Bottle rocket construction*. Retrieved from https://eprints .kfupm.edu.sa/1092/1/waterrocketconstruction.pdf

Amaral, O., Garrison, L., & Klentschy, M. (2002). Helping English learners increase achievement through inquiry-based science instruction. *Bilingual Research Journal, 26,* 213–239.

Arens, W. (2004). *Contemporary advertising*. New York, NY: McGraw-Hill.

Ashworth, J., Clark, J., & Lawday, C. (1996). *I-spy English*. Oxford, England: Oxford University Press/La Nuova Italia.

Assaad, R., & Roudi-Fahimi, F. (2007). *Youth in the Middle East and North Africa: Demographic opportunity or challenge?* Washington, DC: Population Reference Bureau. Retrieved from http://www.prb.org/pdf07/YouthinMENA.pdf

Atkin, J. M., & Karplus, R. (1962). Discovery or invention? *Science Teacher, 29*(5), 45–47.

Atkinson, D. (1997). A critical approach to critical thinking in TESOL. *TESOL Quarterly, 31,* 71–94.

Auerbach, E. R. (1992). *Making meaning, making change: Participatory curriculum development for adult ESL literacy*. McHenry, IL: Center for Applied Linguistics and Delta Systems.

Baker, C. (2000). *The care and education of young bilinguals: An introduction for professionals*. Clevedon, England: Multilingual Matters.

Becher, T. (1989). *Academic tribes and territories: Intellectual enquiry and the cultures of disciplines*. Buckingham, England: Open University Press.

Benesch, S. (1996). Needs analysis and curriculum development in EAP: An example of a critical approach. *TESOL Quarterly, 30,* 723–738.

Benesch, S. (2001). *Critical English for academic purposes: Theory, politics, and practice*. Mahwah, NJ: Lawrence Erlbaum.

Bereiter, C., & Scardamalia, M. (1987). *The psychology of written composition*. Hillsdale, NJ: Lawrence Erlbaum.

Bernier, A. (1997). The challenge of language and history terminology from the student optic. In M. A. Snow & D. M. Brinton (Eds.), *The content-based classroom: Perspectives on integrating language and content* (pp. 95–103). White Plains, NY: Longman.

bit10. (2003). *Science across the world*. Retrieved from http://www.scienceacross.org/

Blip Networks. (2009). *Blip.tv*. Retrieved from http://blip.tv/

Blumenfeld, W. J., & Raymon, D. (2000). Prejudices and discrimination. In M. Adams, W. J. Blumenfeld, R. Castañeda, H. W. Hackman, M. L. Peters, & X. Zúñiga (Eds.), *Readings for diversity and social justice* (pp. 21–20). New York, NY: Routledge.

Board of Regents of the University of Wisconsin-Madison. (2007). *ACCESS for ELLs*. Retrieved from http://www.wida.us/assessment/ACCESS/index.aspx

Braine, G. (1988). A reader reacts . . . . *TESOL Quarterly, 22,* 700–709.

Breiner-Sanders, K. E., Lowe, P., Jr., Miles, J., & Swender, E. (2000). ACTFL proficiency guidelines—speaking: Revised 1999. *Foreign Language Annals, 33,* 13–18. doi:10.1111/j.1944-9720.2000.tb00885.x

Brinton, D. M., Snow, M. A., & Wesche, M. B. (1989). *Content-based second language instruction*. Boston, MA: Heinle & Heinle.

Brown, H. D. (2007). *Teaching by principles: An interactive approach to language pedagogy*. New York, NY: Pearson.

Brufee, K. (1984). Collaborative learning and the "conversation of mankind." *College English, 46,* 635–652.

Burlington School District annual report. (2007). Burlington, VT: Burlington School District.

Bush, R. B., & Folger, J. (2005). *The promise of mediation: The transformative approach to conflict.* San Francisco, CA: Jossey-Bass.

Bybee, R. W. (2002a). *Learning science and the science of learning.* Arlington, VA: NSTA Press.

Bybee, R. W. (2002b). Scientific inquiry, student learning, and the science curriculum. In R. W. Bybee (Ed.), *Learning science and the science of learning* (pp. 25–35). Arlington, VA: NSTA Press.

Bybee, R., & Landes, N. M. (1990). Science for life and living: An elementary school science program from biological sciences curriculum study. *American Biology Teacher, 52*(2), 92–98.

California Department of Education. (2003). *Science content standards for California public schools: Kindergarten through grade 12.* Sacramento, CA: Author. Retrieved from http://www.cde.ca.gov/be/st/ss/documents/sciencestnd.pdf

Carr, J., Sexton, U., & Lagunoff, R. (2007). *Making science accessible to English learners: A guidebook for teachers.* San Francisco, CA: WestEd.

Carrasquillo, A., & Rodriguez, V. (2002). *Language minority students in the mainstream classroom* (2nd ed.). Clevedon, England: Multilingual Matters.

Castro, P., Sercu, L., & Garcia, M. D. C. M. (2004). Integrating language-and-culture teaching: An investigation of Spanish teachers' perceptions of the objectives of foreign language education. *Intercultural Education, 15*, 91–104. doi:10.1080/1467598042000190013

CLIL Compendium. (n.d.). *CLIL types.* Retrieved from http://www.clilcompendium.com/clilexpertise.htm

CLIL in Yemen. (n.d.). Retrieved from http://www.factworld.info/yemen

Cofer, J. O. (2001). The myth of the Latin woman: I just met a girl named Maria. In I. Reed (Ed.), *MultiAmerica: Essays on cultural wars and cultural peace* (pp. 325–327). New York, NY: Penguin Books.

Collier, V. P. (1987). Age and rate of acquisition of second language for academic purposes. *TESOL Quarterly, 21*, 617–641.

Collier, V. P. (1995a). Acquiring a second language for school. *Directions in Language and Education, 1*(4), 1–12.

Collier, V. P. (1995b). *Promoting academic success for ESL students.* New York, NY: Bastos Educational.

Columbia University School of Nursing. (n.d.). *Health literacy assessment tool.* Retrieved from http://www.nursing.columbia.edu/ebp/HealthLitRes/assessTool.html

Columbia University School of Nursing, Center for Evidence-Based Practice in the Underserved. (n.d.). *Health literacy overview.* Retrieved from http://www.nursing.columbia.edu/ebp/HealthLitRes/litResources.html

Council of Europe. (2001). *The common European framework of reference for languages.* Cambridge, England: Cambridge University Press.

Coxhead, A. (2006). *Essentials of teaching academic vocabulary.* Boston, MA: Houghton Mifflin.

Coyle, D. (1999). Supporting students in content and language integrated learning contexts: Planning for effective classrooms. In J. Masih (Ed.), *Learning through a foreign language: Models, methods and outcomes* (pp. 46–62). London, England: Centre for Information on Language Teaching and Research.

Coyle, D. (2002). Relevance of CLIL to the European Commission's language learning objectives. In D. Marsh (Ed.), *CLIL/EMILE the European dimension: Actions, trends and foresight potential* (pp. 27–28). Jyväskylä, Finland: University of Jyväskylä, Continuing Education Centre.

Crookes, G., & Chaudron, C. (2001). Guidelines for language classroom instruction. In M. Celce-Murcia (Ed.), *Teaching English as a second or foreign language* (3rd ed., pp. 29–42). Boston, MA: Heinle & Heinle.

Crystal, D. (1997). *English as a global language.* Cambridge, England: Cambridge University Press.

Cummins, J. (1980). The construct of language proficiency in bilingual education. In J. E. Ablates (Ed.), *Current issues in bilingual education: Georgetown University Round Table on Languages and Linguistics, 1980* (pp. 81–104). Washington, DC: Georgetown University Press.

Cummins, J. (1981a). Age on arrival and immigrant second language learning in Canada: A reassessment. *Applied Linguistics, 2,* 132–149.

Cummins, J. (1981b). The role of primary language development in promoting educational success for language minority students. In *Schooling and language minority students: A theoretical framework* (pp. 3–49). Los Angeles: California State University, Los Angeles, Evaluation, Dissemination, and Assessment Center.

Cummins, J. (2000). *Language, power and pedagogy: Bilingual children in the crossfire.* Clevedon, England: Multilingual Matters.

Cummins, J. (2001). Linguistic interdependence and the educational development of bilingual children. In C. Baker & N. H. Hornberger (Eds.), *An introductory reader to the writings of Jim Cummins* (pp. 63–95). Clevedon, England: Multilingual Matters Press.

Curtain, H. A., & Pesola, C. A. (1994). *Languages and children: Making the match* (2nd ed.). New York, NY: Longman.

Dale, T. C., & Cuevas, G. J. (1995). Integrating language and mathematics learning. In J. Crandall (Ed.), *ESL through content-area instruction: Mathematics, sciences, social studies* (pp. 9–54). Washington, DC: ERIC Clearinghouse on Languages and Linguistics.

Darling-Hammond, L. (2002). Who are our students and what do they need? In L. Darling-Hammond, J. French, & S. P. Garcia-Lopez (Eds.), *Learning to teach for social justice* (pp. 89–91). New York, NY: Teachers College Press.

Davidson, P., & Spring, J. (2008). Rhetorical patterns in academic writing: Re-examining conventional wisdom. In C. Coombe, A. Jendli, & P. Davidson (Eds.), *Teaching writing skills in EFL: Theory, research and pedagogy* (pp. 27–40). Dubai, United Arab Emirates: TESOL Arabia.

Davies, W. M. (2006). An "infusion" approach to critical thinking: Moore on the critical thinking debate. *Higher Education Research and Development, 25,* 179–193. doi:10.1080/07294360600610420

Davison, C. (2001). Current policies, programs and practices in school ESL. In B. Mohan, C. Leung, & C. Davison (Eds.), *English as a second language in the mainstream: Teaching, learning and identity* (pp. 30–50). Harlow, England: Pearson.

Davison, C., & Williams, A. (2001). Integrating language and content: Unresolved issues. In B. Mohan, C. Leung, & C. Davison (Eds.), *English as a second language in the mainstream: Teaching, learning and identity* (pp. 51–70). Harlow, England: Pearson.

Delpit, L. (1995). *Other people's children: Cultural conflict in the classroom.* New York, NY: New Press.

Deutsch, M. (2000). Cooperation and competition. In M. Deutsch & P. Coleman (Eds.), *The handbook of conflict resolution: Theory and practice* (pp. 21–40). San Francisco, CA: Jossey-Bass.

Deutsch, M., Coleman, P., & Marcus, E. (Eds.). (2006). *The handbook of conflict resolution: Theory and practice* (2nd ed.). San Francisco, CA: Jossey-Bass.

Dobb, F. (2004). *Essential elements of effective science instruction for English learners* (2nd ed.). Los Angeles: California Science Project.

Donald, J. (2002). *Learning to think: Disciplinary perspectives.* San Francisco, CA: Jossey-Bass.

Douglas, R., Klentschy, M. P., Worth, K., & Binder, W. (2006). *Linking science and literacy in the K–8 classroom.* Arlington, VA: NSTA Press.

Dunne, F., Nave, B., & Lewis, A. (2000). Critical friends groups: Teachers helping teachers to improve student learning. *Research Bulletin, 28,* 9–12.

Echevarria, J., Vogt, M. E., & Short, D. (2004). *Making content comprehensible to English learners: The SIOP model* (2nd ed.). Boston, MA: Pearson/Allyn & Bacon.

Echevarria, J., Vogt, M. E., & Short, D. (2008). *Making content comprehensible for English learners: The SIOP Model* (3rd ed.). Boston, MA: Pearson/Allyn & Bacon.

Edwards, H. P., Wesche, M. B., Krashen, S., Clement, R., & Kruidenier, B. (1984). Second language acquisition through subject matter learning: A study of sheltered psychology classes at the University of Ottawa. *Canadian Modern Language Review, 41,* 268–282.

ELT course book. (n.d.). Retrieved from http://coursebookelt.wetpaint.com/

Europees Platform. (2008). *European platform for Dutch education in the Netherlands.* Retrieved from http://www.europeesplatform.nl

Eurydice. (2006). *Content and language integrated learning (CLIL) at school in Europe.* Brussels, Belgium: Author. Retrieved from http://eacea.ec.europa.eu/ressources/eurydice/pdf/0_integral/071EN.pdf

Evans, R. (1973). *Jean Piaget: The man and his ideas.* New York, NY: E. P. Dutton.

Fathman, A., & Crowther, D. (Eds.). (2006). *Science for English language learners.* Arlington, VA: NSTA Press.

Fishman, S. (1989). Writing and philosophy. *Teaching Philosophy, 12,* 261–374.

Freeman, D. (2005). Teaching in the context of English-language learners: What do we need to know? In M. Sadowski (Ed.), *Teaching immigrant and second-language students: Strategies for success* (pp. 7–20). Cambridge, MA: Harvard Education Press.

Freire, P. (1970). *Pedagogy of the oppressed*: New York, NY: Continuum.

Fry, R. (2007). *How far behind in math and reading are English language learners?* Washington, DC: Pew Hispanic Center.

Fuller, R. G. (Ed.). (2002). *A love of discovery: Science education—The second career of Robert Karplus.* New York, NY: Kluwer Academic.

Gaffield-Vile, N. (1996). Content-based second language instruction at the tertiary level. *ELT Journal, 50,* 108–114. doi:10.1093/elt/50.2.108

Gardner, H. (1993). *Multiple intelligences: The theory in practice.* New York, NY: Basic Books.

Genesee, F. (1994). *Integrating language and content: Lessons from immersion* (Educational Practice Report 11). Santa Cruz, CA: National Center for Research on Cultural Diversity and Second Language Learning.

Goodman, A. (2004). *Basic skills for the new mediator* (2nd ed.). Rockville, MD: Solomon.

Google. (1999–2009). *Blogger.* Retrieved from http://www.blogger.com/

Google. (2009). *Google docs.* Retrieved from http://docs.google.com/

Government Accountability Office. (2006). *No Child Left Behind Act: Assistance from education could help states better measure progress of students with limited English proficiency.* Washington, DC: Author.

Govoni, N. (2004). *Dictionary of marketing communications.* London, England: Sage.

Grabe, W., & Stoller, F. L. (1997). Content-based instruction: Research foundations. In M. A. Snow & D. M. Brinton (Eds.), *The content-based classroom: Perspectives on integrating language and content* (pp. 5–21). New York, NY: Longman.

Graddol, D. (2006). *English next.* London, England: British Council.

Haansoft. (2009). *ThinkFree.* Retrieved from http://thinkfree.com/

Hayhurst, P. (2004). *Mr. Hayhurst's quick and easy bottle rocket.* Retrieved from http://www.lnhs.org/hayhurst/rockets/

Health literacy resources for adult education. (n.d.). Retrieved from http://www.qlhealthlit.blogspot.com/

Heinich, R., Molenda, M., Russell, J., & Smaldino, S. (2002). *Instructional media and technologies for learning* (7th ed.). Englewood Cliffs, NJ: Prentice Hall.

Herrera, S. G., & Murry, K. G. (2005). *Mastering ESL and bilingual methods: Differentiated instruction for culturally and linguistically diverse (CLD) students.* New York, NY: Pearson.

Hirvela, A. (1997). "Disciplinary portfolios" and EAP writing instruction. *English for Specific Purposes, 16,* 83–100.

Hobbes, T. (1986). *Leviathan.* Harmondsworth, England: Penguin Books.

hooks, b. (1994). *Teaching to transgress: Education as the practice of freedom.* New York, NY: Routledge.

hooks, b. (2001). Feminism: A movement to end sexist oppression. In M. Adams, W. J. Blumenfeld, R. Castañeda, H. W. Hackman, M. L. Peters, & X. Zúñiga (Eds.), *Readings for diversity and social justice* (pp. 238–240). New York, NY: Routledge.

Hubbard, R. (2001). The politics of women's biology. In P. Rothenberg (Ed.), *Race, class, and gender in the United States* (pp. 47–56). New York, NY: Worth.

Hyland, K. (2002). Specificity revisited: How far should we go now? *English for Specific Purposes, 21,* 385–395. doi:10.1016/S0889-4906(01)00028-X

Jenkins, W. L. (2005). *How to audition for commercials: From the ad agency point of view.* New York, NY: Allworth Press.

Johns, A. M. (1990). Coherence as a cultural phenomenon: Employing ethnographic principles in the academic milieu. In U. Connor & A. M. Johns (Eds.), *Coherence in writing: Research and pedagogical perspectives* (pp. 209–226). Alexandria, VA: TESOL.

Johnson, M. (Producer), & Levinson, B. (Director). (1988). *Rain man* [Motion picture]. United States: United Artists.

Joint Committee on National Health Education Standards. (1995). *National health education standards: Achieving health literacy.* New York, NY: American Cancer Society. (ERIC Document Reproduction Service No. ED 386418)

Kant, I. (1998). *Groundwork of the metaphysics of morals.* Cambridge, England: Cambridge University Press.

Kasper, L. (1997). Assessing the metacognitive growth of ESL student writers. *TESL E-J, 3*(1). Retrieved from http://www.tesl-ej.org/wordpress/

Katz, A., & Olsen, J. K. (2006). Strategies for assessing English language learners. In A. Fathman & D. Crowther (Eds.), *Science for English language learners: K–12 custom strategies* (pp. 61–77). Arlington, VA: NSTA Press.

Kember, D. (2004). Interpreting student workload and the factors which shape students' perceptions of their workload. *Studies in Higher Education, 29,* 165–184. doi:10.1080/0307507042000190778

Kember, D., & Leung, D. Y. P. (2006). Characterising a teaching and learning environment conducive to making demands on students while not making their workload excessive. *Studies in Higher Education, 31,* 185–198. doi:10.1080/03075070600572074

Kinsella, K. (2006, October). *Essential features of structured, inclusive academic discussions.* Keynote address at the Office of English Acquisition Summit, Washington, DC.

Krashen, S. D. (1981). *Second language acquisition and second language learning.* Oxford, England: Oxford University Press.

Krashen, S. (1982). *Principles and practice in second language acquisition.* Oxford, England: Pergamon Press.

Krashen, S., & Terrell, T. D. (1983). *The natural approach: Language acquisition in the classroom.* Oxford, England: Pergamon Press.

Kressel, K. (2000). Mediation. In M. Deutsch & P. Coleman (Eds.), *The handbook of conflict resolution: Theory and practice* (pp. 522–545). San Francisco, CA: Jossey-Bass.

Kutner, M., Greenberg, E., Jin, Y., & Paulsen, C. (2006). *The health literacy of America's adults: Results from the 2003 National Assessment of Adult Literacy.* Washington, DC: U.S. Department of Education, National Center for Education Statistics. Retrieved from http://nces.ed.gov/pubs2006/2006483.pdf

Langston, D. (2001). Tired of playing monopoly? In M. Andersen & P. Collins (Eds.), *Race, class, and gender* (pp. 125–134). Belmont, CA: Wadsworth.

Larsen-Freeman, D. (2000). *Techniques and principles in language teaching.* Oxford, England: Oxford University Press.

Larsen-Freeman, D. (2001). Teaching grammar. In M. Celce-Murcia (Ed.), *Teaching English as a second or foreign language* (3rd ed., pp. 251–266). Boston, MA: Heinle & Heinle.

Larsen-Freeman, D. (2003). *Teaching language from grammar to grammaring*. Boston, MA: Heinle & Heinle.

Lasseter, J. (Producer), & Bird, B. (Director). (2004). *The Incredibles* [Motion picture]. United States: Pixar Animation Studios.

LeBaron, M. (2002). *Bridging troubled waters: Conflict resolution from the heart*. San Francisco, CA: Jossey-Bass.

Leedy, L. (2000). *Mapping Penny's world*. New York, NY: Henry Holt.

LeNoir, M. (1997). Image distortion disorder. In I. Reed (Ed.), *MultiAmerica: Essays on cultural wars and cultural peace* (pp. 325–327). New York, NY: Penguin Books.

Leung, C., Harris, R., & Rampton, B. (1997). The idealised native speaker, reified ethnicities, and classroom realities. *TESOL Quarterly, 31,* 543–560.

Lewis, M. (1993). *The lexical approach: The state of ELT and the way forward*. Hove, England: Language Teaching.

Ligon, F., & Tannenbaum, E. (1990). *Picture stories: Language and literacy activities for beginners*. New York, NY: Longman.

Locke, J. (1703). *The Works of John Locke in Nine Volumes (Vol. 2)*. London, England: Rivington.

Lorber, J. (1994). "Night to his day": The social construction of gender. In *Paradoxes of gender* (pp. 13–36). New Haven, CT: Yale University Press.

Mantsios, G. (2000). Class in America: Myths and realities. In P. Rothenberg (Ed.), *Race, class, and gender in the United States* (pp. 168–181). New York, NY: Worth.

Marsh, D. (Ed.). (2002). *CLIL/EMILE the European dimension: Actions, trends and foresight potential*. Jyväskylä, Finland: University of Jyväskylä, Continuing Education Centre.

Marsh, D., Cenoz, J., & Hornberger, N. H. (Eds.). (2007). *Encyclopedia of language and education. Volume 6: Knowledge about language* (2nd ed., pp. 233–246). Boston, MA: Springer.

Martinich, A. (1996). *Philosophical writing* (2nd ed.). Oxford, England: Blackwell.

Maslow, A. (1954). *Motivation and personality*. New York, NY: Harper.

McIntosh, P. (1989, July/August). White privilege: Unpacking the invisible knapsack. *Peace and Freedom,* 10–12.

McIntosh, P. (2001). White privilege: Unpacking the invisible knapsack. In P. Rothenberg (Ed.), *Race, class, and gender in the United States* (pp. 163–168). New York, NY: Worth.

Met, M. (1991). Learning language through content: Learning content through language. *Foreign Language Annals, 24,* 281–295. doi:10.1111/j.1944-9720.1991 .tb00472.x

Met, M. (1999). *Content-based instruction: Defining terms, making decisions.* Washington, DC: National Foreign Language Center.

Mill, J. S. (1978). *On liberty.* Indianapolis, IN: Hackett.

Mohan, B. (1986). *Language and content.* Reading, MA: Addison-Wesley.

Mohan, B. (2001). The second language as a medium of learning. In B. Mohan, C. Leung, & C. Davison (Eds.), *English as a second language in the mainstream: Teaching, learning and identity* (pp. 107–126). Harlow, England: Pearson.

Mohan, B., Leung, C., & Davison, C. (Eds.). (2001). *English as a second language in the mainstream: Teaching, learning and identity.* Harlow, England: Pearson.

Moll, L. C., Amanti, C., Neff, D., & Gonzalez, N. (1992). Funds of knowledge for teaching: Using a qualitative approach to connect homes and classrooms. *Theory Into Practice, 31,* 132–141.

Moore, T. (2004). The critical thinking debate: How general are general thinking skills? *Higher Education Research and Development, 23,* 3–18. doi:10.1080/0729436032000168469

Morrison, T. (1994). *The bluest eye.* New York, NY: Plume.

Myers, J. (2001). *Holidays and special days in the USA.* London, England: Mary Glasgow Magazines.

National Center for Educational Statistics. (2003). *National assessment of adult literacy.* Washington, DC: U.S. Department of Education.

National Clearinghouse for English Language Acquisition and language instruction educational programs. (n.d.). *The growing numbers of limited English proficient students, 1995/96–2005/06.* Retrieved from http://www.ncela.gwu.edu/files/ uploads/4/GrowingLEP_0506.pdf

National Council of Teachers of Mathematics. (1998). *The nature and role of algebra in the K–14 curriculum: Proceedings of a national symposium May 27 and 28, 1997.* Washington, DC: National Academy Press.

National Council of Teachers of Mathematics. (2000). *Principles and standards for school mathematics.* Reston, VA: Author.

National Research Council. (1996). *National science education standards.* Washington DC: National Academy Press.

Nevada Department of Education. (2008). *Nevada state science standards.* Available at http://www.doe.nv.gov/Standards_Science.html

New York City Department of Planning. (2004). *The newest New Yorkers 2000: Immigrant New York in the new millennium.* New York, NY: Author. Available from http://www.nyc.gov/html/dcp/html/census/nny.shtml

Nielsen-Bohlman, L., Allison, M., Panzer, D., & Kindig, A. (Eds.). (2004). *Health literacy: A prescription to end confusion.* Washington, DC: National Academies Press.

Norton, B. (2000). *Identity and language learning: Gender, ethnicity and educational change.* Harlow, England: Longman/Pearson Education.

Nuove Indicazioni per il curricolo della scuola dell'infanzia e del primo ciclo di istruzione [Italian national curriculum: 6- to16-year-old students]. (2007). Retrieved from http://www.pubblica.istruzione.it/news/2007/indicazioni_nazionali.shtml

Nurss, J. R., Parker, R., Williams, M., & Baker, D. (2003). *STOFHLA teaching edition: (English).* Snow Camp, NC: Peppercorn Books.

Pally, M. (1997). Critical thinking in ESL: An argument for sustained content. *Journal of Second Language Writing, 6,* 293–311. doi:10.1016/S1060-3743(97) 90016-3

Pally, M. (Ed.). (2000). *Sustained content teaching in academic ESL/EFL: A practical approach.* Boston, MA: Houghton Mifflin.

Patel, E. (2007). We are each other's business. In J. Allison & D. Gediman (Eds.), *This I believe: The personal philosophies of remarkable men and women* (pp. 178–180). New York, NY: Henry Holt.

Plato. (1992). *The republic* (Trans. G. M. Grube). Indianapolis, IN: Hackett.

Plato. (2002). *Five dialogues* (Trans. G. M. Grube). Indianapolis, IN: Hackett.

Raimes, A. (1991). Out of the woods: Emerging traditions in the teaching of writing. *TESOL Quarterly, 25,* 407–430.

Ramsden, P. (1992). *Learning to teach in higher education.* London, England: Routledge.

Rauscher, L., & McClintock, M. (1997). Ableism curriculum design. In M. Adams, L. Bell, & P. Griffin (Eds.), *Teaching for diversity and social justice* (pp. 198–216). New York, NY: Routledge.

Reppy, J., & Adames, J. (2000). English as a second language. In J. W. Rosenthal (Ed.), *Handbook of undergraduate second language education* (pp. 73–92). Mahwah, NJ: Lawrence Erlbaum.

Rudd, R., Kirsch, I., & Yamamoto, K. (2004). *Literacy and health in America.* Princeton, NJ: Educational Testing Service. Retrieved from http://www.ets.org/ Media/Research/pdf/PICHEATH.pdf

Savignon, S. J. (2001). Communicative language teaching for the twenty-first century. In M. Celce-Murcia (Ed.), *Teaching English as a second or foreign language* (3rd ed., pp. 13–28). Boston, MA: Heinle & Heinle.

Schmidt, R. (2001). Attention. In P. Robinson (Ed.), *Cognition and second language instruction* (pp. 3–32). Cambridge, England: Cambridge University Press.

Secada, W. G. (1998). School mathematics for language enriched pupils. In S. H. Fradd & O. Lee (Eds.), *Creating Florida's multilingual global work force: Educational policies and practices for students learning English as a new language* (pp. IV-1–IV-9). Tallahassee: Florida Department of Education.

Short, D., & Echevarria, J. (1999). *The sheltered instruction observation protocol: A tool for teacher-researcher collaboration and professional development.* Santa Cruz: University of California, Center for Research on Education, Diversity and Excellence.

Short, D., & Fitzsimmons, S. (2007). *Double the work: Challenges and solutions to acquiring language and academic literacy for adolescent English language learners.* Washington, DC: Alliance for Excellent Education.

Silko, L. (2001). The border patrol state. In I. Reed (Ed.), *MultiAmerica: Essays on cultural wars and cultural peace* (pp. 325–327). New York, NY: Penguin Books.

Singleton, K. (n.d.). *Picture stories for adult ESL health literacy.* Retrieved from http://www.cal.org/caela/esl_resources/Health/healthindex.html

SlideShare. (2009). *SlideShare.* Retrieved from http://www.slideshare.net/

Snow, C. (1990). Rationales for native language instruction: Evidence from research. In A. M. Padilla, H. H. Fairchild, & C. M. Valdez (Eds.), *Bilingual education: Issues and strategies* (pp. 47–59). Newbury Park, CA: Sage.

Snow, M. A. (2005). A model of academic literacy for integrated language and content instruction. In E. Hinkel (Ed.), *Handbook of research in second language teaching and learning* (pp. 693–712). Mahwah, NJ: Lawrence Erlbaum.

Snow, M. A. (2007, March). *Language and content.* Presentation at the 41st Annual TESOL Convention and Exhibit, Seattle, WA.

Snow, M. A., Met, M., & Genesee, F. (1989). A conceptual framework for the integration of language and content in second/foreign language instruction. *TESOL Quarterly, 23,* 201–217.

Solano-Flores, G., & Trumbull, E. (2003). Examining language in context: The need for new research and practice paradigms in the testing of English-language learners. *Educational Researcher, 32*(2), 3–13. doi:10.3102/0013189X032002003

Spack, R. (1988). Initiating ESL students into the academic discourse community: How far should we go? *TESOL Quarterly, 22,* 29–51.

Spanos, G., Rhodes, N. C., Dale, T. C., & Crandall, J. (1988). Linguistic features of mathematical problem solving. In R. R. Cocking & J. P. Mestre (Eds.). *Linguistic and cultural influences on learning mathematics* (pp. 221–340). Hillsdale, NJ: Lawrence Erlbaum.

Speaking and writing rubrics of the WIDA Consortium. (n.d.). Retrieved from http://www.wida.us/standards/RG_Speaking%20Writing%20Rubrics.pdf

State of Vermont Department of Education. (2008). *Grade expectations (GEs) and teacher support materials*. Retrieved from http://education.vermont.gov/new/html/pgm_curriculum/mathematics/gle.html

Stillwell, C. (2009). Authentic video as passport to cultural participation and understanding. In S. Rilling and M. Dantas-Whitney (Eds.), *Authenticity in the language classroom and beyond: Adult learners* (pp. 181–189). Alexandria, VA: TESOL.

Stoller, F. (2002, April). *Content-based instruction: A shell for language teaching or a framework for strategic language and content learning?* Plenary address at the 36th Annual TESOL Convention and Exhibit, Salt Lake City, UT. Retrieved from http://www.carla.umn.edu/cobaltt/modules/strategies/Stoller2002/SELECTION.html

Student Oral Language Observation Matrix (SOLOM). (n.d.). Retrieved from http://www.cal.org/twi/EvalToolkit/appendix/solom.pdf

Stryker, S., & Leaver, B. (1997). Content-based instruction: Some lessons and implications. In S. Stryker & B. Leaver (Eds.), *Content-based instruction in foreign language education: Models and methods* (pp. 285–312). Washington, DC: Georgetown University Press.

Sysoyev, P. V. (2003). *Theory of foreign language multicultural education*. Moscow, Russia: Euroschool Press.

Sysoyev, P. V., & Donelson, L. (2003). Teaching cultural identity through a modern language: Discourse as a marker of an individual's cultural identity. *Journal of Eurasian Research, 2*, 65–70.

Tatum, B. (1997). *Why are all the black kids sitting together in the cafeteria?* New York, NY: Basic Books.

Tatum, B. D. (2000). The complexity of identity: "Who Am I?" In M. Adams, W. J. Blumenfeld, R. Castañeda, H. W. Hackman, M. L. Peters, & X. Zúñiga (Eds.), *Readings for diversity and social justice* (pp. 9–14). New York, NY: Routledge.

TESOL. (2006). *PreK–12 English language proficiency standards*. Alexandria, VA: Author.

There once was a daisy. (2007). Retrieved from http://www.nps.gov/glac/forteachers/daisy-chain.htm

Thier, M. (2002). *The new science literacy*. Portsmouth, NH: Heinemann.

Thomas, C., & Thomas, V. (2005). *Exploring questions in religious education*. Tewkesbury, England: Nelson Thornes.

Thomas, W. P., & Collier, V. P. (1999). Accelerated schooling for English language learners. *Educational Leadership, 56*(7), 46–49.

Thomas, W. P., & Collier, V. (2002). *A national study of school effectiveness for language minority students' long-term academic achievement.* Washington, DC: Center for Research on Education, Diversity and Excellence & Center for Applied Linguistics.

Tomlinson, C. A. (1999). *The differentiated classroom: Responding to the needs of all learners.* Alexandria, VA: Association for Supervision and Curriculum Development.

Trigwell, K., Prosser, M., & Waterhouse, F. (1999). Relations between teachers' approaches to teaching and students' approaches to learning. *Higher Education, 37,* 57–70. doi:10.1023/A:1003548313194

Trowbridge, L., & Bybee, R. (1996). *Teaching secondary school science.* Columbus, OH: Merrill.

Tsui, A. (2003). *Understanding expertise in teaching: Case studies of ESL teachers.* Cambridge, England: Cambridge University Press.

United Nations Development Programme. (n.d.). *Human development report 2009: Yemen.* Retrieved from http://hdrstats.undp.org/en/countries/country_fact_sheets/cty_fs_YEM.html

U.S. Department of Agriculture. (2009). *MyPyramid.gov.* Retrieved from http://www.mypyramid.gov

Vanosdall, R., Klentschy, M., Hedges, L., & Weisbaum, K. (2007, April). *A randomized study of the effects of scaffolded guided inquiry instruction on student achievement in science.* Paper presented at the American Educational Research Association national conference, Chicago, IL.

Vastag, B. (2004). Low health literacy called a major problem. *Journal of the American Medical Association, 291,* 2181–2182.

Vygotsky, L. (1962). *Thought and language* (E. Hanfman & G. Vakar, Trans.). Cambridge, MA: Harvard University Press. (Original work published 1934)

Vygotsky, L. (1978). *Mind in society: The development of higher psychological processes.* Cambridge, MA: Harvard University Press. (Original work published 1934)

Wallace, S. (2007). *Getting the buggers motivated in FE.* London, England: Continuum International.

Wallstrum, R., & Crowther, D. (2009, August). *Comparing different vocabulary instruction models for teaching inquiry to English language learners.* Paper presented at the Association for Teacher Education, Reno, NV.

Walqui, A. (2000). *Access and engagement: Program design and instructional approaches for immigrant students in secondary school.* McHenry, IL: Delta Systems.

Walters, G. (Producer), & Stanton, A. (Director). (2003). *Finding Nemo* [Motion picture]. United States: Walt Disney Pictures/Pixar Animation Studios.

WIDA Consortium. (2007). *WIDA English language proficiency standards, prekindergarten through grade 12, 2007 edition*. Madison: Board of Regents of the University of Wisconsin System. Retrieved from http://www.wida.us/standards/elp.aspx

Wikipedia. (n.d.). Retrieved from http://www.wikipedia.org/

Wildman, A., & Davis, A. (2000). Language and silence: Making system privilege visible. In M. Adams, W. J. Blumenfeld, R. Castañeda, H. W. Hackman, M. L. Peters, & X. Zúñiga (Eds.), *Readings for diversity and social justice* (pp. 50–60). New York, NY: Routledge.

Wisconsin Department of Public Instruction. (n.d.). *Social studies, standard A: Geography performance standards—Grade 8*. Retrieved from http://dpi.state.wi.us/standards/ssa8.html

Woodward, T. (1991). *Models and metaphors in language teacher training: Loop input and other strategies*. Cambridge, England: Cambridge University Press.

Woodward, T. (2003). Loop input. *ELT Journal, 57*, 301–304. doi:10.1093/elt/57.3.301

Wooten, D. (Ed.). (1993). *The political writings of John Locke*. Harmondsworth, England: Penguin Books.

World Bank. (2008). *The road not travelled: Education reform in the Middle East and North Africa*. Retrieved from http://siteresources.worldbank.org/INTMENA/Resources/EDU_Flagship_Full_ENG.pdf

World studies: Asia and the Pacific. (2005). Boston, MA: Pearson.

Yahoo! (2008). *Yahoo! groups*. Retrieved from http://groups.yahoo.com/

Yeh, A. (2007). Learner autonomy in blended learning. In J. Egbert & E. Hanson-Smith (Eds.), *CALL environments: Research, practice, and critical issues* (2nd ed., pp. 404–420). Alexandria, VA: TESOL.

YouTube. (2009). *YouTube*. Retrieved from http://www.youtube.com/

Zimmerman, J., & Coyle, V. (1996). *The way of council*. Ojai, CA: Bramble Books.

Zormeier, S., & Samovar, L. (2009). Language as a mirror of reality: Mexican American proverbs. In L. A. Samovar, R. E. Porter, & E. R. McDaniel (Eds.), *Intercultural communication: A reader* (pp. 235–239). Belmont, CA: Wadsworth.

Index

Page numbers followed by an *f* or *t* indicate figures or tables.

C

Geometry course. *See also* Mathematics
    instruction
  context of, 210–211
  curriculum, tasks and materials for, 211–
      216, 212*f*, 213*f*
  introduction to, 209
  reflections regarding, 216–218
Grammar
  American Cultural Studies course and, 198
  English Advertising course and, 185–186
  geography instruction and, 164–170, 166*f*,
      167*f*, 168*f*, 169*f*
Group discussions, 24–27, 204
Guided inquiry. *See also* Inquiry-based science
    programs
  online tasks and, 118
  overview, 130
  scaffolding and sequencing and, 125, 126*t*

H

Health literacy
  context of, 43–45
  curriculum, tasks and materials for, 45–49,
      47*f*
  introduction to, 43
  reflections regarding, 49–52
  resources regarding, 52–53
Home contexts, 20
Homophobia, 195, 196*t*
hooks, bell, 29
Hot seating activity, 143–145. *See also*
    Religious education

I

I statements, 35–36
ICT, 59
Idiom files, 138
Information projects, 78–79
Inquiry-based science programs
  context of, 118–119, 151–152
  curriculum, tasks and materials for, 119–
      125, 120*f*, 122*f*, 123*f*, 124*f*, 152–158,
      153*f*, 156*f*
  introduction to, 117–118, 151
  reflections regarding, 125–130, 125*t*, 126*t*,
      158–159
  rocket unit, 151–159, 153*f*, 156*f*

Instructional planning, 115
Instructions, following, 64, 64*f*, 65*f*, 66*f*
Instructors, 91, 228. *See also* Teachers
International Center for Cooperation and
        Conflict Resolution (ICCCR), 32
Italian education, 58

J

Journal writing. *See also* Writing activities
    Academic Informant Project and, 78
    American Cultural Studies course and, 196
    inquiry-based science programs and, 127
    personal idiom file, 138
Journalog, 78

L

Language toolkit project
    context of, 90–93
    curriculum, tasks and materials for, 93–98,
        95*f*, 96*f*, 97*f*, 98*f*
    example of, 101–106, 102*f*, 103*f*, 105*f*
    introduction to, 89–90
    reflections regarding, 98–101, 99*t*
    resources regarding, 107–108
Language/content continuum, 4–6, 5*f*, 7–8
Language-driven curricula, 6*f*, 7
Lectures, interactive, 93
Lesson planning, 161
Lexical approach, 93, 96–97, 97*f*
Listening skills, 38–40, 60–61, 177*t*
Loop input techniques, 90

M

"Mapping Penny's World" (Leedy, 2000), 165
Mapping skills, 170–171
Matching tasks, 95, 101–106, 102*f*, 103*f*
Materials
    Academic Informant Project, 78–83
    American Cultural Studies course, 194–204,
        196*t*, 200*f*
    business English curriculum and, 19–28
    conflict resolution techniques, 32–41, 36*t*,
        37*f*
    content and language integrated learning
        (CLIL), 57–68, 60*f*, 61*f*, 62*f*, 63*f*, 64*f*,
        65*f*, 66*f*, 67*f*

Probing questions, 39–40
Problem-solving approach, 229–230
Proficiency standards, 7
Project-centered approach, 59
Public service announcement (PSA) project
    context of, 175–179, 177*t*, 179*f*
    course content, 190
    curriculum, tasks and materials for, 180–
        186, 183*f*, 185*f*, 187*f*, 188*f*
    example of, 192
    introduction to, 175
    reflections regarding, 186–189, 188*f*
    scoring rubric used in, 191

Q

Queens Health Network (QHN), 48–49
Questioning, 155
Questions, probing, 39–40

R

Race, 195, 196*t*
Racism, 20–21, 24–25, 195, 196*t*
Rationales for integration, 4–8, 5*f*, 6*f*
Reading skills, 22, 65
Reading strategies
    American Cultural Studies course and,
        195–196, 196*t*
    English Advertising course and, 177*t*
    language toolkit project and, 94, 98*f*
Reflection activities, 179*f*, 196
Reflective projects, 82–83, 87
Religious education
    context of, 134–136
    curriculum, tasks and materials for, 136–
        145, 139*f*, 140*f*, 141*f*, 142*f*, 143*f*
    introduction to, 133–134
    reflections regarding, 145–146
    task sheets for, 146–148
Resources
    Academic Informant Project and, 87
    content and language integrated learning
        (CLIL) and, 74
    health literacy curriculum and, 52–53
    language toolkit project and, 107–108
    Science Across the World (SAW) approach,
        238–239

Rocket unit
    context of, 151–152
    curriculum, tasks and materials for, 152–
        158, 153*f*, 156*f*
    introduction to, 151
    reflections regarding, 158–159
Role-plays, 36–38, 37*f*

S

Scaffolding
    inquiry-based science programs and, 125,
        126*t*
    religious education and, 144–145, 146
    rocket unit and, 157, 159
Science Across the World (SAW) approach
    context of, 231–234
    curriculum, tasks and materials for, 234–237
    reflections regarding, 237–238
    resources regarding, 238–239
*Science Content Standards for California
    Public Schools* (California Department of
    Education, 2003), 153, 153*f*
Science instruction
    content and language integrated learning
        (CLIL) and, 58, 72–73
    context of, 118–119, 151–152, 231–234
    curriculum, tasks and materials for, 119–
        125, 120*f*, 122*f*, 123*f*, 124*f*, 152–158,
        153*f*, 156*f*, 234–237
    introduction to, 117–118, 151, 231
    reflections regarding, 125–130, 125*t*, 126*t*,
        158–159, 237–238
    resources regarding, 238–239
    rocket unit, 151–159, 153*f*, 156*f*
    sample lesson plan for, 72–73
    student motivation and, 231–238
    Yemeni instruction and, 231–238
Sensitive topics, 205
Sequencing, 125, 126*t*
Sexism, 195, 196*t*
Sexuality, 195, 196*t*
Short Test of Functional Health Literacy in
    Adults (S-TOFHLA), 49–50, 51
Sikhism storyboard activity, 138–143, 139*f*,
    140*f*, 141*f*, 142*f*, 143*f*. *See also* Religious
    education
Small-group work, 197, 204–205

Also Available From TESOL

TESOL Classroom Practice Series
Maria Dantas-Whitney, Sarah Rilling, and Lilia Savova, Series Editors

Authenticity in the Classroom and Beyond: Children and Adolescent Learners
Maria Dantas-Whitney and Sarah Rilling, Editors

Language Games: Innovative Activities for Teaching English
Maureen Snow Adrade, Editor

Authenticity in the Classroom and Beyond: Adult Learners
Sarah Rilling and Maria Dantas-Whitney, Editors

Adult Language Learners: Context and Innovation
Ann F. V. Smith and Gregory Strong, Editors

Applications of Task-Based Learning in TESOL
Ali Shehadeh and Christine Coombe, Editors

Explorations in Second Language Reading
Roger Cohen, Editor

Insights on Teaching Speaking in TESOL
Tim Stewart, Editor

Multilevel and Diverse Classrooms
Bradley Baurain and Phan Le Ha, Editors

Effective Second Language Writing
Susan Kasten, Editor

Using Textbooks Effectively
Lilia Savova, Editor

Classroom Management
Thomas S. C. Farrell, Editor

T E S O L